THE UNTAPPED
HUMAN RESOURCE:

THE UNTAPPED
HUMAN RESOURCE:

The Urban Negro
and Employment Equality

MARVIN J. LEVINE

A d.h. mark publication
of General Learning Press

THIS BOOK IS IN THE D.H. MARK SERIES IN MANAGEMENT

Consulting Editor:
Max S. Wortman, Jr.

Printed in the United States of America.

Library of Congress Card Number 72-77772

To my Mother and Father

LIST OF TABLES

Contents

Preface

The most salient facets of the employment relationships and status of urban Negroes, the dominant numerical minority group, will be examined in this book, since the writer feels that employment experience is the crucial factor in the determination of economic welfare. There is no intention to downgrade the plight of the other disadvantaged minorities but rather a belief that material benefits for other minorities are inexorably linked to the degree of economic progress attained by the largest minority.

This book will describe in practical, nontechnical terms to the concerned personnel manager in private industry, the public adminstrator, the academic observer, and the concerned citizen the reasons why the disadvantaged worker is a poor employment risk and what measures can be taken to insure a higher job retention rate. For those harboring the conventional stereotypes of Negro employment deficiencies — that the urban black is a lazy, shiftless individual whose educational and skill shortcomings make him virtually unemployable — the writer will attempt to explain why the inner city job seeker lacks the requisite vocational incentive and is in dire need of motivational redirection.

The corporate personnel executive, as well as the owner or manager of a small or medium-sized business should be interested in understanding fully how and why cultural differences are translated all too often into substandard job performance on the part of the ghetto employee. In fact, those firms located in or near the inner city should be particularly interested in learning how to exploit the unmeasured potential of the black labor market. Relaxing hiring standards by doing away with the requirement for holding a high school diploma; no longer considering an arrest record as necessarily disqualifying a black job applicant; revising employment tests to eliminate cultural bias — these policies only insure a rudimentary adherence to the goal of equal employment opportunity spelled out in Title VII of the Civil Rights Act of 1964. It is true that these practices will ease the recruiting problem but much more must be done to insure that the Negro employee, once on the job, does not become discouraged and return to the streets to become a potentially explosive social problem. To put it bluntly, the employer must do considerably more than post a notice to the effect that he is an "equal opportunity employer." The nature of what affirmative action he should take, as well as the possible legal liability he faces, should he continue to discriminate, will be spelled out in substantial detail.

This study could not have been completed without the assistance of other individuals. I would like to thank all the employers and personnel managers who responded to the two questionnaire surveys, making the empirical findings possible, and allowing the reader, if he is a businessman, to compare his minority group employment policies and practices with those described in the text. My research assistant, Edward Geckle, rendered invaluable assistance in obtaining important tabular data. Essential typing and proofreading services were efficiently provided by Isabel Thompson, Ann Berzinski, Catherine Conners, and Connie Jennings. I am also grateful to the Bureau of Business and Economic Research at the University of Maryland for a research grant that helped finance part of this study. Perhaps most significantly, the constant encouragement of my wife, Dina, engendered the tenacity of purpose essential to the completion of the project.

Needless to say, the writer assumes full responsibility for all errors of omission or commission.

Marvin J. Levine
College Park, Maryland

March, 1972

Chapter 1
The Economic Variables
of Negro Employment

INTRODUCTION

An essential element in the prevalent ferment in American society has been the increased militancy of various minority groups — Negroes, Puerto Ricans, Mexican-Americans, and American Indians — in their determined striving to achieve equality through economic, social, and political parity with their white fellow citizens. It is the opinion of the writer that improvement in the economic status of minorities deserves the most urgent consideration in terms of public and private planning, policy, and program priorities, and that social and political advances will inevitably follow material gains in living standards.

Acknowledging the broad-gauged economic gains made by Negroes during the past decade, this book will nevertheless focus on the continuing economic problem areas confronting urban Negroes, with deliberate concern for the residents of the central cities, confined by a vicious cycle of discrimination and limited opportunity to lives characterized by inferior education and vocational training resulting in persistent unemployment with its concomitant low earning power and substandard incomes. Put another way, the writer is impressed with the need to explore fully the dilemma of the ghetto dweller, who has thus far been largely unsuccessful in his efforts to enter the economic mainstream.

Both politicians and government planners agree that one of the most important, if not *the* most important, contributions toward the alleviation of Negro employment problems can be forthcoming through the continued efforts of the business community and the federal government. In this context, empirical evidence demonstrating that the private sector is favorably disposed toward such objectives is essential prior to the formulation and implementation of requisite policies.

In an earlier study published in 1969, the author evaluated employer attitudes toward, and experiences with, Negro employment problems by means of a closed-end questionnaire mailed in the fall of 1967 to 100 large corporations scattered throughout the United States. Findings were based on information furnished by 63 usable responses.[1] Integrated into the textual material in the present study will be the responses of 228 small and medium-sized firms (out of 600 contacted by mail) to the same questionnaire, which was administered in the fall of 1968. Comparisons will be drawn, when appropriate, between the earlier data supplied by the corporate respondents and the present sample. Urban centers surveyed were Detroit, Houston, Baltimore, and Los Angeles, all with representative black populations and located in the Northern, Southern, Border, and Western regions, thereby constituting a cross-sectional investigation possessing national validity. Tables 1 through 3 describe the size of the firms sampled, their industrial classifications and the gross average hourly earnings of blue-collar workers in most of the industries represented.

DEMOGRAPHIC OVERVIEW

Baltimore, Detroit, Houston, and Los Angeles have all experienced rapid increases in Negro population since 1950, and, according to recent statistics, contained the following percentages of Negro inhabitants: 34.7 per cent, 28.9 per cent, 23.0 per cent, and 13.5 per cent, respectively.[2] A continuation of recent trends would cause Baltimore to become over 50 per cent Negro by 1972 and Detroit would have a black majority by 1979.[3]

Moreover, the recent decennial census indicates that Negroes, to a greater extent than whites, have become metropolitan Americans. As of 1969, it was estimated that 70 per cent of the black population was living in metropolitan areas. The figure for the white population was just under 65 per cent. The main stream of this Negro migration was to the central cities, where 55 per cent of the black population now lives. The white population of the central cities dropped by 2.1 million between 1960 and 1969, while the Negro population in these cities grew by 2.6 million. The proportion of Negro families earning upwards of $8,000 more than doubled in the 1960-1968 period, from 15 per cent in 1960 to 32 per cent in 1968. The number earning more than $15,000 a year tripled from 2 to 6 per cent. These income gains were reflected in the changing Negro employment pattern. The number of Negroes in professional and technical jobs more than doubled from 1960 to 1969, compared to a gain of only 41 per cent for whites. The number of Negro managers, officials, and proprietors went up 43 per cent in the same period, compared with a 12 per cent increase for whites. All across the spectrum of higher-paying, white-collar and skilled jobs, Negro gains in the 1960s were dramatic — 114 per cent in the clerical field, 61 per cent in sales, 70 per cent in the craftsman-foreman group. At the same time, there was an absolute decline in the number and percentage of Negroes in most unskilled and low-paying job categories. The number of black farmers and farm workers dropped 56 per cent in the first nine years of the past decade; the number of nonfarm laborers declined 8 per cent. The number of private household workers dropped 28 per cent, which meant that in 1969 there were more white maids and housekeepers and cooks (900,000) than blacks in the same jobs (712,000). Overall, the final figures from the 1970 Census are expected to show that median Negro family incomes in current dollars have nearly doubled in the past ten years and, in the past five years, have been increasing at a faster rate than the incomes of white families. The figures will also show substantial gains in both Negro and white housing and educational levels. Not all the figures on the 1960s, however, will be quite that rosy. They will show that while more than 16 million people got out of "poverty," as defined by the government, more than 20 million are still poverty stricken. They will indicate that despite impressive economic gains, the average Negro family still earns less than two-thirds of the average white family's income although this disparity is not even throughout the country. The ratio of Negro to white family income ranged from 54 per cent in the South to 80 per cent in the West in 1968. Negroes, the interim reports show, were three times as likely as whites to be poor in 1969, less likely to be in college and more likely to be unemployed. All of these measures of discrimination and disadvantage, however, were more pronounced at the beginning than at the end of the 1960s. In 1960, 40 per cent of the blacks and 65 per cent of the whites in the 20 to 29 age group had completed high school or had attended college; the figures for March, 1970 were 61 per cent and 80 per cent, respectively.[4]

EARNINGS IN URBAN POVERTY CENTERS

Due to a long-term trend, wages in the semiskilled, unskilled, and service classifications have increased faster than earnings for skilled, professional, and managerial employees. With Negroes clustered in the lower-rated job categories, it appears that their relative income position compared to whites has shown far greater improvement.[5]

Nevertheless, weekly earnings data in urban poverty areas of three cities, as shown in Table 4, graphically illustrate the degree to which many of the workers in urban ghetto areas are underpaid. Figures for Baltimore were not available. Substantial proportions of the full-time workers, especially females, in the poverty areas earned less than $65 a week, the weekly equivalent of the current Federal minimum wage. Approximately 70 per cent of the Negro women, compared to 45 per cent of the white females, in the Houston poverty area earned less than $65 a week working at full-time jobs. Large proportions of Negro and white men in Houston earned less than $100 weekly at full-time jobs, 55 and 43 per cent, respectively. Earnings were considerably higher in Detroit and Los Angeles, with about 1 of 4 whites and 1 of 5 Negro males earning less than $100 weekly.

Median weekly earnings for full-time workers in the poverty areas even more deeply reflected the interurban differentials. Average weekly earnings for whites and Negroes were substantially lower in Houston than in the other two cities. In Detroit and Los Angeles, moreover, Negro males earned more than white men. Only in Los Angeles did Negro women earn more than their white counterparts.

Although large percentages of poverty area workers received low earnings, a significant proportion of the employed persons in each urban center had substantial weekly earnings. In Detroit, where overall earnings were highest, about 40 per cent of both Negro and white men earned $150 or more weekly. However, in Houston, only 1 of 10 Negro males and 1 of 5 white men averaged this much.[6]

INCOME AS A MEASURE OF ECONOMIC STATUS

The labor force experience and earnings of individuals are not complete or sufficient measures of a family's economic health. Nor is having a job a guarantee of financial independence for many families. A more comprehensive measure of family economic well-being is the level of annual family income, which includes incomes from all sources: earnings, welfare payments, rents, social security, and other sources. Despite significant differences among the poverty areas, average incomes of all families in the three cities were sharply lower than for families in the nation as a whole. As Table 5 shows, the median income of white families (2 or more persons) was highest in Los Angeles ($6,600), and lowest in Houston ($6,000), with Detroit in the middle ($6,300). These levels are in sharp contrast to the annual incomes of white families in large central cities, which averaged $9,300 in 1968. White families in the United States averaged about $8,900 in 1968. The income levels for Negro families ranged from $4,700 in Houston to $6,200 in Detroit, with Los Angeles ranking second with $5,600. These statistics are far below the $8,600 median income received by all of the nation's families in 1968 and are less than the average income level of all Negro families in large central cities in 1968 — $6,600. The proportion of poverty area families with very low or "poverty level" incomes (less than $3,500 annual income for a nonfarm family of four) varied from city to city and between Negro and white families. In Houston 1 of 3 Negro families had this level of income, a proportion well above both Negro and white families in the other cities. Conversely, less than 1 of 5 Negro families in Houston reported income of $8,000 or more annually compared to at least 1 out of 3 for both white and Negro families in Detroit and Los Angeles.[7] These figures indicate that a substantial gap in family incomes between the races remains, although some inroads on poverty have been made in recent years. General prosperity has left the remaining poor families actually worse off in relation to the rest of the community. Poor Negroes in the big city slums are falling farther behind. The successful and lucky fight their way out of the slums. Left behind, trapped in poverty and hopelessness, are large numbers of Negroes for whom life is growing worse.[8] Special censuses in 1965 and 1966 of the Watts area in Los Angeles and the predominantly Negro tract that surrounds this ghetto area found no improvement from 1960 in the socioeconomic condition of the residents. Another cautionary note is the lack of a perceptible rise in the relative share of income and earnings received by families in the lowest fifth of the national income distribution.[9]

Negroes at the bottom of the social ladder have not shared in the general postwar economic progress to the degree that other Negroes have. The significant point to bear in mind here is that lower income Negroes are increasing both in number and as a proportion of the total Negro population in the United States. Dependency is virtually imposed on a good many slum residents. Lack of meaningful job opportunities that provide an adequate income reinforces a belief that it is futile to strive — a belief that often becomes irreversible. The sizable proportion of slum residents who live on welfare payments is a hard fact of slum life, a fact which is both an influence on and a result of the complex pressures operating in the urban ghettos. In the Watts area of Los Angeles, 30 per cent of the population — 94,000 persons — are welfare recipients.[10]

Discrimination, rather than deficiencies in education or training, is the basic reason for income disparity between the nation's black and white populations, according to several studies commissioned by the federal government in recent years. Nonetheless, the government continues to emphasize education and training rather than enforcement of antidiscrimination laws. A study by the Equal Employment Opportunities Commission in 1969 concluded, on the basis of several statistical studies, that lower educational levels of some minority groups account only for about one-third of the difference in occupational ranking between black and white men. The remaining two-thirds of the cases "must be atrributed to discrimination." Similar findings were reported in two independent reports, one by Professor Lester Thurow of the Massachusetts Institute of Technology, and the other by A. L. Nellum and Associates of Washington, D.C. Thurow's report concludes that the government's policy won't work. He characterizes the policy as an acknowledgement that discrimination is responsible for lower incomes among blacks than whites, but calls it ineffectual because it is difficult to stop focusing attention on education and training. The real problem, according to Thurow, is the advancement of blacks after they have been hired. The Nellum study centered on Concentrated Employment Programs in eight cities. It said that the "racist" employment system discriminates particularly against the poor who have gone through training programs. It concludes that no training will be successful until the "realities of racism" are taken seriously and dealt with.[11]

OCCUPATIONAL INEQUITIES

The higher an individual's position in the occupational hierarchy, the more likely he is to experience satisfaction in his employment. Regarding this not unexpected conclusion, the findings of job satisfaction studies have been consistent and generally unequivocal. Satisfaction is greater among white-collar than blue-collar workers as a whole, and typically is found to be highest among professionals and businessmen and lowest among unskilled laborers. This general relationship between satisfaction and occupational level is confirmed both by independent studies of limited occupational samples and by the few broad-gauge, multi-occupational studies thus far undertaken.[12]

Table 6 illustrates that even in the poverty areas of three large urban centers, Negroes fare badly compared to whites. With the exception of Negro males in Los Angeles, who held more high status occupations than whites due mainly to the large numbers of Mexican-Americans in the latter category, both white men and women in Detroit and Houston were bracketed in more desirable occupations. A large proportion of adult men, particularly Negro men, was employed in nonfarm laborer or service jobs, many of which are low skilled. The problem was greatest in Houston, where more than 1 out of 3 employed Negro men held these low-skill jobs. White men in these areas, many of whom were Spanish-American, were also disproportionately employed in low-skill occupations, although less so than Negro men. Working men in these areas were less likely to be employed in white-collar professional or managerial jobs. Compared with about 30 per cent of the employed men in the United States, only 7 to 13 per cent of the white men and about 6 to 11 per cent of Negro males had professional or managerial jobs. Adult women in these urban centers were also more likely to be working in less desirable occupations than women in the nation as a whole. For example, about 2 out of 3 Negro women in Houston worked in service occupations, mostly private household work. About 1 out of 3 in Detroit and Houston were employed as domestics and in other service jobs, but only 1 out of 8 white women in Los Angeles, where a large proportion were Mexican-Americans, held these low-paying jobs.[13]

It is apparent that improvement in the economic position of Negroes will be significantly affected by the progress made toward occupational parity with whites. Hiestand has stated:

Purely from the point of view of occupational equality, the advances of Negroes relative to whites cannot be considered remarkable, even if we consider only the period since 1940. The remaining discrepancies . . . are so great that the prospects of substantial equality during the present century are not particularly promising. . . .[14]

A survey of six major New York City banks showed that although the banks have increased the number of minority group members hired, this increase has primarily been in low-level jobs. The net increase in minority hiring for the period 1966-68 has been 7 to 13 per cent. Between January 1967 and January 1969, the proportion of nonwhite bank employees rose from 16 per cent to 26 per cent. Minorities comprised 4 to 6 per cent of the total number of officers and managers. In office and clerical categories, the percentages range from 29 to 38 per cent. Banks also suffer from the embarrassment that their supervisory personnel are almost all white, while in many departments most employees are nonwhites. The study also noted that no minorities have been placed in the money departments of banks — the trust, credit, or finance divisions — which are widely regarded as the quickest and best routes to success in banking. Instead, more than half of all minority placements have been made in the metropolitan branch systems where they can move into branch management positions. Interviews at the banks studied "suggest that virtually all supervisory personnel are hostile to accelerated promotion of minority personnel."[15]

At the corporate level, a federal judge ruled on April 13, 1970 that Bethlehem Steel Company must offer every employee hired before October 1, 1967, the opportunity to transfer from his present department. The decision denied a suit started in December, 1967, but it also forced Bethlehem to take more than a dozen steps to improve its employment policies and working conditions for blacks. The original action would have given black employees the chance to transfer without loss of seniority or present rates of pay. About one-third of the plant's work force, as of the 1967 date, including 2160 black workers, would have been affected had the relief sought been granted. The court rejected the plea for continuous seniority and pay rates on the grounds that it would "result in considerable inequities to other plant employees, and would create an unwarranted preference for Negroes over whites in 11 departments." The ruling included the finding that Bethlehem had discriminatorily assigned blacks to hotter, dirtier, less desirable jobs and departments than it had given to whites. Bethlehem admitted discriminating against blacks but maintained that such practices are no longer followed. Future standards to be met by the defendant included the following:

1. Bethlehem will not assign black job applicants to less desirable jobs because of their race.

2. The company must hire, recall, assign, transfer or refuse employment without discrimination.

3. Preference will not be given to job applicants with relatives working in the plant.

4. There must be programs to recruit blacks.

5. Qualifications for jobs newly available to blacks because of the transfer order must not be higher than those required for the least qualified person assigned to the new department since January 1, 1964.

6. Non-craft employees must be notified of admissions standards for apprenticeship programs. 1968 contract provisions for the selection of apprentices shall be suspended for five years.

7. Everyone who applied for the apprenticeship programs between January 1, 1964 and October 1, 1967, and who meets the standards applied to the least qualified white applicant accepted in that period, must be hired immediately without further testing.

8. The elctronic repair training program may not be restricted to employees of the electrical division or a related department.

9. Blacks who transfer or enter apprenticeship programs must be provided with on-the-job and formal training.

10. There can be no retaliation against employees who participated in the investigation for this suit.

11. Pool agreements between the company and union must be renegotiated to make transferring easier.

12. The company must file a report with the court every 90 days, for three years, to show promotions, firings and new apprentices.

13. The Department of Justice must have access to records used as the basis for the reports.[16]

The United States Civil Rights Commission heard allegations of racial discrimination by McDonnell-Douglas Corporation in January, 1970. When the company was awarded the F-15 fighter plane contract in December of 1969, its affirmative action plans did not meet with federal government approval, supposedly a requirement for receiving a contract. McDonnell has 2700 minority group employees out of a total work force of 33,000, or about 8.1 per cent of the total force. About 14 per cent of the combined population of St. Louis and St. Louis County is black. Forty-one of the company's 4898 officials (0.008%) and 60 of its 6700 (0.008%) professionals are black.[17]

Tables 7 through 10 furnish evidence that there has been a noticeable movement into better jobs by nonwhites since 1962, but that the rate of advancement must accelerate even more rapidly in the future to produce occupational equality.

Approximately 58,000 companies with 100 or more employees were required to report the number of their white, Negro, Spanish-American, and other minority employees in 1966, as were all government contractors employing 50 persons or more. Tables 11 through 14 describe the 1969 employment situation in almost all the industries represented in the four city sample, and illustrate the restrictive pattern of Negro employment which is pervasive throughout the statistics. The occupational distribution and participation rate of Negroes and all other employees is compared. With total employment in a group as a base, the occupational distribution indicates the percentage of persons employed in a particular job category (*e.g.,* of all Negro employes, $x\%$ are technicians). The participation rate refers to the minority employment percentage of total employment in each job category (*e.g.,* of all clerical workers in an industry or area, $y\%$ are Negroes).

At the white-collar level, black workers are virtually excluded from managerial and professional jobs, are rarely significant in sales positions, are under-represented among technicians and clerical workers. At the blue-collar level, they are conspicuous by their absence in skilled craft jobs and instead are overly visible in low-status laborer and service worker jobs. There was consistently high Negro employment in personal services, food processing, and primary metals production, where the low-paying occupations are clustered. Where they do participate significantly in the white-collar category, it is generally in industries where white-collar positions enjoy salaries and status below those usually accompanying such jobs. White-collar Negroes are usually clerks, sales persons, or technicians. In Detroit, for example, while Negroes comprised 7.6 per cent of the reporting labor force, they hold 6.0 per cent of the white-collar jobs and 5.6 per cent of higher paying skilled craftsmen positions. One need merely look at the transportation equipment industry — including auto, truck, ships, and airplane manufacturing — where Negroes hold 4.4 per cent of all jobs but only 3.3 per cent of white-collar jobs and 4.7 per cent of skilled craftsmen positions.

Regardless of reason, if a city has 20 per cent Negro employment and the number of Negroes working at a particular plant in that city is only two-tenths of 1 per cent of the work force, a case for blatant discrimination is easily constructed. The mass of statistical evidence and practical experience since the Civil Rights Act of 1964 became effective July 2, 1965, has demonstrated that the practice of discrimination in employment knows bounds of neither region nor tradition, trade nor position.

Perhaps the single best recent empirical field study of urban Negroes is Liebow's work on a street corner society of Washington, D.C. Liebow rejects the notion of a lower-class or "poverty" culture. He does not see the street corner world as a self-sustaining social system with its own value system, or as a valued cultural pattern, but, rather, as a modification of the larger society, created by repeated failure. It involves, not self-realization in relation to goals, but an outcome of failures in many types of effort.[18]

Since many of the hard-core unemployed have a history of welfare dependency, motivating them to work is a major task — sometimes unsuccessful. Many of them simply see no logic in giving up a steady — albeit low — income for the vagaries of a job they are pretty well convinced won't be much. They perceive greater stability in welfare than in marginal jobs. Yet, there is increasing evidence that many industries are opening up positions for Negroes who have the proper skills. Many of these positions are near the bottom of the skill ladder, but many are also among the higher rungs. Nonetheless, because many Negroes lack appropriate skills — and in some cases adequate self-confidence and motivation — job openings may remain unfilled and Negroes may not be hired. Also, because of educational and skill deficiencies, companies find it more costly to recruit and train Negro workers than white employees.

OBSTACLES TO EMPLOYMENT EQUALITY

For complete equal employment opportunity a firm should have at every skill level the same percentage of Negroes as is in the urban area population. Unfortunately, this goal is presently unattainable due to a variety of factors. In the first place, to the obstacles which bar slum residents from satisfactory employment — and often from any job — must be added problems associated directly with the job search. In general, employers do not recruit people from these areas, most of them members of minority groups, for any but the most low-skilled, menial jobs. Furthermore, inner city residents generally lack information on available job openings and on the most effective ways of looking for jobs. Really effective methods of communicating job information do not yet exist in many slum districts. Newspaper, radio and television advertisements, and placement offices all fail to reach out sufficiently into the urban core areas and the principal form of communication about jobs is personal contacts. Since people living in poverty areas generally have contact only with their friends and neighbors in low-level occupations, this kind of communication does little to widen their knowledge of job openings or their job seeking activities. Labor mobility studies show that few jobs are located from newspaper advertisements, employment offices, and the like. Workers most frequently learn of jobs from friends, by passing the place of work and seeing help wanted signs, and by other casual association. Since nonwhites have few associations with white areas distant from the ghetto and since few of their friends and neighbors are employed there or make frequent trips there, the chances of their learning of distant job opportunities may be significantly lessened. Specifically, communication has had to be made with the Negro community to convince people to apply. This, companies often find, is hard and discouraging work. Negroes are often fearful of leaving the accepted avenues of travel to look for jobs. Once the word gets around, potential employees do apply. Meanwhile, the experience of those already on the payroll, their treatment, and their opportunities for promotion, all determine the number of future applicants. Some firms never get Negro applicants because of long-standing reputations for discrimination.

However, a 1968 survey, which drew upon comparative data from matched samples of 200 black and 144 white labor force members in Boston, Massachusetts, suggested that the black worker actually searches more intensively for a job than does his white counterpart, despite higher rejection rates and widespread anticipation that discrimination would occur if a black person attempted to secure a position normally held by whites.[19]

Secondly, in hiring the hard-core unemployed, firms may find that a lowering of selection standards may be necessary. Special training programs and additional supervisory help can enable the disadvantaged employee to achieve production standards and to establish good work habits. However, smaller, specialized firms may be unable to do this because of stringent skill requirements, unavailability of additional supervisory help, and inability to finance special training programs. A number of recent studies have pointed up the barriers to equal employment opportunity presented by institutional processes built into traditional hiring and promotion policies. One such study was that of the application of equal employment practices in twenty companies and their impact on minority group employment. While all of the firms reported some progress in equalizing opportunities, the general feeling was that shortages of adequately trained Negroes hindered any dramatic change. There was a pronounced tendency to blame the inferior educational and social background of the Negro for his job difficulties and thus to see the community rather than industry, as responsible.[20]

Because many of them are high-cost employees, ghetto workers are often rejected by preferred (high-wage) employers and relegated to employment in less preferred (low-wage) firms, where their higher costs are discounted in the wage rate, or to nonmarket activities. In fact experience has shown a definite pattern of reservation wages differing by city, below which it is difficult to attract JOBS (Job Opportunities in the Business Sector) applicants: $1.60 in Dallas and Houston; $1.75 in Atlanta and Portland; $1.80 in Baltimore; $2.00 and over in Boston, Buffalo, Chicago, Los Angeles, Philadelphia, and St. Louis.[21]

Unions in skilled trades demand qualified persons and often engage in discriminatory hiring policies. By almost any standard, most of the major A.F.L.-C.I.O. construction trades unions are among the nation's most important remaining strongholds of racial discrimination. Among the construction unions' 1,300,000 members, about 106,000 or 8.4 per cent are blacks. The overall figures are misleading; 81,000 of the blacks belong to the lowest-paid laborer's union, where they form 30 per cent of the membership. The latest compilation by the EEOC indicates that only 1.6 per cent of the union carpenters are black; among electricians the figure is 0.6 per cent; among plumbers 0.2 per cent.[22]

Finally, attitudes of union members and traditional procedures of unions may work to shut out minority group members from employment for which they are otherwise qualified. For example, unions and frequently employers as well, have often opposed changes in apprenticeship programs, since such changes may conflict with established job rights.

RECENT TRENDS IN URBAN UNEMPLOYMENT

Since this study will concentrate on employment problems of the nation's largest urban minority group, it is important to determine the nature and extent of urban joblessness in the United States. The magnitude of the problem becomes apparent with the realization that disproportionate Negro unemployment rates are accompanied by substantive underemployment and restricted opportunities for the 8.4 million working nonwhites, who are predominantly Negroes.

In its report the National Advisory Commission on Civil Disorders underlined the importance of steady work with adequate pay not only in providing purchasing power and social status, but also in developing the capabilities, confidence and self-esteem and individual needs to insure responsible citizenship. Even more important than the fact that the rates of Negro unemployment were still double those for whites in all corresponding age and sex categories, the Commission said, is that employed Negroes are all too often in low-status and low-paying jobs with little opportunity. Negro males, in particular, are more than twice as likely as white men to be in low-paid, unskilled, or service jobs.[23]

The Commission found in its survey of cities where racial disorders occurred in 1967, that Negroes were twice as likely as whites to hold unskilled jobs — which were often seasonal, part-time and dead-end. More than 20 per cent of the rioters were unemployed, and many of those with jobs were only marginally employed, and in jobs which the rioters believed were below their level of ability. The Department of Labor uses the term "subemployment rate" to include both the unemployed and the underemployed and it provides some measure of the enormous disparity between employment conditions in most of the nation and those prevalent in disadvantaged Negro areas in the large cities. Table 15 illustrates the scope of the problem.

Two Department of Labor studies of persons involved in rioting found the same kind of relationship between rioting and unemployment and employment in low-paying jobs. A survey of 1,000 persons arrested during the April, 1968 riots in Washington, D.C. indicated that about 11 per cent were unemployed.[24] By comparison Washington's unemployment rate was less than 3 per cent. Of the persons arrested who were working, 2 of every 3 had semiskilled, unskilled, or service jobs. Average take-home pay was $83 a week. Another study of the Detroit riots showed that about 80 per cent of the rioters were employed in relatively low-paying occupations.[25]

Recent data collected by the Bureau of Labor Statistics describes the employment characteristics of urban poverty neighborhoods in the 100 largest metropolitan areas including somewhat over six million workers. In the fourth quarter of 1969, for example, the jobless rate of this labor force segment was 4.9 per cent, compared with 3.1 per cent for the remainder of the civilian labor force. For whites the unemployment rate in urban poverty areas was 3.9 per cent; for nonwhites it was 6.4 per cent (compared with 3.0 per cent and 4.4 per cent, respectively, for other urban nonpoverty neighborhoods).[26] Three fourths of the small 40,000 decline in unemployment in the poverty neighborhoods between 1968 and 1969 occurred among white workers, who made up three-fifths of the poverty neighborhood labor force. Their jobless rate, at 4.2 per cent, was eight-tenths of a percentage point below the 1968 rate. In contrast, the jobless rate for Negroes (7.2 per cent) was not significantly changed during the one-year period.[27]

In 1967 the following were estimated annual average unemployment rates for central city residents, white and nonwhite, in the four metropolitan areas: Los Angeles — white 6.0, nonwhite 9.1; Detroit — white 2.9, nonwhite 9.8; Baltimore — white 3.3, nonwhite 8.0; Houston — white, 2.4, nonwhite 6.3.[28] The 1968 unemployment rates for the same areas were as follows: Los Angeles — white 4.2, nonwhite 8.5; Detroit — white 3.0, nonwhite 7.5; Baltimore — white 3.7, nonwhite 6.5; Houston — white 2.5, nonwhite 5.8.[29]

During the July 1968-June 1969 period poverty areas surveyed in Detroit, Houston, and Los Angeles indicated unemployment rates well above comparable national figures. The highest jobless rates for Negro workers were 15.2 per cent in Los Angeles and 13.5 per cent in Detroit, more than double the 6.5 per cent rate for Negro workers nationally. The figure for Houston was 9.5 per cent. Jobless rates for Negro teenagers were highest for individuals in Los Angeles — 45 per cent, Detroit — 40 per cent, and

Houston — 38 per cent. The national unemployment rate for Negro teenagers for the same period was 25 per cent. Negro males who were household heads in poverty areas had an unemployment rate of 7.2 per cent in Los Angeles and 4.9 per cent in Detroit, sharply higher than the 2.8 per cent rate nationally. About 1 out of 3 Negro workers in the Detroit and Los Angeles area was unemployed at some time during the year, compared to 1 out of 4 Negro employees in the nation. In Houston 27 per cent of the Negro workers were without work at some time during the twelve-month period, which was twice the proportion for the entire nation's work force.[30] The proportion of Negro jobless experiencing long-term unemployment — 15 weeks or more — ranged from 22 per cent in Detroit to 24.8 per cent in Houston to 28.4 per cent in Los Angeles. In each of the urban poverty areas, jobless adult men were more likely to have experienced 15 weeks or more of unemployment during the year than other age and sex groups. A further subdivision of the long-term unemployed may be made between those who are out of work from 15 to 26 weeks, and those who are out of work for 27 weeks or more, who are considered to be the persistent or "hard-core" unemployed. Those in the 15-26 week category were as follows: Detroit, 12.3 per cent; Los Angeles, 15.0 per cent; and Houston, 15.6 per cent. While some persons suffering extremely long-term unemployment may have been cyclically unemployed, many of them no doubt had been permanently displaced from their jobs by the relocation or liquidation of their former places of employment, technological change, employment cutbacks due to shifts in demand, or other changes in our economy which create persistent unemployment. The urban percentages were: Houston, 9.4; Detroit, 9.7; and Los Angeles, 13.4

Against 1969's low 3.5 per cent unemployment rate overall, the following selected group of rates for the same year emphasizes the more serious impact on teenagers, women, and blacks: All teenagers — 12.2 per cent; black male teenagers — 21.2 per cent; adults, aged 20-44 — 3.2 per cent; black females, 20-44 — 7.2 per cent; white, total — 3.1 per cent; black, total — 6.4 per cent. Recently, the real effort being made by industry to create and extend job opportunities to blacks seemed to be narrowing the gap slightly between white and black unemployment rates; the slow increase in the jobless total from the beginning of 1969 to the end of the year was mostly at the expense of whites. But whether this trend will persist with a further substantial boost in unemployment is problematical. The Council of Economic Advisors devoted a special section of a recent report to minority group employment problems. It showed that of 2,831,000 persons out of work in 1969, 570,000 were black. Fully half of these — 290,000 — needed jobs in order to have made the Negro jobless rate equal to that of the white.[31]

In February, 1970, the unemployment rate for whites was 3.6 per cent, for nonwhites, 6.3 per cent. The rate for whites had changed little since 1967 while the nonwhite rate dipped a full point. It is not certain, however, whether this represents real improvement; it could reflect the fact that more nonwhites are simply dropping out of the labor force altogether.[32] The NAACP has estimated that Detroit's inner city unemployed number 30,000, only about one-third of whom actually are registered as unemployed.[33]

However, in the Labor Department's employment report covering June, 1970, at the height of a business slump, jobless rates for traditionally disadvantaged workers, which had risen relatively slowly earlier in the business slowdown, were shown to be rising more rapidly. The rate for Negroes and other minorities jumped from 8.0 to 8.7 per cent in June while the white rate slipped from 4.6 to 4.2 per cent and the former returned to its long-term ratio to the white rate of more than 2 to 1.[34] In fact, layoffs threatened nationwide efforts to rehabilitate people once thought unemployable. Many of the so-called hard-core unemployed lost new jobs in auto and farm equipment plants, and others stood to lose their jobs in steel and other industries if the industrial slowdown continued. Beyond the layoffs, however, was something worse for the campaign to put the ghetto people into jobs: new hiring was at a low level, with fewer and fewer starting jobs for those recruited from the ghettos and trained to work. Also, losses of newly gained jobs can have a debilitating effect on the hard-core workers, who may drop out of the productive labor force and go back to the streets. The further importance of economic expansion as a prerequisite for the employment stability of the hard-core worker is seen in the fact that the employment status of disadvantaged groups seems to improve more than proportionately during cyclical upswings. For instance, it has been determined that a decrease of 1 percentage point in the overall unemployment rate is associated on the average with a decrease of 1.7 percentage points in the nonwhite rate.[35]Moreover a 1 per cent increase in adult white male employment may be associated with as high as a 3.3 per cent increase in adult nonwhite male employment.[36]

TABLE 1.   Standard Industrial Classifications of Firms, by City.

	Sample Totals	Baltimore	Los Angeles	Detroit	Houston
Food & kindred products	15	12	2	0	1
Fabricated metal products	20	9	3	4	4
Apparel & other finished products	13	9	3	1	0
Lumber & wood products, except furniture	1	1	0	0	0
Textile mill products	4	3	0	1	0
Paper & allied products	3	2	1	0	0
Chemicals & allied products	10	4	3	2	1
Furniture & fixtures	11	7	2	2	0
Printing, publishing & allied industries	18	15	1	2	0
Miscellaneous manufacturing industries	9	5	3	1	0
Primary metal industries	4	2	0	1	1
Machinery, except electrical	13	5	0	8	0
Stone, clay, glass, & concrete products	5	1	2	2	0
Rubber & miscellaneous plastic products	3	1	2	0	0
Retail trade	16	2	8	4	2
Banking	2	0	0	0	2
Contract construction	9	0	2	1	6
Wholesale trade	38	0	12	17	9
Crude petroleum & natural gas	4	0	1	0	3
Pipe line transportation	1	0	0	0	1
Transportation equipment	7	0	6	1	0
Electrical machinery, equipment & supplies	5	0	3	2	0
Motor freight transportation	3	0	2	1	0
Professional, scientific & controlling instruments	2	0	1	1	0
Miscellaneous business services	4	0	3	1	0
Transportation services	1	0	1	0	0
Personal services	0	1	0	0	0
Petroleum refining & related industries	1	0	0	1	0
Real estate	1	0	0	0	1

Source: Negro Employment Questionnaire.

TABLE 2.   Gross Average Hourly Earnings of Production or Nonsupervisory Workers on Payrolls of 24 Industries in Sample: Annual Average 1967.

Food & kindred products	$2.64
Fabricated metal products	$2.97
Apparel & other finished products	$2.03
Lumber & wood products, except furniture	$2.38
Textile mill products	$2.06
Paper & allied products	$2.87
Chemicals & allied products	$3.10
Furniture & fixtures	$2.32
Printing, publishing & allied industries	$3.28
Miscellaneous manufacturing industries	$2.34
Primary metal industries	$3.34
Machinery, except electrical	$3.19
Stone, clay, glass & concrete products	$2.83
Rubber & miscellaneous plastics products	$2.74
Retail trade	$2.01
Banking	$2.61
Contract construction	$4.09
Wholesale trade	$2.88
Crude petroleum & natural gas	$3.41
Transportation equipment	$3.43
Electrical machinery, equipment, & supplies	$2.77
Professional, scientific, & controlling instruments	$2.84
Petroleum refining & related industries	$3.58
Real estate	$2.61
Total average hourly earnings $2.85	

Source: U. S. Department of Labor. *Manpower Report of the President, 1968*. Washington, D.C.: U. S. Government Printing Office, April, 1968, p. 275.

TABLE 3.   Size of Firms (Number of Employees) by City.

	Sample Totals		Baltimore		Los Angeles		Detroit		Houston	
	No.	*%*	*No.*	*%*	*No.*	*%*	*No.*	*%*	*No.*	*%*
0–5	10	4.4	10	12.7	0	0.0	0	0.0	0	0.0
6–10	17	7.5	16	20.3	0	0.0	0	0.0	1	3.1
11–25	38	16.8	20	25.3	5	8.2	7	13.0	6	18.8
26–50	53	23.5	14	17.7	13	21.3	20	37.0	6	18.8
51–100	46	20.4	4	5.1	20	32.8	14	25.9	8	25.0
101–250	46	20.4	10	12.7	17	27.9	11	20.4	8	25.0
251–500	9	4.0	1	1.3	5	8.2	1	1.8	2	6.2
501–1000	6	2.7	3	3.8	1	1.6	1	1.8	1	3.1
Over 1000	1	0.3	1	1.3	0	0.0	0	0.0	0	0.0
Range	1–1250		1–1250		12–900		11–550		8–800	
Mean	100		79		130		87		117	

Source: Negro Employment Questionnaire.

TABLE 4. Weekly Earnings for Fully-Employed Persons by Race and Sex, by City, July 1968-June 1969 (Per Cent Distribution).

	Detroit	*Houston*	*Los Angeles*
White Male			
0–$64	8.8	11.6	3.4
$65–$99	14.7	31.4	25.3
$100–$149	36.8	37.2	46.0
$150 or more	39.7	19.8	25.3
Median Weekly Earnings	$135.00	$107.00	$117.00
White Female			
0–$64	31.3	44.4	18.4
$65–$99	37.5	38.9	57.1
$100–$149	21.9	13.9	20.4
$150 or more	9.4	2.8	4.1
Median Weekly Earnings	$77.00	$70.00	$78.00
Negro Male			
0–$64	5.4	13.0	0.0
$65–$99	13.2	42.6	18.7
$100–$149	42.6	33.9	44.2
$150 or more	38.8	10.4	37.2
Median Weekly Earnings	$139.00	$95.00	$136.00
Negro Female			
0–$64	34.8	71.1	13.4
$65–$99	39.1	20.5	50.0
$100–$149	20.3	6.0	30.0
$150 or more	5.8	2.4	6.7
Median Weekly Earnings	$73.00	$55.00	$87.00

Source: *Employment Situation in Poverty Areas of Six Cities, July 1968-June 1969*, Washington, D.C.: U. S. Department of Labor, Bureau of Labor Statistics Report No. 370, October, 1969.

TABLE 5.   Annual Money Income of Families (2 or more Members) by Race and City, July 1968–June 1969 (Per Cent Distribution).

	Detroit	*Houston*	*Los Angeles*
White			
0–$3,499	26.2	18.6	17.9
$3,500–$4,999	13.1	17.6	14.9
$5,000–$7,999	25.0	33.0	32.8
$8,000–$9,999	14.3	13.7	14.2
$10,000 or more	21.4	16.7	20.1
Median Income	$6,300	$6,000	$6,600
Negro			
0–$3,499	27.8	35.3	21.9
$3,500–$4,999	13.0	17.9	21.9
$5,000–$7,999	24.3	28.8	21.9
$8,000–$9,999	15.2	8.7	14.1
$10,000 or more	19.6	9.2	20.3
Median Income	$6,200	$4,700	$5,600

Source: *Employment Situation in Poverty Areas of Six Cities, July 1968–June 1969*, Washington, D.C.: U. S. Department of Labor, Bureau of Labor Statistics Report No. 370, October, 1969.

TABLE 6. Distribution of Employed Persons by Occupation, Race, Age, and Sex, July 1968-June 1969 (Per Cent Distribution).

Occupation Males, 20 years and Over	Detroit White	Detroit Negro	Houston White	Houston Negro	Los Angeles White	Los Angeles Negro
White-collar workers	21.3	11.1	16.6	13.8	15.5	21.3
Prof., techn. & managerial	12.6	5.7	9.1	6.9	6.5	10.4
Clerical workers	6.9	4.4	6.2	5.8	7.5	7.9
Sales workers	1.8	1.0	1.3	1.1	1.6	3.0
Blue-collar workers	67.1	77.1	73.2	71.4	78.1	61.1
Craftsmen and foremen	15.6	12.4	27.6	12.9	21.0	15.8
Operatives	40.1	47.6	30.1	34.0	45.5	34.7
Nonfarm laborers	11.4	17.2	15.4	24.5	11.7	10.5
Service workers	11.6	11.8	10.0	13.9	6.2	16.5
Private household workers	.2	–	–	.1	.2	–
Other service workers	11.4	11.8	10.0	13.8	6.0	16.5
Farm workers	–	–	.2	.9	.2	1.1
Females, 20 years and Over						
White-collar workers	50.1	29.4	45.6	19.0	33.8	34.4
Prof., techn. & managerial	18.8	6.6	12.8	7.6	5.3	10.0
Clerical workers	24.5	19.8	28.1	9.4	24.5	21.4
Sales workers	6.8	3.0	4.8	2.1	4.1	2.1
Blue-collar workers	18.9	18.2	22.1	12.9	53.7	27.9
Craftsmen and foremen	1.1	.8	1.5	.8	2.8	1.4
Operatives	16.8	16.1	20.1	11.4	48.9	25.6
Nonfarm laborers	1.0	1.3	.5	.8	1.9	.9
Service workers	31.0	52.4	32.3	68.0	12.5	37.7
Private household workers	1.8	19.0	5.8	35.0	3.2	14.8
Other service workers	29.2	33.3	26.5	33.0	9.3	22.8
Farm workers	–	–	–	–	–	–

Source: *Employment Situation in Poverty Areas of Six Cities, July 1968-June 1969*, Washington, D.C.: U. S. Department of Labor, Bureau of Labor Statistics Report No. 370, October 1969.

TABLE 7. Nonwhite Workers as a Percentage of Total Employment by Occupation, Annual Averages. (Numbers in thousands)

Occupation Group	1957[1,2]		1962[1]		1967	
	Total employment	Per cent nonwhite	Total employment	Per cent nonwhite	Total employment	Per cent nonwhite
Total	65,100	10.4	67,846	10.5	74,372	10.8
Professional, technical, and kindred	6,476	3.8	8,040	4.6	9,879	6.0
Medical and health	1,157	3.6	1,353	5.3	1,578	7.6
Teachers, excluding college	1,351	6.5	1,713	8.1	2,159	9.4
Other	3,968	2.9	4,974	3.3	6,143	4.4
Managers, officials, and proprietors	6,705	2.1	7,408	2.5	7,495	2.8
Salaried	3,045	1.1	4,053	1.9	5,284	2.2
Self employed—retail trade	1,835	3.3	1,583	3.7	1,074	4.7
Self employed—excluding retail trade	1,825	2.4	1,773	2.9	1,137	3.8
Clerical	9,172	4.4	10,107	5.1	12,333	7.3
Stenographers, typists, and secretaries	2,170	3.7	2,511	3.8	3,190	5.1
Other	7,002	4.6	7,596	5.5	9,144	8.0
Sales	4,137	1.9	4,346	2.6	4,525	3.0
Retail trade	2,495	2.5	2,529	3.0	2,761	3.6
Other	1,642	1.0	1,817	2.1	1,765	2.2
Craftsmen and foremen	8,663	4.4	8,678	4.9	9,845	6.3
Carpenters	899	3.9	812	5.4	840	6.2
Construction, excluding carpenters	1,673	5.5	1,705	6.5	1,923	8.2
Mechanics and repairmen	2,032	5.9	2,145	6.2	2,539	7.6
Metal crafts, excluding mechanics	1,182	3.0	1,046	3.4	1,260	5.5
Other craftsmen	1,709	4.4	1,751	4.3	1,858	5.4
Foremen, not elsewhere classified	1,168	2.0	1,218	2.2	1,427	3.4
Operatives and kindred	12,542	11.3	12,041	11.7	13,884	13.6
Drivers and deliverymen	2,330	13.5	2,352	12.9	2,511	14.1
Other	10,212	10.7	9,689	11.5	11,372	13.4

Table 7 continued

Occupation Group	1957[1,2] Total employment	1957[1,2] Per cent nonwhite	1962[1] Total employment	1962[1] Per cent nonwhite	1967 Total employment	1967 Per cent nonwhite
Durable goods manufacturing	3,805	9.0	3,611	9.9	4,751	12.1
Nondurable goods manufacturing	3,458	8.3	3,314	9.2	3,761	12.9
Other industries	2,949	15.9	2,764	16.1	2,861	16.4
Nonfarm laborers	3,682	27.3	3,559	27.0	3,533	25.4
Construction	N.A.	N.A.	747	30.1	732	26.9
Manufacturing	N.A.	N.A.	1,017	26.0	1,107	25.7
Other industries	N.A.	N.A.	1,796	26.3	1,694	24.6
Service workers	7,653	28.2	8,802	26.4	9,325	25.3
Private household	2,108	47.8	2,341	44.4	1,769	47.2[3]
Service workers excluding private household	5,545	20.8	6,461	19.9	7,556	20.1
Protective service workers	742	4.3	805	4.6	954	7.0
Waiters, cooks, bartenders	1,593	15.0	1,774	14.3	2,061	14.8
Other service workers	3,210	27.4	3,882	25.7	4,541	25.3
Farm workers	6,070	15.3	4,866	16.1	3,554	11.9
Farmers and farm managers	3,326	8.3	2,595	7.5	1,970	5.4
Farm laborers and foremen	2,744	23.7	2,271	25.8	1,584	20.0
Paid	1,495	31.0	1,382	32.1	1,049	26.8
Unpaid family workers	1,249	15.1	889	16.1	536	6.7

[1] Beginning in 1967, occupational data cover persons 16 years of age and over. Prior to 1967, persons 14 years of age and over are included.

[2] 1957 averages based on observations for January, April, July, and October.

[3] The change in definition of employment eliminating persons 14 and 15 years of age affects comparisons of white–nonwhite employment in this category. If allowances are made for these changes, the proportion of Negroes in this occupation would be slightly lower in 1967 than in 1962.

N.A.–Not available.

Source: Hodge, Claire C. "The Negro Job Situation: Has It Improved?" *Monthly Labor Review,* Washington, D.C.: U. S. Department of Labor, Bureau of Labor Statistics, January, 1969, p. 27.

TABLE 8. Employed Persons by Occupation and Color, Annual Averages, 1962 and 1967. (Numbers in thousands)

Occupation Group	1962[1] White Number	White Per cent	Nonwhite Number	Nonwhite Per cent	1967 White Number	White Per cent	Nonwhite Number	Nonwhite Per cent
Total	60,749	100.0	7,097	100.0	66,361	100.0	8,011	100.0
Professional, technical, and kindred	7,667	12.6	373	5.3	9,287	14.0	592	7.4
Managers, officials, and proprietors	7,220	11.9	188	2.6	7,287	11.0	209	2.6
Clerical	9,594	15.8	512	7.2	11,435	17.2	899	11.2
Sales	4,231	7.0	115	1.6	4,387	6.6	138	1.7
Craftsmen and foremen	8,250	13.6	427	6.0	9,229	13.9	617	7.7
Operatives and kindred	10,629	17.5	1,412	19.9	12,002	18.1	1,882	23.5
Nonfarm laborers	2,597	4.3	962	13.6	2,635	4.0	899	11.2
Service workers	6,476	10.6	2,326	32.8	6,971	10.5	2,353	29.4
Private household	1,301	2.1	1,040	14.7	934	1.4	835	10.4
Service, excluding private household	5,175	8.5	1,286	18.1	6,037	9.1	1,519	19.0
Farm workers	4,084	6.7	782	11.0	3,130	4.7	423	5.3
Farmers and farm managers	2,400	4.0	195	2.7	1,862	2.8	107	1.3
Farm laborers and foremen	1,684	2.8	587	8.3	1,268	1.9	317	4.0

[1] Beginning in 1967, occupational data cover persons 16 years of age and over. Prior to 1967, persons 14 years of age and over are included.

Source: Hodge, Negro Job Situation, p. 26.

TABLE 9.   Nonwhite Workers as a Proportion of all Workers in Higher Status Occupations.

| Occupation | Nonwhite workers as a proportion of all workers in the occupation | | | Increase in Proportion of nonwhite workers required to reach 10.8 per cent of all workers in occupation[1] | Actual increase, 1962-67, as a per cent of the increase required to reach 10.8 per cent |
| | Per cent | | Increase, 1962-67 | | |
	1962	1967	(Percentage points)	(Percentage points)	(Percent)
Professional, technical and kindred workers	4.6	6.0	1.4	6.2	23
Medical and health	5.3	7.6	2.3	5.5	42
Teachers, except college	8.1	9.4	1.3	2.7	48
Others	3.3	4.4	1.1	7.5	15
Managers, officials, and proprietors	2.5	2.8	0.3	8.3	4
Salaried	1.9	2.2	0.3	8.9	3
Self-employed, retail trade	3.7	4.7	1.0	7.1	14
Self-employed, other	2.9	3.8	0.9	7.9	11
Clerical and kindred workers	5.1	7.3	2.2	5.7	39
Stenographers, typists and secretaries	3.8	5.1	1.3	7.0	19
Others	5.5	8.0	2.5	5.3	47
Sales workers	2.6	3.0	0.4	8.2	5
Retail trade	3.0	3.6	0.6	7.8	8
Other	2.1	2.2	0.1	8.7	1
Craftsmen, foremen, and kindred workers	4.9	6.3	1.4	5.9	24
Carpenters	5.4	6.2	0.8	5.4	15
Construction craftsmen except carpenters	6.5	8.2	1.7	4.3	40
Mechanics and repairmen	6.2	7.6	1.4	4.6	30
Metal crafts except mechanics	3.4	5.5	2.1	7.4	28
Other craftsmen	4.3	5.4	1.1	6.5	17
Foremen, not elsewhere classified	2.2	3.4	1.2	8.6	14
Protective service workers	4.6	7.0	2.4	6.2	39

[1] Difference between 1962 level and 10.8 percent (the proportion of Negroes in the employed labor force in 1967).
NOTE: Operatives and kindred workers are not included in this table because the nonwhite proportion was greater than 10.8 percent of all workers in the occupation in 1967. (see table 4.)
Source: Hodge, *Negro Job Situation,* p. 24.

TABLE 10. Nonwhite Workers by Occupation, Annual Averages, 1957, 1962, and 1967. (Numbers in thousands)

Occupation Group	1957[1,2]	1962[1]	1967	Change 1957 to 1962 (Per cent)	Change 1962 to 1967 (Per cent)
Total, 16 years of age and over	6,647	7,004	8,011	5.4	14.4
Total, 14 years of age and over	6,749	7,097	—	5.2	12.9[3]
Professional, technical, and kindred	246	373	592	51.6	58.7
Medical and health	42	72	120	71.4	66.7
Teachers, excluding college	88	138	202	56.8	46.4
Other	116	163	271	40.5	66.3
Managers, officials, and proprietors	140	188	209	34.3	11.2
Salaried	35	77	115	120.0	49.4
Self-employed, retail trade	61	59	51	-3.3	-13.6
Self-employed, excluding retail trade	44	52	43	18.2	-17.3
Clerical	401	512	899	27.7	75.6
Stenographers, typists and secretaries	80	95	163	18.8	71.6
Other	321	417	736	29.9	76.5
Sales	78	115	138	47.4	20.0
Retail trade	62	77	99	24.2	28.6
Other	16	38	39	137.5	2.6
Craftsmen and foremen	380	427	617	12.4	44.5
Carpenters	35	44	52	25.7	18.2
Construction excluding carpenters	92	111	157	20.7	41.4
Mechanics and repairmen	119	133	192	11.8	44.4
Metal craftsmen excluding mechanics	35	36	69	2.9	91.7
Other craftsmen	76	76	100	0.0	31.6
Foremen, not elsewhere classified	23	27	49	17.4	81.5
Operatives and kindred workers	1,411	1,412	1,882	0.1	33.3
Drivers and deliverymen	314	303	354	-3.5	16.8

TABLE 10 continued

Occupation Group	1957[1,2]	1962[1]	1967	Change 1957 to 1962 (Per cent)	Change 1962 to 1967 (Per cent)
Other	1,097	1,110	1,528	1.2	37.7
Durable goods manufacturing	342	359	575	5.0	60.2
Nondurable goods manufacturing	286	306	484	7.0	58.2
Other industries	469	445	469	-5.1	5.4
Nonfarm laborers	1,007	962	899	-4.5	-6.5
Construction	–	225	197	–	-12.4
Manufacturing	–	264	285	–	8.0
Other industries	–	473	416	–	-12.1
Service workers	2,159	2,326	2,353	7.7	1.2
Private households	1,008	1,040	835	3.2	-19.7
Service workers, excluding private household	1,151	1,286	1,519	11.7	18.1
Protective service workers	32	37	67	15.6	81.1
Waiters, cooks, bartenders	239	253	304	5.9	20.2
Other service workers	880	996	1,149	13.2	15.4
Farm workers	927	782	423	-15.6	-45.9
Farmers and farm managers	276	195	107	-29.3	-45.1
Farm laborers and foremen	651	587	317	-9.8	-46.0
Paid	463	444	281	-4.1	-36.7
Unpaid family workers	188	143	36	-23.9	-74.8

[1] Beginning in 1967, occupational data cover persons 16 years of age and over. Prior to 1967, occupational data have not been revised to exclude persons 14–15 years of age except for the figures on total employment shown here for comparison with 1967 total employment.

[2] 1957 averages based on observations for January, April, July, and October; 1962 and 1967 are based on 12-month averages.

[3] Based on change between 1962 including persons 14 years of age and over, and 1967 including persons 16 years and over.

Note: Dashes indicate data not available.

Source: Hodge, *Negro Job Situation*, p. 22.

TABLE 11.   Negro Employment by Occupation and Industry in the Baltimore Standard Metropolitan Statistical Area (SMSA), 1969.

	Total Employment	White-Collar Occupations						Blue-Collar Occupations				
		Total White-Collar Employment	Officials & Managers	Professionals	Technicians	Sales Workers	Office & Clerical	Total Blue-Collar Employment	Craftsmen	Operatives	Laborers	Service Workers
Primary metal industries												
Negro												
Total	10,227	296	127	4	36	0	129	9,635	705	5,450	3,480	296
Occupational distrib.	100.0	2.9	1.2	0.1	0.4	0.0	1.3	94.2	6.9	53.3	34.0	2.9
Participation rate	30.3	4.0	3.9	0.6	5.7	0.0	4.7	37.4	9.9	41.0	64.9	52.3
All employees												
Total (19 estab.)	33,803	7,455	3,263	678	627	128	2,759	25,782	7,134	13,282	5,366	566
Occupational distrib.	100.0	22.1	9.7	2.0	1.9	0.4	8.2	76.3	21.1	39.3	15.9	1.7
Printing & publishing etc.												
Negro												
Total	753	162	10	6	0	49	97	523	80	344	99	68
Occupational distrib.	100.0	21.5	1.3	0.7	0.0	6.5	12.9	69.5	10.6	45.7	13.1	9.0
Participation rate	10.4	5.4	1.9	1.2	0.0	5.7	9.2	12.7	3.9	20.8	22.8	53.5
All employees												
Total (27 estab.)	7,252	2,994	517	502	55	866	1,054	4,131	2,044	1,653	434	127
Occupational distrib.	100.0	41.3	7.1	6.9	0.8	11.9	14.5	57.0	28.2	22.8	6.0	1.8
Paper & allied products												
Negro												
Total	1,563	37	14	1	2	1	19	1,482	237	676	569	44
Occupational distrib.	100.0	2.4	0.8	0.1	0.1	0.1	1.2	94.8	15.2	43.3	36.4	2.8
Participation rate	22.3	2.3	2.5	1.4	2.2	0.4	3.0	27.8	17.7	26.4	39.7	56.4
All employees												
Total (37 estab.)	6,998	1,593	563	72	91	229	638	5,327	1,337	2,557	1,433	78
Occupational distrib.	100.0	22.8	8.0	1.0	1.3	3.3	9.1	76.1	19.1	36.5	20.5	1.1
Retail trade												
Negro												
Total	3,657	1,735	126	26	15	1,023	545	1,074	209	352	513	848
Occupational distrib.	100.0	47.4	3.4	0.7	0.4	28.0	14.9	29.5	5.7	9.6	14.0	23.2
Participation rate	18.9	11.7	6.0	17.3	6.8	11.8	14.8	37.0	25.7	33.6	49.4	52.9
All employees												
Total (52 estab.)	19,314	14,812	2,096	150	219	8,661	3,686	2,899	812	1,048	1,039	1,603
Occupational distrib.	100.0	76.7	10.9	0.8	1.1	27.6	19.1	15.0	4.2	5.4	5.4	8.3

Table 11 continued

	Total Employment	White-Collar Occupations						Blue-Collar Occupations				
		Total White-Collar Employment	Officials & Managers	Professionals	Technicians	Sales Workers	Office & Clerical	Total Blue-Collar Employment	Craftsmen	Operatives	Laborers	Service Workers
Food & kindred products												
Negro												
Total	2,551	331	42	8	11	210	60	2,031	264	748	1,019	189
Occupational distrib.	100.0	13.0	1.6	0.3	0.4	8.2	2.4	80.0	10.3	29.3	40.0	7.4
Participation rate	19.6	6.7	3.2	5.3	8.6	9.8	4.9	26.4	14.8	23.2	37.9	57.1
All employees												
Total (51 estab.)	12,988	4,960	1,322	151	128	2,137	1,222	7,697	1,787	3,220	2,690	331
Occupational distrib.	100.0	38.2	10.2	1.2	1.0	16.5	9.4	59.3	13.8	24.8	20.7	2.5
Textile mill products												
Negro												
Total	252	17	2	0	1	0	14	225	7	133	85	10
Occupational distrib.	100.0	6.7	1.0	0.0	0.4	0.0	5.6	89.3	2.8	52.8	33.7	4.0
Participation rate	12.7	3.7	1.3	0.0	5.3	0.0	6.3	15.1	6.7	12.6	25.2	27.8
All employees												
Total (9 estab.)	1,989	459	153	19	19	45	223	1,494	105	1,052	337	36
Occupational distrib.	100.0	23.1	7.7	1.0	1.0	2.3	11.2	75.1	5.3	52.9	17.0	1.8
Rubber & plastic products												
Negro												
Total	848	36	6	3	13	0	14	785	54	517	214	27
Occupational distrib.	100.0	4.2	0.7	0.4	1.5	0.0	1.7	92.6	6.4	61.0	25.2	3.2
Participation rate	30.3	6.5	2.7	4.3	23.2	0.0	8.0	35.7	18.9	37.0	41.7	57.4
All employees												
Total (15 estab.)	2,800	556	219	70	56	35	176	2,197	286	1,398	513	47
Occupational distrib.	100.0	19.9	7.8	2.5	2.0	1.3	6.3	78.5	10.2	49.9	18.3	1.7
Stone, clay, & glass products												
Negro												
Total	1,611	16	6	1	2	0	7	1,553	113	1,095	345	42
Occupational distrib.	100.0	1.0	0.3	0.1	0.1	0.0	0.4	96.4	7.0	68.0	21.4	2.6
Participation rate	32.3	1.7	1.4	1.1	1.7	0.0	2.9	38.7	11.9	45.3	53.2	73.7
All employees												
Total (20 estab.)	4,991	916	422	95	120	35	244	4,018	953	2,417	648	57
Occupational distrib.	100.0	18.4	8.5	1.9	2.4	0.7	4.9	80.5	19.1	48.4	13.0	1.1

Table 11 continued

	Total Employment	White-Collar Occupations						Blue-Collar Occupations				
		Total White-Collar Employment	Officials & Managers	Professionals	Technicians	Sales Workers	Office & Clerical	Total Blue-Collar Employment	Craftsmen	Operatives	Laborers	Service Workers
Fabricated metal products												
Negro												
Total	2,102	58	9	2	4	3	40	1,997	205	1,126	666	47
Occupational distrib.	100.0	2.8	0.4	0.1	0.2	0.1	1.9	95.0	9.8	53.6	31.7	2.2
Participation rate	17.8	1.9	1.0	0.7	1.2	0.7	3.6	23.2	7.8	25.7	41.2	34.8
All employees												
Total (35 estab.)	11,816	3,073	866	305	329	450	1,123	8,608	2,612	4,380	1,616	135
Occupational distrib.	100.0	26.0	7.3	2.6	2.8	3.8	9.5	72.9	22.1	37.1	13.7	7.4
Apparel & related products												
Negro												
Total	727	95	11	0	1	0	83	589	116	427	46	43
Occupational distrib.	100.0	13.1	1.5	0.0	0.1	0.0	11.4	81.0	16.0	58.7	6.3	5.9
Participation rate	12.8	7.5	3.4	0.0	2.9	0.0	11.4	13.5	9.9	14.4	22.2	53.1
All employees												
Total (27 estab.)	5,695	1,263	326	69	35	103	730	4,351	1,176	2,968	207	81
Occupational distrib.	100.0	22.2	5.7	1.2	0.6	1.8	12.8	76.4	20.6	52.1	21.8	1.4
Machinery (Non-electrical)												
Negro												
Total	1,325	173	12	45	23	0	93	1,091	25	390	676	61
Occupational distrib.	100.0	13.1	0.9	3.4	1.7	0.0	7.0	82.3	1.9	29.4	51.0	4.6
Participation rate	13.2	5.8	1.6	8.1	4.8	0.0	8.5	15.9	0.9	14.4	47.5	37.9
All employees												
Total (28 estab.)	10,008	2,964	746	555	483	89	1,091	6,883	2,750	2,710	1,423	161
Occupational distrib.	100.0	29.6	7.5	5.5	4.8	0.9	10.9	68.8	27.5	27.1	14.2	1.6
Chemicals & allied products												
Negro												
Total	1,944	143	27	16	61	2	37	1,715	215	867	633	86
Occupational distrib.	100.0	7.4	1.4	0.8	3.1	0.1	0.2	88.2	11.1	44.6	32.6	4.4
Participation rate	19.7	3.6	2.7	2.1	9.1	0.5	3.4	30.2	15.1	30.3	45.4	37.2
All employees												
Total (43 estab.)	9,871	3,966	1,015	759	674	423	1,095	5,674	1,420	2,860	1,394	231
Occupational distrib.	100.0	40.2	10.3	7.7	6.8	4.3	11.1	57.5	14.4	29.0	14.1	2.3

Table 11 continued

	Total Employ-ment	White-Collar Occupations						Total Blue-Collar Em-ployment	Blue-Collar Occupations			Service Workers
		Total White-Collar Em-ployment	Officials & Managers	Profes-sionals	Techni-cians	Sales Workers	Office & Clerical		Crafts-men	Opera-tives	Laborers	
Totals												
Negro employment	27,560	3,099	392	112	169	1,288	1,138	22,700	2,230	12,125	8,345	1,761
All employees	127,525	45,011	11,508	3,425	2,836	13,201	14,041	79,061	22,416	39,545	17,180	3,453
Negro participation rate	21.6	6.9	3.4	3.3	6.0	9.8	8.1	28.7	9.9	30.7	48.6	51.0

Note: Because of rounding, sums of individual items may not equal totals.

Source: Equal Employment Opportunity Report No. 1. Washington, D.C.: Equal Opportunity Employment Commission, 1969.

TABLE 12.   Negro Employment by Occupation and Industry in the Detroit SMSA, 1969.

	Total Employ-ment	White-Collar Occupations						Blue-Collar Occupations				
		Total White-Collar Em-ployment	Officials & Managers	Profes-sionals	Techni-cians	Sales Workers	Office & Clerical	Total Blue-Collar Em-ployment	Crafts-men	Opera-tives	Laborers	Service Workers
Contract construction												
Negro												
Total	835	47	6	3	5	1	32	765	189	167	409	23
Occupational distrib.	100.0	5.6	0.7	0.4	0.6	0.1	3.8	91.6	22.6	20.0	49.0	2.8
Participation rate	10.7	2.4	0.8	0.8	2.9	0.4	5.0	14.0	5.4	9.7	40.2	46.4
All employees												
Total (56 estab.)	8,972	1,957	582	387	235	111	642	7,551	1,216	1,315	985	106
Occupational distrib.	100.0	21.8	6.5	4.3	2.6	1.2	7.2	84.2	13.6	14.7	11.0	1.2
Furnitures & fixtures												
Negro												
Total	162	4	1	0	1	0	2	155	20	58	77	3
Occupational distrib.	100.0	2.5	0.6	0.0	0.6	0.0	1.2	95.7	12.3	35.8	47.5	1.9
Participation rate	21.4	2.6	2.0	0.0	9.1	0.0	3.8	26.2	17.1	19.3	44.3	33.3
All employees												
Total (6 estab.)	756	155	50	19	11	22	53	592	117	301	174	9
Occupational distrib.	100.0	20.5	6.6	2.5	1.5	2.9	7.0	78.3	15.5	39.8	23.0	1.2
Printing & publishing industries												
Negro												
Total	897	412	9	13	10	40	340	334	83	158	93	151
Occupational distrib.	100.0	45.9	1.0	1.4	1.1	4.5	37.9	37.2	9.3	17.6	10.4	16.8
Participation rate	9.7	8.5	1.0	2.5	5.0	3.2	17.3	8.0	4.1	9.5	18.0	58.8
All employees												
Total (33 estab.)	9,264	4,831	876	530	201	1,259	1,965	4,176	2,002	1,658	516	257
Occupational distrib.	100.0	52.1	9.5	5.7	2.2	13.6	21.2	45.1	21.6	17.9	5.6	2.8
Chemicals & allied products												
Negro												
Total	1,043	216	22	20	46	14	114	747	55	342	350	80
Occupational distrib.	100.0	20.7	2.1	1.9	4.4	1.3	10.9	71.6	5.3	32.8	33.6	7.7
Participation rate	7.1	2.8	1.2	1.6	5.9	0.8	5.5	11.1	3.3	9.5	23.6	17.9
All employees												
Total (51 estab.)	14,769	7,597	1,826	1,233	778	1,679	2,081	6,724	1,642	3,599	1,483	448
Occupational distrib.	100.0	51.4	12.4	8.3	52.7	11.4	14.1	45.5	11.1	24.4	10.0	3.0

Table 12 continued

	Total Employment	White-Collar Occupations						Blue-Collar Occupations				
		Total White-Collar Employment	Officials & Managers	Professionals	Technicians	Sales Workers	Office & Clerical	Total Blue-Collar Employment	Craftsmen	Operatives	Laborers	Service Workers
Stone, clay, & glass products												
Negro												
Total	814	31	8	3	5	0	15	768	81	357	330	15
Occupational distrib.	100.0	3.8	1.0	0.4	0.6	0.0	1.8	94.3	10.0	43.9	40.5	1.8
Participation rate	13.4	2.1	1.6	1.2	2.9	0.0	3.2	17.2	11.5	14.4	25.9	16.5
All employees												
Total (31 estab.)	6,057	1,509	490	243	172	135	469	4,457	705	2,477	1,275	91
Occupational distrib.	100.0	24.9	8.1	4.0	2.8	2.2	7.7	73.6	11.6	40.9	21.1	1.5
Primary metal industries												
Negro												
Total	5,476	150	75	10	23	0	42	5,227	387	3,696	1,144	99
Occupational distrib.	100.0	2.7	1.4	0.2	0.4	0.0	0.8	95.5	7.1	67.5	20.9	1.8
Participation rate	24.6	3.3	4.2	2.0	4.0	0.0	3.1	30.0	8.7	37.4	37.1	34.0
All employees												
Total (62 estab.)	22,233	4,536	1,780	496	569	323	1,368	17,406	4,441	9,878	3,087	291
Occupational distrib.	100.0	20.4	8.0	2.2	2.6	1.5	6.2	78.3	20.0	44.4	13.9	1.3
Fabricated metal products												
Negro												
Total	2,977	82	24	2	14	0	42	2,825	143	1,857	825	70
Occupational distrib.	100.0	2.8	0.8	0.1	1.4	0.0	1.4	94.9	4.8	62.4	27.7	2.4
Participation rate	12.5	1.7	1.4	0.5	2.4	0.0	2.2	15.3	4.4	17.7	17.6	17.0
All employees												
Total (109 estab.)	23,798	4,937	1,688	392	595	346	1,916	18,450	3,243	10,512	4,695	411
Occupational distrib.	100.0	20.7	7.1	1.6	2.5	1.5	8.1	77.5	13.6	44.2	19.7	1.7
Machinery (non-electrical)												
Negro												
Total	2,104	373	18	23	98	4	230	1,521	199	925	397	210
Occupational distrib.	100.0	17.7	0.8	1.1	4.7	0.2	11.0	72.2	9.5	44.0	18.9	10.0
Participation rate	4.7	2.2	0.5	0.7	2.8	0.4	4.3	5.6	1.8	7.3	13.3	24.3
All employees												
Total (159 estab.)	44,800	17,000	3,806	3,408	3,447	992	5,347	26,936	11,319	12,626	2,991	864
Occupational distrib.	100.0	37.9	8.5	7.6	7.7	2.2	11.9	66.8	25.3	28.2	6.7	1.9

Table 12 continued

	Total Employment	White-Collar Occupations						Blue-Collar Occupations				
		Total White-Collar Employment	Officials & Managers	Professionals	Technicians	Sales Workers	Office & Clerical	Total Blue-Collar Employment	Craftsmen	Operatives	Laborers	Service Workers
Electrical machinery, equipment & supplies												
Negro												
Total	2,762	317	62	23	28	3	201	2,349	125	1,917	307	96
Occupational distrib.	100.0	11.5	2.2	0.8	1.0	0.1	7.3	85.0	4.5	69.4	11.1	3.5
Participation rate	26.2	10.4	7.2	6.0	5.9	1.9	17.3	32.3	8.5	38.8	35.8	46.6
All employees												
Total (31 estab.)	10,527	3,042	864	386	474	158	1,160	7,279	1,476	4,946	857	206
Occupational distrib.	100.0	28.9	8.2	3.7	4.5	1.5	11.0	69.1	14.0	47.0	8.1	2.0
Transportation equipment												
Negro												
Total	41,308	1,745	487	167	160	1	930	37,774	1,086	34,307	2,381	1,789
Occupational distrib.	100.0	4.2	1.2	0.4	0.4	0.0	2.3	91.4	2.6	83.1	5.8	4.3
Participation rate	24.4	3.3	3.3	1.3	1.8	0.3	6.0	33.9	4.7	41.8	38.3	34.3
All employees												
Total (105 estab.)	169,572	52,900	14,873	13,201	8,987	369	15,470	111,453	23,136	82,102	6,215	5,219
Occupational distrib.	100.0	31.2	8.8	7.8	5.3	0.2	9.1	65.7	13.6	48.4	3.7	3.1
Instruments & related products												
Negro												
Total	92	17	0	1	4	1	11	60	2	23	35	15
Occupational distrib.	100.0	18.5	0.0	1.1	4.3	1.1	12.1	65.2	2.2	25.0	38.0	16.3
Participation rate	5.9	2.3	0.0	1.4	3.8	0.7	4.2	7.7	0.6	7.2	24.1	40.5
All employees												
Total (14 estab.)	1,565	747	173	70	105	140	259	781	318	318	145	37
Occupational distrib.	100.0	47.7	11.1	4.5	6.7	8.9	16.5	49.9	20.3	20.3	9.3	6.5
Motor freight transportation												
Negro												
Total	650	167	28	0	7	3	129	450	58	239	153	33
Occupational distrib.	100.0	25.7	4.3	0.0	1.1	0.5	19.8	69.2	8.9	36.8	23.5	5.1
Participation rate	4.5	3.5	2.0	0.0	2.4	1.2	4.8	4.8	4.4	3.8	8.9	18.3
All employees												
Total (98 estab.)	14,302	4,818	1,367	210	294	260	2,687	9,304	1,329	6,254	1,721	180
Occupational distrib.	100.0	33.7	13.1	1.5	20.6	1.8	18.8	65.1	9.3	43.7	12.0	1.3

Table 12 continued

	Total Employment	White-Collar Occupations						Blue-Collar Occupations				
		Total White-Collar Employment	Officials & Managers	Professionals	Technicians	Sales Workers	Office & Clerical	Total Blue-Collar Employment	Crafts-men	Opera-tives	Laborers	Service Workers
Wholesale trade												
Negro												
Total	2,727	812	51	51	70	268	372	1,767	164	873	730	148
Occupational distrib.	100.0	29.8	1.9	1.9	2.6	9.8	13.6	64.8	22.6	32.0	26.8	5.4
Participation rate	10.7	4.9	1.7	2.6	4.2	5.9	6.7	21.6	7.5	22.6	34.0	26.1
All employees												
Total (345 estab.)	25,491	16,734	3,033	1,942	1,678	4,539	5,542	8,190	2,180	3,866	2,144	567
Occupational distrib.	100.0	65.6	11.9	7.6	6.6	17.8	21.7	26.3	8.6	15.2	8.4	2.2
Retail trade												
Negro												
Total	4,592	2,549	161	10	11	1,633	734	670	129	300	241	1,373
Occupational distrib.	100.0	55.5	3.5	0.2	0.2	35.6	16.0	14.6	2.8	6.5	5.2	29.9
Participation rate	12.2	8.6	4.8	5.2	7.0	8.5	11.1	16.7	9.6	17.9	23.8	33.1
All employees												
Total (59 estab.)	37,714	29,539	3,383	192	158	19,191	6,615	4,024	1,338	1,674	1,012	4,151
Occupational distrib.	100.0	78.3	9.0	0.5	0.4	50.9	17.5	10.7	3.5	4.4	2.7	11.0
Personal services												
Negro												
Total	1,391	98	25	0	2	38	33	1,151	101	438	612	142
Occupational distrib.	100.0	7.0	1.8	0.0	0.1	2.7	2.4	82.7	7.3	31.5	44.0	10.2
Participation rate	59.9	13.1	21.6	0.0	5.4	8.4	23.7	82.9	55.8	76.4	96.5	75.9
All employees												
Total (11 estab.)	2,321	746	116	3	37	451	139	1,388	181	573	634	187
Occupational distrib.	100.0	32.1	5.0	0.1	1.6	19.4	6.0	59.8	7.8	24.7	27.3	8.1
Miscellaneous business services												
Negro												
Total	4,832	2,780	99	148	36	21	2,476	710	447	138	125	1,342
Occupational distrib.	100.0	57.5	2.0	3.1	0.7	0.4	51.2	14.7	9.3	2.9	2.6	27.8
Participation rate	22.3	20.5	4.6	5.7	4.8	3.6	33.1	13.9	12.7	15.3	18.0	45.3
All employees												
Total (103 estab.)	21,625	13,543	2,148	2,587	743	584	7,481	5,119	3,520	903	696	2,963
Occupational distrib.	100.0	62.6	9.9	12.0	3.4	2.7	34.6	23.7	16.3	4.2	3.2	13.7

Table 12 continued

	Total Employ-ment	White-Collar Occupations						Blue-Collar Occupations				Service Workers
		Total White-Collar Em-ployment	Officials & Managers	Profes-sionals	Techni-cians	Sales Workers	Office & Clerical	Total Blue-Collar Em-ployment	Crafts-men	Opera-tives	Laborers	
Totals												
Negro employment	72,662	9,800	1,076	474	520	2,027	5,703	57,273	3,269	45,795	8,209	5,589
All employees	413,766	164,591	37,055	25,299	18,484	30,559	53,194	233,830	58,163	143,002	28,630	15,987
Negro participation rate	17.6	6.0	2.9	1.9	2.8	6.6	10.7	24.5	5.6	32.0	28.7	35.0

Note: Because of rounding, sums of individual items may not equal totals.

Source: Equal Employment Opportunity Report No. 1 Washington, D.C.: Equal Employment Opportunity Commission, 1969.

TABLE 13. Negro Employment by Occupation and Industry in the Houston SMSA, 1969.

	Total Employment	White-Collar Occupations						Blue-Collar Occupations				
		Total White-Collar Employment	Officials & Managers	Professionals	Technicians	Sales Workers	Office & Clerical	Total Blue-Collar Employment	Craftsmen	Operatives	Laborers	Service Workers
Crude petroleum & natural gas												
Negro												
Total	631	200	3	16	47	2	132	328	63	208	57	103
Occupational distrib.	100.0	31.6	0.4	2.5	7.4	0.3	20.9	51.9	9.9	32.9	9.0	16.3
Participation rate	5.0	2.4	0.2	0.6	3.1	1.1	4.9	8.5	3.9	12.1	11.0	64.8
All employees												
Total (95 estab.)	12,538	8,505	1,484	2,621	1,505	188	2,707	3,874	1,636	1,719	519	159
Occupational distrib.	100.0	67.8	11.8	20.9	12.0	1.4	21.5	30.8	13.0	13.7	4.1	1.2
Contract construction												
Negro												
Total	1,392	68	3	13	22	0	30	1,295	176	283	836	29
Occupational distrib.	100.0	4.8	0.2	0.9	1.5	0.0	2.1	93.0	12.6	20.3	60.0	2.0
Participation rate	10.8	1.3	0.3	1.0	1.5	0.0	2.5	16.3	3.4	23.8	50.1	34.5
All employees												
Total (94 estab.)	12,854	4,867	984	1,254	1,388	70	1,171	7,903	5,048	1,189	1,666	84
Occupational distrib.	100.0	37.8	7.6	9.7	10.7	0.5	9.1	61.4	39.2	9.2	12.9	0.6
Food & kindred products												
Negro												
Total	2,647	200	41	3	24	92	40	2,320	189	1,115	1,016	127
Occupational distrib.	100.0	7.6	1.5	0.1	0.9	3.5	1.5	87.6	7.1	42.1	38.4	4.7
Participation rate	23.8	4.4	3.5	0.9	11.3	5.3	3.6	36.9	15.1	38.9	47.0	47.2
All employees												
Total (57 estab.)	11,117	4,565	1,169	332	212	1,744	1,108	6,283	1,252	2,870	2,161	269
Occupational distrib.	100.0	41.0	10.5	2.9	1.9	15.6	9.9	56.5	11.3	25.8	19.4	2.4
Chemicals & allied products												
Negro												
Total	1,398	138	16	16	43	3	60	1,166	142	655	369	94
Occupational distrib.	100.0	9.9	1.1	1.1	3.1	0.2	4.3	83.4	10.2	46.9	26.4	6.7
Participation rate	6.0	1.2	0.5	0.6	2.4	0.5	2.4	10.1	3.3	10.3	42.0	20.9
All employees												
Total (102 estab.)	23,153	11,144	3,388	2,860	1,820	579	2,497	11,560	4,334	6,348	878	449
Occupational distrib.	100.0	48.1	14.6	12.4	7.9	2.5	10.8	49.9	18.7	27.4	3.8	1.9

Table 13 continued

	Total Employment	White-Collar Occupations						Blue-Collar Occupations				
		Total White-Collar Employment	Officials & Managers	Professionals	Technicians	Sales Workers	Office & Clerical	Total Blue-Collar Employment	Crafts-men	Opera-tives	Laborers	Service Workers
Primary metal industries												
Negro												
Total	2,378	40	16	1	5	1	17	2,306	487	1,455	364	32
Occupational distrib.	100.0	1.7	0.7	0.0	0.2	0.0	0.7	97.0	20.5	61.2	15.3	1.3
Participation rate	29.0	1.8	1.7	0.5	1.7	0.9	2.5	38.8	20.0	52.2	50.1	41.6
All employees												
Total (25 estab.)	8,209	2,185	924	183	286	116	676	5,947	2,433	2,787	727	77
Occupational distrib.	100.0	26.6	11.3	2.2	3.5	1.4	8.2	72.4	29.6	34.0	8.9	0.9
Fabricated metal products												
Negro												
Total	1,581	38	9	1	7	0	21	1,516	147	910	459	27
Occupational distrib.	100.0	2.4	0.6	0.1	0.4	0.0	1.3	95.9	9.3	57.6	29.0	1.7
Participation rate	17.7	1.5	1.2	0.6	2.1	0.0	2.1	24.1	7.1	28.0	46.9	47.4
All employees												
Total (57 estab.)	8,953	2,602	746	162	341	374	979	6,294	2,066	3,249	979	57
Occupational distrib.	100.0	29.1	8.3	1.8	3.8	4.2	11.0	70.3	23.1	36.3	11.0	0.6
Pipeline transportation												
Negro												
Total	65	23	0	3	8	0	12	42	0	7	35	0
Occupational distrib.	100.0	35.4	0.0	4.6	12.3	0.0	18.5	64.6	0.0	10.8	53.8	0.0
Participation rate	4.0	2.2	0.0	1.0	6.2	0.0	3.4	7.5	0.0	2.5	25.0	0.0
All employees												
Total (16 estab.)	1,613	1,051	258	294	128	22	349	562	144	278	140	0
Occupational distrib.	100.0	65.2	16.0	18.2	7.9	1.4	21.6	34.8	8.9	17.2	8.7	0.0
Wholesale trade												
Negro												
Total	2,647	285	15	7	38	36	189	2,289	425	1,291	573	73
Occupational distrib.	100.0	10.8	0.6	0.3	1.4	1.4	7.1	86.5	16.1	48.8	21.6	2.8
Participate rate	12.8	2.2	0.6	0.5	3.3	1.2	3.8	31.8	16.9	37.0	48.2	21.2
All employees												
Total (315 estab.)	20,673	13,133	2,483	1,405	1,141	3,066	5,038	7,196	2,520	3,487	1,189	344
Occupational distrib.	100.0	63.5	12.0	6.8	5.5	14.8	24.4	34.8	12.2	16.9	5.8	1.7

Table 13 continued

	Total Employment	White-Collar Occupations						Blue-Collar Occupations				
		Total White-Collar Employment	Officials & Managers	Professionals	Technicians	Sales Workers	Office & Clerical	Total Blue-Collar Employment	Craftsmen	Operatives	Laborers	Service Workers
Retail trade												
Negro												
Total	2,252	931	50	2	8	603	268	634	67	287	280	687
Occupational distrib.	100.0	41.3	2.2	0.1	0.4	26.8	11.9	28.2	3.0	12.7	12.4	30.5
Participation rate	12.5	6.6	2.8	3.4	5.8	7.1	7.6	25.6	9.1	30.6	35.1	44.8
All employees												
Total (55 estab.)	18,025	14,021	1,761	59	138	8,519	3,544	2,472	736	939	797	1,532
Occupational distrib.	100.0	77.8	9.8	0.3	0.8	47.3	19.7	13.7	4.1	5.2	4.4	8.5
Real estate												
Negro												
Total	65	3	0	0	0	0	3	6	0	4	2	56
Occupational distrib.	100.0	4.6	0.0	0.0	0.0	0.0	4.6	9.2	0.0	6.1	3.1	86.2
Participation rate	9.9	1.0	0.0	0.0	0.0	0.0	2.1	3.7	0.0	16.0	11.1	27.9
All employees												
Total (15 estab.)	658	295	60	57	16	20	142	162	119	25	18	201
Occupational distrib.	100.0	44.8	9.1	8.7	2.4	3.0	21.6	24.6	18.1	3.8	2.7	30.5
Banking												
Negro												
Total	428	352	5	1	4	0	342	34	0	29	5	42
Occupational distrib.	100.0	82.2	1.1	0.1	1.0	0.0	80.0	8.0	0.0	6.8	1.1	9.8
Participation rate	7.3	6.4	0.6	0.3	2.5	0.0	8.3	44.2	0.0	64.4	100.0	19.0
All employees												
Total (16 estab.)	5,836	5,538	895	349	163	15	4,116	77	27	45	5	221
Occupational distrib.	100.0	81.0	15.3	6.0	2.8	0.1	70.5	1.3	0.1	0.1	0.1	3.8
Totals												
Negro employment	15,484	2,278	416	63	206	737	1,114	11,936	1,696	6,244	3,996	1,270
All employees	123,629	67,906	14,152	9,576	7,138	14,713	22,327	52,330	20,315	22,936	9,079	3,393
Negro participation rate	12.5	3.4	2.9	0.7	2.9	5.0	5.0	22.8	8.3	27.2	44.0	37.4

Note: Because of rounding sums of individual items may not equal totals.

Source: Equal Employment Opportunity Report No 1. Washington, D.C.: Equal Employment Opportunity Commission, 1969.

TABLE 14. Negro Employment by Occupation and Industry in the Los Angeles SMSA, 1969.

	Total Employ-ment	White-Collar Occupations						Blue-Collar Occupations				
		Total White-Collar Employment	Officials & Managers	Profes-sionals	Techni-cians	Sales Workers	Office & Clerical	Total Blue-Collar Employment	Crafts-men	Opera-tives	Laborers	Service Workers
Crude petroleum & natural gas												
Negro												
Total	131	106	0	6	8	0	92	25	11	11	3	0
Occupational distrib.	100.0	80.9	0.0	4.6	6.1	0.0	70.2	19.1	8.4	8.4	2.3	0.0
Participation rate	2.7	3.2	0.0	.5	2.1	0.0	7.6	1.7	1.5	1.8	4.8	0.0
All employees												
Total (38 estab.)	4,777	3,344	565	1,177	373	21	1,208	1,429	746	621	62	4
Occupational distrib.	100.0	70.0	11.8	24.6	7.8	.4	25.3	29.9	15.6	13.0	1.3	.1
Contract construction												
Negro												
Total	1,022	145	4	33	40	1	67	874	305	156	413	3
Occupational distrib.	100.0	14.2	0.4	3.2	3.9	0.1	6.6	85.5	29.8	15.3	40.4	0.4
Participation rate	5.6	1.8	0.3	0.9	3.9	0.5	2.9	8.9	5.9	6.2	19.7	3.3
All employees												
Total (78 estab.)	18,129	8,254	1,297	3,450	1,039	188	2,280	9,784	5,183	2,508	2,093	91
Occupational distrib.	100.0	45.5	7.2	19.0	5.7	0.0	12.6	54.0	28.6	13.8	11.5	0.5
Food & kindred products												
Negro												
Total	1,727	205	23	4	19	104	55	1,396	125	551	720	126
Occupational distrib.	100.0	11.9	1.3	0.2	1.1	6.0	3.2	80.8	7.2	31.9	41.7	7.3
Participation rate	7.4	2.6	1.5	0.7	6.6	2.7	2.9	9.4	3.9	8.2	14.5	23.8
All employees												
Total (121 estab.)	23,431	8,029	1,499	553	289	3,814	1,874	14,872	3,210	6,696	4,966	530
Occupational distrib.	100.0	34.3	6.4	2.4	1.2	16.3	8.0	63.5	13.7	28.6	21.2	2.3
Apparel & related products												
Negro												
Total	345	55	4	0	6	11	34	247	86	106	55	43
Occupational distrib.	100.0	15.9	1.2	0.0	1.7	3.2	9.9	71.6	24.9	30.7	15.9	12.5
Participation rate	6.2	4.3	1.3	0.0	9.7	2.8	7.5	5.9	5.0	5.0	14.7	39.4
All employees												
Total (34 estab.)	5,596	1,288	314	60	62	396	456	4,199	1,704	2,120	375	109
Occupational distrib.	100.0	23.0	5.6	1.1	1.1	7.1	8.2	75.0	30.5	37.9	6.7	1.9

Table 14 continued

	Total Employment	White-Collar Occupations						Blue-Collar Occupations				
		Total White-Collar Employment	Officials & Managers	Professionals	Technicians	Sales Workers	Office & Clerical	Total Blue-Collar Employment	Craftsmen	Operatives	Laborers	Service Workers
Furniture & fixtures												
Negro												
Total	712	28	11	1	5	0	11	675	89	402	184	9
Occupational distrib.	100.0	4.0	1.5	0.1	0.7	0.0	1.5	94.8	12.4	56.5	25.8	1.3
Participation rate	13.0	2.1	2.6	1.1	7.6	0.0	2.0	16.5	9.3	18.5	18.9	22.5
All employees												
Total (31 estab.)	5,482	1,341	418	95	66	207	555	4,101	958	2,170	973	40
Occupational distrib.	100.0	24.5	7.6	1.7	1.2	3.5	10.1	74.8	17.5	39.6	17.7	0.7
Paper & allied products												
Negro												
Total	1,093	39	6	3	3	3	24	999	169	515	315	55
Occupational distrib.	100.0	3.5	0.5	0.2	0.2	0.2	2.1	91.3	15.4	47.1	28.8	5.0
Participation rate	9.7	1.6	0.7	1.9	2.2	0.7	2.5	11.6	7.0	12.8	14.5	42.6
All employees												
Total (58 estab.)	11,217	2,502	817	162	139	407	977	8,586	2,408	4,012	2,166	129
Occupational distrib.	100.0	22.3	7.3	1.4	1.2	3.6	8.7	76.5	21.4	35.7	19.3	1.1
Printing & pub. industries												
Negro												
Total	774	396	6	17	155	22	196	251	75	136	40	127
Occupational distrib.	100.0	51.1	0.7	2.1	20.0	2.8	25.3	32.4	9.6	17.5	5.1	16.4
Participation rate	4.9	4.5	0.6	1.5	6.8	2.1	6.1	3.8	2.4	5.2	4.7	35.3
All employees												
Total (51 estab.)	15,738	8,718	1,077	1,105	2,281	1,056	3,199	6,660	3,184	2,620	856	360
Occupational distrib.	100.0	•55.3	6.8	7.0	14.4	6.7	20.3	42.3	20.2	16.6	5.4	2.2
Chemicals & allied products												
Negro												
Total	1,288	188	26	26	43	15	78	1,053	105	680	268	47
Occupational distrib.	100.0	14.5	2.0	2.0	3.3	1.1	6.0	81.7	8.1	52.7	20.8	3.6
Participation rate	6.9	2.1	1.1	1.8	4.6	1.2	2.5	11.3	5.0	13.7	11.8	20.3
All employees												
Total (136 estab.)	18,595	9,036	2,303	1,428	932	1,281	3,092	9,327	2,102	4,949	2,276	232
Occupational distrib.	100.0	48.5	12.3	7.6	5.0	6.8	16.6	50.1	11.3	26.6	12.2	1.2

Table 14 continued

	Total Employment	White-Collar Occupations						Blue-Collar Occupations				
		Total White-Collar Employment	Officials & Managers	Professionals	Technicians	Sales Workers	Office & Clerical	Total Blue-Collar Employment	Craftsmen	Operatives	Laborers	Service Workers
Rubber & plastic products												
Negro												
Total	1,696	87	36	7	8	0	36	1,549	99	1,218	232	60
Occupational distrib.	100.0	5.1	2.1	0.4	0.4	0.0	2.1	91.3	5.8	71.8	13.6	3.5
Participation rate	13.2	2.6	3.3	1.9	2.9	0.0	2.8	16.6	5.8	22.4	10.6	24.8
All employees												
Total (53 estab.)	12,885	3,292	1,093	373	278	256	1,292	9,351	1,718	5,435	2,198	242
Occupational distrib.	100.0	25.5	8.4	2.8	2.1	1.9	10.0	72.5	13.3	42.1	17.0	1.8
Stone, clay, & glass products												
Negro												
Total	737	46	6	3	8	2	27	659	102	346	211	32
Occupational distrib.	100.0	6.2	0.8	0.4	1.0	0.2	3.6	89.4	13.8	46.9	28.6	4.3
Participation rate	6.1	1.3	0.6	0.6	2.4	0.5	2.1	8.0	5.6	7.2	12.8	25.0
All employees												
Total (55 estab.)	12,004	3,596	1,076	528	335	399	1,258	8,280	1,807	4,819	1,654	128
Occupational distrib.	100.0	29.9	8.9	4.3	2.7	3.3	10.4	68.9	15.0	40.1	13.7	1.0
Fabricated metal products												
Negro												
Total	1,414	95	15	5	15	4	56	1,265	215	839	211	54
Occupational distrib.	100.0	6.7	1.0	0.3	1.0	0.2	3.9	89.4	15.2	59.3	14.9	3.8
Participation rate	6.1	1.5	0.8	0.9	2.1	0.5	2.3	7.7	3.7	10.1	9.0	20.1
All employees												
Total (136 estab.)	23,167	6,422	1,936	554	700	796	2,436	16,476	5,869	8,269	2,338	269
Occupational distrib.	100.0	27.7	8.3	2.3	3.0	3.4	10.5	71.1	25.3	35.6	10.0	1.1
Electrical machinery, equipment, supplies												
Negro												
Total	4,680	1,288	104	326	402	9	447	3,099	435	2,117	547	293
Occupational distrib.	100.0	27.5	2.2	6.9	8.5	0.1	9.5	66.2	9.2	45.2	11.6	6.2
Participation rate	5.2	2.2	1.0	1.6	4.2	0.7	2.9	9.5	4.3	11.6	13.0	28.0
All employees												
Total (192 estab.)	90,822	57,315	10,161	20,958	9,577	1,244	15,375	32,459	10,011	18,228	4,220	1,048
Occupational distrib.	100.0	63.1	11.1	23.0	10.5	1.3	16.9	35.7	11.1	20.0	4.6	1.1

Table 14 continued

	Total Employment	White-Collar Occupations						Blue-Collar Occupations				
		Total White-Collar Employment	Officials & Managers	Professionals	Technicians	Sales Workers	Office & Clerical	Total Blue-Collar Employment	Craftsmen	Operatives	Laborers	Service Workers
Transportation equipment												
Negro												
Total	5,675	663	97	161	105	0	300	4,825	1,385	3,102	338	187
Occupational distrib.	100.0	11.6	1.7	2.8	1.8	0.0	5.2	85.0	24.4	54.6	5.9	3.2
Participation rate	7.5	1.9	1.4	1.2	3.3	0.0	2.9	11.9	7.3	16.0	16.8	17.7
All employees												
Total (92 estab.)	75,635	34,142	6,929	13,375	3,182	413	10,243	40,436	18,981	19,448	2,007	1,057
Occupational distrib.	100.0	45.1	9.1	17.6	4.2	0.5	13.5	53.4	25.0	25.7	2.6	1.3
Instruments & related products												
Negro												
Total	791	99	10	19	32	2	36	661	73	276	312	31
Occupational distrib.	100.0	12.5	1.2	2.4	4.0	0.2	4.5	83.5	9.2	34.8	39.4	3.9
Participation rate	5.2	1.3	0.6	1.0	2.3	0.6	1.7	8.5	3.2	8.9	13.0	17.8
All employees												
Total (59 estab.)	15,298	7,364	1,685	1,854	1,386	355	2,084	7,760	2,272	3,087	2,401	174
Occupational distrib.	100.0	48.1	11.0	12.1	9.0	2.3	13.6	50.7	14.8	20.1	15.6	1.1
Miscellaneous mftg. industries												
Negro												
Total	1,604	171	21	2	25	8	115	1,424	40	385	999	9
Occupational distrib.	100.0	10.6	1.3	0.1	1.5	0.4	7.1	88.7	2.4	24.0	62.2	0.5
Participation rate	18.4	5.6	2.5	0.4	8.0	2.1	11.0	25.5	5.3	17.2	38.6	15.8
All employees												
Total (26 estab.)	8,698	3,056	853	460	311	383	1,049	5,585	754	2,242	2,589	57
Occupational distrib.	100.0	35.1	9.8	5.2	3.5	4.4	12.0	64.2	8.6	25.7	29.7	0.6
Motor freight transportation												
Negro												
Total	1,171	137	8	4	0	3	122	965	67	532	366	69
Occupational distrib.	100.0	11.6	0.6	0.3	0.0	0.2	10.4	82.4	5.7	45.4	31.2	5.8
Participation rate	6.4	3.0	0.6	2.6	0.0	0.8	4.8	7.2	3.7	5.9	14.2	22.9
All employees												
Total (80 estab.)	18,295	4,524	1,355	154	89	364	2,562	13,470	1,804	9,082	2,584	301
Occupational distrib.	100.0	24.7	7.4	0.8	0.4	1.9	14.0	73.6	9.8	49.6	14.1	1.6

Table 14 continued

	Total Employment	White-Collar Occupations						Blue-Collar Occupations				
		Total White-Collar Employment	Officials & Managers	Professionals	Technicians	Sales Workers	Office & Clerical	Total Blue-Collar Employment	Craftsmen	Operatives	Laborers	Service Workers
Transportation services												
Negro												
Total	97	18	1	0	0	1	16	77	0	34	43	2
Occupational distrib.	100.0	18.5	1.0	0.0	0.0	1.0	16.4	79.3	0.0	35.0	44.3	2.0
Participation rate	6.3	1.7	0.7	0.0	0.0	0.5	2.3	15.9	0.0	14.8	17.6	100.0
All employees												
Total (24 estab.)	1,537	1,052	145	15	0	196	696	483	8	230	245	2
Occupational distrib.	100.0	68.4	9.4	0.9	0.0	12.7	45.2	31.4	0.5	14.9	15.9	0.1
Wholesale trade												
Negro												
Total	2,484	1,028	56	55	163	217	537	1,317	196	780	341	139
Occupational distrib.	100.0	41.3	2.2	2.2	6.5	8.7	21.6	53.0	7.8	31.4	13.7	5.5
Participation rate	5.2	3.2	1.1	2.1	4.9	2.2	4.8	8.8	4.4	10.0	12.9	22.9
All employees												
Total (564 estab.)	47,808	32,302	5,220	2,682	3,318	9,992	11,090	14,898	4,476	7,784	2,638	608
Occupational distrib.	100.0	67.5	10.9	5.6	6.9	20.9	23.1	31.1	9.3	16.2	5.5	1.2
Retail trade												
Negro												
Total	3,988	2,338	143	9	63	1,361	762	815	132	334	349	835
Occupational distrib.	100.0	58.6	3.5	0.2	1.5	34.1	19.1	20.4	3.3	8.3	8.7	20.9
Participation rate	7.2	5.2	2.6	2.3	19.8	4.9	7.1	11.8	6.3	10.7	20.2	21.0
All employees												
Total (74 estab.)	55,510	44,617	5,499	386	318	27,721	10,693	6,920	2,079	3,112	1,729	3,973
Occupational distrib.	100.0	80.3	9.9	0.6	0.5	49.9	19.2	12.4	3.7	5.6	3.1	7.1
Miscellaneous business services												
Negro												
Total	5,924	1,081	80	206	327	5	463	1,589	442	1,014	133	3,254
Occupational distrib.	100.0	18.2	1.3	3.4	5.5	0.1	7.8	26.8	7.4	17.1	2.2	54.9
Participation rate	11.3	3.4	1.8	1.6	7.3	0.9	4.8	13.0	7.1	19.3	19.7	38.8
All employees												
Total (143 estab.)	52,588	32,010	4,353	13,072	4,457	557	9,571	12,185	6,265	5,245	675	8,393
Occupational distrib.	100.0	60.8	8.2	24.8	8.4	1.0	18.1	23.1	11.9	9.9	1.2	15.9

Table 14 continued

		White-Collar Occupations						Blue-Collar Occupations				
	Total Employment	*Total White-Collar Employment*	*Officials & Managers*	*Professionals*	*Technicians*	*Sales Workers*	*Office & Clerical*	*Total Blue-Collar Employment*	*Craftsmen*	*Operatives*	*Laborers*	*Service Workers*
Totals												
Negro employment	37,353	8,213	657	887	1,427	1,768	3,474	23,755	4,151	13,534	6,080	5,375
All employees	517,202	272,204	48,595	62,441	29,132	50,046	81,990	227,261	75,539	112,767	39,035	17,747
Negro participation rate	7.2	3.0	1.4	1.4	4.9	3.5	4.2	10.5	5.5	12.0	15.6	30.3

Note: Because of rounding, sums of individual items may not equal totals.

Source: Equal Employment Opportunity Report No. 1. Washington, D.C.: Equal Employment Opportunity Commission, 1969.

TABLE 15.   Nonwhite Subemployment in Disadvantaged Areas of All Central Cities, 1967.

Group	Unemployment	Underemployment	Subemployment
Adult men	102,000	230,000	332,000
Adult women	118,000	266,000	384,000
Teenagers	98,000	220,000	318,000
Total	318,000	716,000	1,034,000

Source: Report of the National Advisory Commission on Civil Disorders, New York: Bantam Books, Inc., 1968, p. 257.

REFERENCES

1. Levine, Marvin J. "The Private Sector and Negro Employment Problems," *MSU Business Topics,* Winter 1969, pp. 63-70.

2. Statistics for these cities taken from *Manpower Report of the President, 1963,* (transmitted to the Congress, March, 1964), Washington, D.C.: U.S. Government Printing Office, 1964, p. 271.

3. *Report of the National Advisory Commission on Civil Disorders.* New York: Bantam Books, Inc., 1968, p. 391.

4. "Census Officials Expect Most Accurate Count in U.S. History," *The Washington Post,* July 20, 1970, p. A-4.

5. Hiestand, Dale L. *Economic Growth and Employment Opportunities for Minorities.* New York and London: Columbia University Press, 1964, pp. 56-57.

6. *Employment Situation in Poverty Areas of Six Cities, July 1968-June 1969.* Washington, D.C.: U.S. Department of Labor, Bureau of Labor Statistics Report No. 370, October, 1969.

7. *Ibid.*

8. "Gap Between Negro and White Jobless Rated Undented Despite Crash Efforts," *The Washington Post,* December 31, 1967, p. E-8.

9. *Current Population Reports,* Series P-23, Nos. 18 & 21. Washington, D.C.: U.S. Bureau of the Census, 1966 and 1967.

10. *Manpower Report of the President, op.cit.,* p. 83.

11. "Discrimination Blamed for Black/White Income Disparities," *Urban Employment,* March 15, 1970, p. 5.

12. See, for example: (1) Herzberg, Frederick and others. *Job Attitudes: Review of Research and Opinion.* Pittsburgh: Psychological Service of Pittsburgh, 1957. (2) Blauner, Robert. "Work Satisfaction and Industrial Trends in Modern Society. In *Labor and Trade Unionism,* edited by Walter Galenson and Seymour Martin Lipset. New York: John Wiley and Sons, Inc., 1960, pp. 339-360. (3) Wilensky, Harold. "Varieties of Work Experience." In *Man in a World at Work,* edited by Henry Borow. Boston: Houghton-Mifflin, 1964, pp. 125-154.

13. *Employment Situation In Poverty Areas of Six Cities, op. cit.,* p. 3.

14. Hiestand, *op. cit.,* p. 57.

15. *Urban Employment,* August 15, 1970, p. 2.

16. *Ibid.,* pp. 5-6.

17. *Urban Employment,* May 1, 1970, p. 6.

18. Liebow, E. *Tally's Corner.* Boston: Little, Brown & Co. Inc., 1967.

19. Kidder, Alice Handsaker. "Racial Differences in Job Search and Wages." *Monthly Labor Review,* July, 1968, p. 25.

20. Ferman, Louis A. *The Negro and Equal Employment Opportunities: A Review of Management Experiences in Twenty Companies.* Ann Arbor: University of Michigan Press, 1968.

21. Mangum, Garth L. *The Emergence of Manpower Policy.* New York: Holt, Rinehart & Winston, Inc., 1969, p. 127.

22. "A Narrow Victory for Blacks." *Time,* January 5, 1970, p. 50.

23. *Report of the National Advisory Commission on Civil Disorders, op. cit.,* p. 391.

24. Strasel, Harold C. and Larken, Paul G. *Rioters in Washington: A Study of People and Employment.* Washington, D.C.: U.S. Department of Labor, Manpower Administration, 1968.

25. Lachman, Sheldon J. and Singer, Benjamin D. *The Detroit Riot of July 1967 — A Psychological, Social, and Economic Profile of 500 Arrestees.* Washington, D.C.: U.S. Department of Labor, Manpower Administration, 1968.

26. "What the unemployment rate means." *Business Week,* Feb. 14, 1970, p. 88.

27. "The Employment Situation in Urban Poverty Neighborhoods: Fourth Quarter 1969." *News,* U.S. Department of Labor, Bureau of Labor Statistics, January 29, 1970, p. 2.

28. U.S. Census Bureau. *Current Population Surveys.* Washington, D.C.: U.S. Government Printing Office, 1967.

29. *Employment and Earnings and Monthly Report on the Labor Force.* Washington, D.C.: U.S. Department of Labor, Bureau of Labor Statistics, March, 1969, pp. 11, 12, 14, 15.

30. "Job Situation and Earnings Vary Widely, Survey of Six City Poverty Areas Shows." *News,* U.S. Department of Labor, Bureau of Labor Statistics, October 24, 1969, pp. 1-2.

31. Rowen, Hobart. "The Jobless 'Rate' is Like an Iceberg." *The Washington Post,* Feb. 19, 1970, p. A-18.

32. "What the unemployment rate means," *op cit.,* p. 88.

33. Samuels, Gertrude. "Help Wanted. The Hard-Core Unemployed." *The New York Times Magazine,* Jan. 28, 1968, p. 27.

34. "Joblessness in Poverty Areas Rising More Slowly Than Nationwide Rate." *The Washington Post,* July 14, 1970, p. A-6.

35. Bowen, W. G. "Unemployment in the United States: Quantitative Dimensions." In *Unemployment in a Prosperous Economy,* Princeton, N.J.: Industrial Relations Section, Princeton University, 1965.

36. Thurow, Lester. "Employment Gains and the Determinants of the Occupational Distribution of Negroes." Paper presented to a conference on the Education and Training of Racial Minorities, May, 1967, University of Wisconsin, Madison, Wisconsin.

Chapter 2
Business Perceptions of
Negro Employment Status

BUSINESS ATTITUDES TOWARD 1964 CIVIL RIGHTS ACT

Since small and medium-sized firms have not participated to any meaningful extent in minority hiring and training programs sponsored by the government or private sector, it is important initially to investigate the potential for participation in this vital area. A basic consideration is the attitude of the business community toward cooperation with the federal government in the alleviation of Negro employment problems. Evidence of widespread racial discrimination in employment led to the inclusion of Title VII in the 1964 Civil Rights Act, banning such exclusionary policies, as well as those based on religion, nationality, sex and creed. The respondents were asked several questions regarding their viewpoints toward that piece of landmark legislation. Generally negative responses would indicate that government efforts to implement the concept of equal employment opportunity could anticipate widespread resistance due to lack of acceptance of the basic legislative objectives. An initial inquiry sought to determine the degree of acceptance of the Act. As Table 16 shows, although less than a majority of the firms surveyed expressed unqualified support, taken together with those who indicated qualified approval, approximately 8 of 10 employers had adopted positive attitudes toward the legislation. On a sample basis, only roughly 12 per cent were in opposition. In the earlier corporate survey, 9 of 10 large firms were positive with only 3 per cent taking a negative stance toward civil rights principles. Not unexpectedly, Houston firms were decidedly more opposed to the law.

Table 17 describes the nature of the negative comments. As indicated, on an overall basis, nearly 1 of 4 individuals preferred not to disclose the nature of their complaints against the law. The most undesirable feature with more than 1 of 3 respondents was their perception that the Act was simply another manifestation of unnecessary government intervention in private enterprise. Houston employers again were most adamant in voicing displeasure with government action, expressing the more conservative philosophy prevalent in the South.

An interesting feature of the comments in the "Others" category is that there seemed to be no middle ground. Responses could hardly be classified as moderate in tone. Also, surprisingly, a number of the criticisms centered on inadequacies in enforcement. The following are specimen reactions from the four cities:

Baltimore "Nothing to back it up. No teeth in it. Unenforceable. Politically unenforceable."
"Only 100 years too late."

Detroit "Disapprove because it shouldn't be necessary."
"Some Negroes take 'It's my right' attitude."
"Too much out of proportion; Negro must help himself — by himself."

Houston "Not strong enough in certain respects."
"News media is our biggest trouble-maker!"
"Inflexibility with civil servants; many situations must be weighed on merits of case."
"Undue pressure brought to bear, without proper reasoning or discussion taking place."

Los Angeles "Not being enforced."
"Financing and inducing revolution that is not needed."
"It is not enforced strongly enough."
"Not being enforced in all areas."
"These rights were already given in our Bill of Rights."
"More gradual approach would have been better."

The most common criticism among the corporate respondents was that the requirement of equal treatment for women would create problems. Nearly 4 of 10 replies mentioned that problem. This is understandable since many large firms employ substantial numbers of female employees in comparison to the smaller businesses. Thirty-two per cent of the large firms complained of unnecessary government intervention, a figure close to that of the smaller firms.

Tables 18 and 19 measure the potential impact of the law on company practices. The first table shows that approximately 15 per cent of the firms would encounter some problem areas in complying with the legal requirements. Twice that percentage of large firms had indicated that certain adjustments would be necessary. Once again, the Houston companies led the field in terms of their subjective judgments that the law would be more disruptive of the status quo. Nevertheless, the Southern employers did not intend to make more changes in operating procedures, proportionally, than the businesses in the other cities. This might be interpreted as meaning that they had not been practicing employment discrimination prior to the law's enactment and saw no need for changing their policies after its passage, or that they would continue their standard procedures in spite of their illegalities. Of course, the same evaluation can be made of the responses from the other regions.

A marked difference existed, however, between the two surveys in perceptions of the need to change existing practices. Seven of ten small enterprises contended that the Civil Rights law would occasion no need for modifications compared to only 44 per cent of the corporations, of whom 3 of 8 believed accomodations would have to be made to insure female equality, and 1 of 6 foresaw changes in Southern subsidiaries. This may be due to the fact that the larger firms are more aware of the need for strict adherence to employment equality since they are most often exposed to the glare of publicity when inequities are discovered.

Only two employers cared to elaborate further on the possible problems caused by compliance, and changes in business practices. A Houston respondent indicated that the law would "motivate us to do more in the office," and a Detroit employer stated that compliance would force them to hire women salesmen.

Another question specifically asked if the new legislation would "make it difficult for you to employ the people you want to employ in your firm?" One of the five large firms had admitted that they either definitely would or might encounter obstacles in applying such hiring standards. Table 20 indicates that nearly 3 of 10 small employers anticipated possible problems. The higher incidence of "maybe" and "no" responses from Houston again suggests that firms in that Southern center either have been conforming to equal employment opportunity standards all along or intend to continue discriminatory hiring programs. The weight of existing experience tends to confer a higher validity quotient upon the more pessimistic appraisal.

The following additional comments that were forthcoming from each of the sample cities can be classified as examples of outright defiance, general opposition, and a wait-and-see attitude.

Baltimore   An executive maintained, "In the interest of my company, I would, if necessary, violate the Act."

Los Angeles   Several employers presented these views:
"Compulsion cannot be handled emotionally for desired results."
"Yes, however, if the government doesn't tell us who to employ, the unions do. In both cases, they are more concerned with who needs the job than in who does it best."

Houston   "Government regulations should not require or prevent anyone from employing anyone he wishes, assuming that all are citizens free of court restraints."

Detroit A respondent reserved judgment in stating "Maybe, it depends upon its administration."

Table 21 identifies the values that the sample participants recognized in the 1964 law. The ranking of items in the earlier study followed along quite closely with that of the smaller firms. Houston firms were least enthusiastic in believing that the law "reaffirmed our basic concept of justice" and more emphatic in maintaining that it was valueless. Only 1.4 per cent of the corporations viewed it in that manner compared to nearly five times that percentage of small businesses. In this respect, the small employers maintained their overall less sanguine opinion of the legislation.

The only employer who elaborated further on this question was a Houston man who stated, "I do not believe the law is concerned with justice but only with the practical opening of opportunities for Negroes, which in many cases has worked to the injustice of non-Negro persons." It should be noted that although the Houston firms questioned the worth of the law, they did agree that as a practical matter, it would smooth the path to equality employment.

A final inquiry sought to elicit appraisals of whether the remedial legislation by itself would be sufficient to eliminate discrimination or if additional efforts would be required. Six of ten corporate respondents were of the opinion that more than the law would be necessary to insure equality. Table 22 demonstrates that a majority, albeit a less substantial one, of the smaller enterprises agreed with that judgment.

Relevant additional remarks ran the gamut from blaming the federal government for Negro reliance on welfare to the need for additional education to promote upward mobility:

Detroit "The Negro problem seems to get the most publicity, and probably rightly so. I think that programs that are initiated should not be limited strictly to the Negro race. We have underemployment throughout our population. Many of the problems we have today were probably caused by government programs started in the '30s. Until the generation that was raised under these programs has a change of initiative or addition of attainable goals, we will be in a period of unrest. The sociological climate or environment that these people adapted for themselves in order to gain government money would seem to be the cause of their problems today. I would hope this problem will be solved soon, but I realize it took a long time to create it, and it will take a long time to improve it — even when it seems to be solved, it will exist to some extent — man is not a forgiving being, there are times when he has to hate someone — and what easier way is there to identify your enemy but by color? This holds true on all sides, it's not only whites that are bigots."

Los Angeles   Several employers added:
"Wisdom is not the criterion at present."
"And Negroe does more for himself, education primarily."

Houston   A decidedly negative criticism came from Houston:
"Solve nothing except to put a lot of lazy, incompetent Negroes on jobs where they can loaf and hold their jobs with government help."

Baltimore   Two firms contributed these statements:
"Additional efforts on the part of Negroes to become properly equipped to do the jobs available."
"Additional efforts — such as education is necessary."

COMPANY PERCEPTIONS OF NEGRO ECONOMIC PROGRESS

The overall economic position of Negroes relative to whites as described in Table 23 merits investigation, since it is an aggregative measure of the earnings and income experience of each ethnic group. In the earlier survey, 1 of 4 corporate employers expressed the view that the gap in economic status between the two races during the past decade had widened, while 56 per cent maintained that Negroes had improved their position vis-a-vis whites. As Table 24 shows, the smaller firms were even more sanguine concerning Negro economic progress, with almost 3 of 4 respondents contending the economic disparity had narrowed, and only 8 per cent stating that Negroes had fallen even farther behind in economic terms. No more than 1 of 10 employers in any city believed that the differential had worsened during the past ten years. More than 8 of 10 Houston firms assessed Negro advancement in positive terms, which may be due to the rapid industrialization in that Southern location and the accompanying improvement in living standards for all residents. Only two firms were willing to elaborate on their responses. A Detroit employer felt the gap had widened, stating, "I only know what I read," and a Houston executive used questionable logic in maintaining that the economic difference had lessened when he wrote, "Negroes and whites in our company today are at a salary level 80-100 per cent over 10 years ago." Since Negro movement toward economic equality is directly related to the rate of white progress, it is conceivable that the disparity would remain constant or even increase despite apparent regional improvement. Another important consideration to note is that if a majority of the smaller businesses perceived a perceptible trend toward income equality, they might be less willing to contribute to remedial programs. As noted earlier, the small firms were more reluctant to participate in private-enterprise sponsored community action programs than had been the large enterprises.

Negro socioeconomic gains, both quantitative and qualitative, have not been achieved without substantial militancy during the past fifteen years. The attitude of the white majority toward present Negro efforts toward social equality may indicate whether the movement will reach its goal smoothly or face continued resistance. Almost 8 of 10 large employers were not willing to generalize on the merits of Negro self-help efforts with only 8 per cent criticizing the activities as overly aggressive and 1 of 10 indicating approval. However, as the data in Table 25 indicate, the smaller employers were much more biased against the nature of advancement measures. Approximately one-half of all responses characterized Negro activities as being pursued too vigorously; slightly more than 1 of 10 considered them as justified; and 1 or 3 were not willing to evaluate their character. Just the opposite of what might have been expected developed in the intercity comparison as slightly more than 4 of 10 firms in Los Angeles and Detroit, where two of the most traumatic urban disorders occurred during the past five years, judged Negro actions as too militant compared to more than 5 of 10 in Houston and Baltimore, where less serious urban outbreaks took place. Again surprisingly, larger percentages in Detroit and Los Angeles were reluctant to rule one way or the other and the largest proportion of employers satisfied with advancement efforts were located in Los Angeles. On the other hand, a possible explanation is that traditional racial bias has always been more pervasive in Houston and Baltimore than in Detroit and Los Angeles due to regional values, and that racial unrest would be less likely to affect attitudes in the latter cities. Had the former urban centers experienced large-scale disorders, it is possible that their responses would have been even more negative in tone. As a corollary, if businessmen thought that the Negro was overly belligerent in pressing for improvement, they might be less enthusiastic in contributing their resources in hiring and training the hard-core unemployables. The interrelationship of these attitudes was borne out since it has been shown that the smaller employers were substantially more negative toward such programs than the corporate employers. The following comments illustrate the diversity of opinions:

Houston
"Too hard, in some areas. Like a child, you have to crawl before you can walk."
"Some groups too hard."

Detroit
"Can't generalize — too hard in some and not enough in others."
"Improperly."
"Negro must improve by own initiative."

Los Angeles
"Too hard — only because at this stage he is incapable of producing adequately to earn it."
"Militants too hard."
"Too hard — Rap Brown. Just about hard enough — NAACP."
"Can't generalize — some groups too hard."

Baltimore
"Too hard — the wrong way."

A Houston employer probably was closest to reality when he said, "... The Negro today is pressing his case with varying degrees of intensity in various locations and areas. Also, various age groups and educational levels are pressing at different rates of intensity."

The comments revealed a marked ambivalence on the part of the small and medium-sized firms. A sense that injustice has been done is evident from many responses, yet reluctance to accept faster progress and its consequences is equally plain.

THE INFLUENCE OF LOCAL EMPLOYMENT CUSTOMS

A qualitative measure demonstrating the influence of community prejudices vis-a-vis tolerable Negro labor force participation rates can be determined by investigating the prevalence of local racial employment customs.

If local customs with respect to racial relations become an important consideration when management develops a Negro employment policy at the firm level, and these customs are discriminatory in nature, serious obstacles would lie in the path of equitable hiring and promotion efforts. Moreover, sectional employment practices leading to conspicuous imbalances in the racial composition of local work forces are prima facie evidence of violations of Title VII of the Civil Rights Act of 1964 banning racial bias in firms with 25 or more employees since July 2, 1968.

On the one hand, whereas two-thirds of the large firms indicated that they would be influenced to a greater or lesser degree by local racial customs toward Negro employment, approximately one-half of the respondents in this study held a similar opinion. On the other hand, nearly 4 of 10 smaller firms would completely overlook regional employment preferences, compared to 27 per cent of the large firms. Thus, it appears that the smaller firms are more liberal in outlook than the corporations. Table 26 provides further insight through an urban comparison which shows that Houston firms, not unexpectedly, were less willing than those in the other cities to discount the importance of locational employment guidelines. The additional comments were few in number and indicated a certain amount of confusion regarding the overall impact of local customs. For example, one employer who would be guided to a great extent by area customs stated, "First to be sure the person qualifies no matter the race," which is clearly contradictory. Another executive admitted by implication the pressures upon business to conform to community practices when he maintained, "It is easy to say 'not at all' when it is someone else's problem. It is easy to have super liberal 'holier than thou' ideals when someone else must pay the price." One employer opposed the use of local preferences but contended that they would nevertheless be utilized. The most enlightened comment paraphrased existing government policy: "How do you expect racial barriers torn down if you make provisions according to section?"

In addition, further to refine business attitudes in this important area, respondents were asked to specify the percentage of Negro employees they would consider acceptable in their operations, thereby providing concrete quantitative evidence of the constraints on hiring and recruitment policies that locality preferences impose. Table 27 furnishes absolute and percentage figures indicating a greater degree of consistency among the small firms than among the large corporations in the earlier study. Again, approximately 4 of 10 small businesses had no specific figure in mind when it came to the determination of Negro employment at the company level. Their oft-quoted opinion was that skill and ability, not race, should be the only important criterion in setting hiring standards. Two-thirds of the large firms had responded similarly, refusing to cite a desired percentage, with many maintaining that any expressed quota would in itself be discriminatory, apparently repudiating their previously held views on the relative importance of selected racial employment customs.

There are several schools of thought when it comes to the question of labor force participation rates in urban areas. One holds to the notion that claims of discrimination are unsupported if the black employment percentage approximates their percentage of the national population, or around 10 per cent. This approach is not acceptable, however, to many Negro leaders who contend that the percentage of Negro employees in a company ought to equal the percentage of Negroes in the community. Realistically, the desired percentage will be a function of past employment experience, favorable or otherwise, and the present racial composition of the urban area; if the population has a sizeable percentage of Negroes combined with favorable work evaluations by employers, the probability exists that company percentages may exceed the national percentage. Moreover, even if employers rate Negroes as poor employees, the percentage clustered in the less attractive, low-wage occupations very often will exceed the national percentage.

A set percentage, or quota approach, can be criticized for its inflexibility. Negro labor force participation rates reflect not only the employer's hiring standards and attitudes but more basically the availability of qualified job applicants in a local labor market. One might contend that local preferences are a consequence of past experience with the qualified job-seekers. Hiring standards for unskilled jobs today in many instances disqualify poorly educated applicants, since a high school diploma exceeds their educational attainment. Employers should be urged to relax unduly stringent hiring standards if at all possible when detrimental consequences for productivity would not ensue. If these standards are deliberately discriminatory, however, then quotas imposed by the government are much less difficult to justify. The determination that discrimination is practiced in certain industries is difficult to refute when these industries contain relatively fewer Negro occupational positions than would be predicted on the basis of the relative educational levels of Negroes in those industries. If a basic disparity exists between the relative educational attainment and the relative occupational position of Negroes, a prima facie case can be made out for discrimination and direct action to reduce the occupational under-representation is justified where Negro capabilities are equal but Negro opportunities are unequal.

There are at least two approaches to utilize in order to ascertain that Negroes have equal abilities but unequal employment opportunities. The first is a comparison of the scope of employment of Negroes in the higher-rated occupations in two companies or industries in close geographical proximity so as to possess equal accessibility to the same pool of Negro labor. Further, if it can be demonstrated that one firm or industry employs different percentages of Negro labor in different occupations relative to the amounts of white workers utilized, a strong presumption of unequal employment opportunities will result.

A more direct method to indicate that equal capabilities are not matched by equal opportunities consists of estimating for a group of firms or industries the average relationship between the relative occupational position and the relative capability of Negroes. Industries which should be the subject of further investigation can be isolated on the premise that they employ relatively less Negro labor in the better paying occupations than would be anticipated on the basis of the relative capability of the Negro labor in the industry.

SUGGESTED MEASURES FOR ALLEVIATING
BLACK UNEMPLOYMENT

As these comments indicate, generally low levels of educational attainment are one factor which contributes to the high jobless levels and low earnings of residents of urban poverty areas. Except for Negroes in Los Angeles and whites in Detroit, fewer than 40 per cent of the workers in each urban center had completed four years of high school or more. Half of the Los Angeles Negroes have completed at least a high school education. In Houston (10.7 years) and Los Angeles (12.0 years), Negro workers have completed more schooling than their white counterparts (9.0 and 9.6 years, respectively). However, in these cities, the white population has a high proportion of Mexican-Americans, some of whom are relatively recent arrivals to the United States and have language difficulties.[1]

One of the Baltimore respondents has a house organ entitled *Type Talk* from which the following column from the September, 1963 edition is taken:

> A recent inspection of both of the major vocational schools in Baltimore leaves one disgusted with those who are not telling the true facts about our public school system. ... At Mergenthaler Vocational School, the enrollment is 98% white and 2% colored — a very *select* colored. The equipment is up-to-date, the physical plant excellent and not even fully utilized. At Carver Vocational School, the enrollment is 100% Negro, and the equipment is that which has been salvaged from obsolete plants, broken and unrepaired. The quarters allotted for departments are crowded and created without any inducement for study. The School Board probably considers this school a necessary evil and that it should be hidden away. In fact, when a good teacher is developed, he or she is taken away and transferred to another school.

On the one hand, small employers complain that many job applicants are unqualified because of lack of requisite skills, training and education. However, they are reluctant, on the other hand, to participate in programs to aid the urban hard-core unemployed. Ironically, the greatest number of responses to the question of what efforts, in addition to legislation, would be required to solve the Negro employment problem, indicated that education and training should have the highest priority, according to Table 28. It should be stressed, however, that the firms ranked direct involvement by business in education and training as the third most needed course of action, following education and training and improved motivation. These were the same priorities the large firms had listed. A possible interpretation is that businessmen recognize the problem areas but would rather let others solve them. The four cities were quite uniform in their ranking of ameliorative measures, with no outstanding differences.

Garth Mangum, a member of the National Manpower Policy Task Force, has stated that the business community still hires blacks in only token numbers. He characterizes training as a treadmill for some youths, who go from one program to another until they are finally hired. Therefore, it is extremely important to review the reasons why a man goes from one job to another. Frequently, the reasons are inadequate training or discriminatory hiring practices.[2] Yet care by companies to eliminate prejudice in hiring was ranked fifth in the urgency of eight remedial policies.

Once again individual comments reinforced the tabular data, and provided further information concerning problem areas.

Baltimore

"We run a small business in a Negro area and have had extensive experience in dealing with problems pertaining to the Negro. My firm hope is that our educational facilities will eventually solve our problems and more important will establish a semblance of a proper 'home' life wherein both parents will raise their children with stability."

"Minority unemployment in this country is basically a problem of education, or the lack of it. Not only the education of the minority but the education of the majority to accept their proper role in our society as pertains to the education, housing and job opportunity. So long as the majority refuses to understand or even recognize the problem, the education of the minority will be frustrated."

"I feel our taxes now are being used too much for welfare. There are both colored and white now on welfare that are strong and healthy to work. I don't object to the old and sick benefitting by welfare. I say give them more. But the others — take them off of welfare; and if you must, force them to work."

"As long as any man, white or black, feels that his situation is the result of other people's actions, he is deluding himself and is rationalizing away his chance to accomplish something on his own!"

"The Negro should try to be better at his job than the white. Also develop a sense of pride in his own living, *i.e.,* be clean, keep a clean house, try to live a clean life."

"The Negro for a number of years has for many reasons been denied the proper education necessary for him to compete in the society. True, the main reasons has been his economical situation that has held him to inadequate schooling, but it has also created a stagnant frame of mind, leaving them very lowly motivated. To simplify this situation, by merely giving them better jobs, seems not the entire answer to the problem. For an example: Take a man whose basic salary is $45.00 a week. He is given a better position and a raise to $100.00 per week. With his lack of knowledge of how to budget his money, what to buy, where to shop, how much to bank for an accumulation of cash, he and his family are worse off. He must be taught to use his new income to the best of the family's needs. Who has taught him? How will he know? How can we completely bring him into community living, which takes us to social training, according to his standard of living. I will end this by saying that it should be all of the people's concern that all low-income individuals be he Negro or other be given a full opportunity to not only earn more money, but be a useful person to himself, as well as to his community."

Los Angeles

"Present welfare program limits job motivation."

"Negroes need to show greater desire for self-betterment."

"Some Negroes have told me that the whites should pay for so-called past injustices by supporting them indefinitely. I see very little chance of improving the racial problem in the U.S. until the multitude of Negroes on welfare are willing to be educated and accept jobs."

"Motivation — by reducing welfare and unemployment benefits."

"It would seem that the major problem is motivation and education. Basically, it is not economical to employ an untrained person, white or black, in a position that requires a certain amount of skill. Therefore, the individual must want to learn; then it's the industry problem to provide this opportunity."

"The only thing any man is entitled to is a fair chance. That means that the most capable man should get the job regardless of any other consideration. Because the Negro has not had the same opportunity to learn, he has not been given an equal chance to compete, and that is the one thing society owes him. Other than that, someone had better explain to the Negro that he has to earn it, not just demand it or try to take it. I who have spent 35 years working from 60 to 100 hours per week cannot accept the theory that I owe every unshaven, unwashed bum in the country an effortless existence. Only those unable to work should be supported."

"They must be made to realize the virtues of hard work and responsibility. The trade unions must open their doors."

"Industry is being overloaded with the faults of others."

"Can't be trained."

Houston

"Education is not training and is currently too mixed up with it. Industry should be involved more in training! Education is not the business of industry."

Detroit

"Motivation — make them want to be educated."

"The pressure on small businesses such as mine seems to indicate that an equal employment opportunity policy really means only hire Negroes. Trends and attitude seem to have no place with the political administrators. In our company, we don't bid certain work, because of this reaction even two of our last four hired have been black."

It is important to note that the education and skill levels of the entire workforce continue to rise, so that the black worker must continue to advance even more rapidly in education and training if he is to make up for past handicaps.

TABLE 16.   Degree of Acceptance of Civil Rights Act of 1964, by City.

	Sample Totals No.	%	Baltimore No.	%	Los Angeles No.	%	Detroit No.	%	Houston No.	%
Unconditional approval	88	38.6	33	41.8	20	32.3	25	45.5	10	31.3
Approval with reservations	98	43.0	32	40.5	28	45.2	23	41.8	15	46.9
Disapproval	27	11.8	5	6.3	9	14.5	6	10.9	7	21.8
No response	15	6.6	9	11.4	5	8.0	1	1.8	0	0.0

Source: Negro Employment Questionnaire.

TABLE 17.   Nature of Criticism of Civil Rights Act of 1964, by City.

	Sample Totals No.	%	Baltimore No.	%	Los Angeles No.	%	Detroit No.	%	Houston No.	%
Unspecified complaints	39	23.8	14	28.6	10	21.7	10	26.3	5	16.6
Objection to public accomodations section	7	4.3	1	2.0	2	4.3	3	7.9	1	3.3
Sex provision may cause trouble	34	20.9	13	26.5	6	13.0	9	23.7	6	20.0
More of government in business	58	35.6	14	28.6	18	39.0	12	31.6	14	46.7
Others	15	9.2	3	6.1	5	10.6	3	7.9	4	13.4
No response	10	6.2	4	4.2	5	10.6	1	2.6	0	0.0

Source: Negro Employment Questionnaire.

TABLE 18. Determination of Whether Compliance with Civil Rights Act of 1964 Would Cause Firms Embarrassment, Annoyance, or Difficulty, by City.

	Sample Totals		Baltimore		Los Angeles		Detroit		Houston	
	No.	*%*	*No.*	*%*	*No.*	*%*	*No.*	*%*	*No.*	*%*
Yes	33	14.4	8	10.7	9	14.5	11	20.8	5	14.3
No	177	77.6	61	76.0	48	77.4	38	71.7	30	85.7
No response	10	8.0	10	13.3	5	8.1	4	7.5	0	0.0

Source: Negro Employment Questionnaire.

TABLE 19. Ways in Which Civil Rights Act Will Affect Company Practices, by City.

	Sample Totals		Baltimore		Los Angeles		Detroit		Houston	
	No.	*%*	*No.*	*%*	*No.*	*%*	*No.*	*%*	*No.*	*%*
None	177	71.4	64	77.9	49	76.6	39	70.9	25	73.5
Sex provisions may create difficulties	33	14.1	11	14.3	9	14.1	9	16.4	4	11.8
Will promote changes at Southern locations	9	8.1	1	1.3	2	3.0	1	1.8	5	4.7
No response	15	6.4	5	6.5	4	6.3	6	10.0	0	0.0

Source: Negro Employment Questionnaire.

TABLE 20. Probability of Difficulty in Applying Preferential Hiring Standards, by City.

	Sample Totals		Baltimore		Los Angeles		Detroit		Houston	
	No.	*%*	*No.*	*%*	*No.*	*%*	*No.*	*%*	*No.*	*%*
Yes	16	7.0	6	7.9	5	8.1	5	9.4	0	0.0
Maybe	49	21.4	14	17.1	14	22.6	16	30.2	5	14.7
No	158	69.0	57	71.1	42	67.7	30	56.6	29	85.3
No response	6	2.6	3	3.9	1	1.6	2	3.8	0	0.0

Source: Negro Employment Questionnaire.

TABLE 21.   Perceived Values in Civil Rights Act of 1964, by City.

	Sample Totals		Baltimore		Los Angeles		Detroit		Houston	
	No.	%	No.	%	No.	%	No.	%	No.	%
Will prod those who otherwise would not act	85	20.0	24	17.8	29	24.4	20	19.8	13	19.1
Will raise living standards of Negroes eventually	99	23.2	36	25.2	25	21.0	20	19.8	18	26.5
Will make it easier for enlightened companies to implement their policies	52	12.2	18	13.3	13	10.9	11	10.9	10	14.7
Will break down regional differences eventually	49	11.5	19	13.7	11	9.2	12	11.9	7	10.3
Reaffirms our basic concept of justice	81	19.0	23	17.0	25	21.0	23	22.8	10	14.7
No values	27	6.4	4	2.2	10	8.4	5	4.9	8	11.8
No response	33	7.7	15	11.1	6	5.0	10	9.9	2	2.9

Source: Negro Employment Questionnaire.

TABLE 22.   Perceived Efficacy of 1964 Civil Rights Act, by City.

	Sample Totals		Baltimore		Los Angeles		Detroit		Houston	
	No.	%	No.	%	No.	%	No.	%	No.	%
Will go a long way if wisely administered	84	36.2	26	30.7	20	32.3	23	41.1	15	42.9
Additional efforts	127	54.7	44	57.3	36	58.1	29	51.8	18	51.4
No response	21	9.1	9	12.0	6	9.6	4	7.1	2	5.7

Source: Negro Employment Questionnaire,

TABLE 23.   Economic Status of Negroes Compared to Whites–1968.

	Black	White
Median family income	$5,359	$8,936
Below poverty level	29%	8%
Below $5,000 a year	46.9%	19.9%
$8,000 and above	29.5%	57.6%
$25,000 and above	.4%	2.8%
Per capita income	$1,348	$2,616
Unemployment overall (February, 1970)	7.0%[*]	3.8%
Unemployment among married men	2.5%[*]	1.4%
Unemployment among teen-agers (February, 1970)	25.3%[*]	11.7%
Receiving welfare	16%	3%
Number of professional workers (doctors, lawyers, teachers, etc.)	692,000[*]	10,031,000
Increase in professional jobs in 1960s	109%	41%
Managerial workers	254,000	7,721,000
Increase in managerial jobs in 1960s	43%[*]	12%
Self-employed (nonfarm)	293,000[*]	4,964,000
Own home	38%[*]	64%
Own car	40.3%[*]	51.8%
Own black-and-white TV	81.9%	77.5%
Own color TV	12.4%	33.5%
Average insurance coverage	$2,750[*]	$6,600

*Includes all "nonwhites": Americans of Indian, Chinese, Japanese, and other origins, as well as blacks who make up about 95% of the total.

Source: "Working in the White Man's World," *Time*, April 6, 1970, p. 94.

TABLE 24.   Perception of Change During Past Decade in Economic Status Differential Between Whites and Negroes, by City.

	Sample Totals No.	%	Baltimore No.	%	Los Angeles No.	%	Detroit No.	%	Houston No.	%
Widened	19	8.3	8	10.0	7	11.3	2	3.6	2	6.3
Lessened	165	72.1	54	67.5	44	71.0	41	74.5	26	81.2
Remained the same	30	13.1	10	12.5	8	12.9	8	14.7	4	12.5
No response	15	6.5	8	10.0	3	4.8	4	7.2	0	0.0

Source: Negro Employment Questionnaire.

TABLE 25.   Evaluation of Negro Advancement Efforts, by City.

	Sample Totals		Baltimore		Los Angeles		Detroit		Houston	
	No.	%	No.	%	No.	%	No.	%	No.	%
Too hard	110	47.8	42	51.9	27	43.5	23	41.8	18	56.3
Not hard enough	6	2.6	3	3.7	1	1.7	0	0.0	2	6.3
Just about hard enough	30	13.0	7	8.6	10	16.1	8	14.6	5	15.6
Can't generalize	76	33.0	21	25.9	24	38.7	24	43.6	7	21.7
No response	8	3.5	8	9.5	0	0.0	0	0.0	0	0.0

Source: Negro Employment Questionnaire.

TABLE 26.   Influence of Local Racial Employment Customs Upon Negro Employment Levels, by City.

Degree of Influence	Sample Totals		Baltimore		Los Angeles		Detroit		Houston	
	No.	%	No.	%	No.	%	No.	%	No.	%
To a great extent	23	10.1	6	7.6	8	12.9	4	7.3	5	15.6
To some extent	96	42.1	32	40.5	24	38.7	22	40.0	18	56.3
Not at all	87	38.2	32	40.5	24	38.7	22	40.0	9	28.1
No response	22	9.6	9	11.4	6	9.7	7	12.7	0	0.0

Source: Negro Employment Questionnaire.

TABLE 27.   Desired Percentage of Negro Employees in Individual Firms, by City.

Acceptable Percentage	Sample Totals		Baltimore		Los Angeles		Detroit		Houston	
	No.	%	No.	%	No.	%	No.	%	No.	%
0 – 10%	30	13.1	6	7.6	15	23.8	3	5.5	6	18.8
11 – 20%	25	10.9	9	11.4	7	11.1	5	9.1	4	12.5
21 – 30%	16	7.0	5	6.3	3	4.8	4	7.3	4	12.5
31 – 40%	7	3.1	4	5.1	0	0.0	2	3.6	1	3.1
41 – 50%	16	7.0	11	13.9	1	1.6	2	3.6	2	6.3
Over 50%	6	2.6	2	2.5	0	0.0	2	3.6	2	6.3
No specific figure	88	38.4	28	35.5	21	33.3	27	49.1	12	37.5
No response	41	17.9	14	17.7	16	25.4	10	18.2	1	3.1

Source: Negro Employment Questionnaire.

TABLE 28.   Appraisal by Firms of Efforts, in Addition to Legislation, Required to Solve Negro Employment Problems, by City.

	Sample Totals		Baltimore		Los Angeles		Detroit		Houston	
	No.	%	No.	%	No.	%	No.	%	No.	%
Education and training	167	28.7	62	32.8	46	27.5	37	18.4	22	27.8
Motivation of Negroes	143	24.6	47	24.9	38	22.8	40	27.2	18	22.8
Emphasis by industry on fact that equal employment opportunity is good business	43	7.4	13	6.9	14	8.4	8	5.4	8	10.1
Involvement by industry in education and training	74	12.7	20	10.6	16	9.6	25	17.0	13	16.5
Community enlightenment and action	56	9.6	20	10.6	16	9.6	13	8.8	7	8.9
Care by companies to eliminate prejudice in hiring	55	9.5	16	8.5	19	11.4	15	10.2	5	6.3
Extra recruiting efforts	21	3.5	4	2.1	10	6.0	3	2.0	4	5.1
Change of situation in southern courts	23	4.0	7	3.7	8	4.8	6	4.1	2	2.5

Source: Negro Employment Questionnaire.

REFERENCES

1. *Employment Situation in Poverty Areas of Six Cities, op cit.,* p. 5.
2. *Urban Employment,* May 1, 1970, p. 5.

Chapter 3
Efforts to Promote Employment Equality

ROLE OF COMPANY HEAD IN POLICY
FORMULATION AND EXECUTION

The comments indicating that there still exists in some firms resistance to completely integrated work forces poses the immediate question of what the role of a company's chief executive officer should be in promoting equal employment opportunities. Despite the pledges of presidents, there are problems with supervisors and other employees. If subordinates perceive that, through his comments and actions, the head of a business is only paying lip-service to equal employment opportunity or meets violations with passivity, those opposing integrated employment may continue efforts to thwart meaningful job equality. However, if the head of a firm makes the policy and sees that it is executed, less defiance by subordinates, due to fear of adverse consequences for their own employment security, can be expected. If top management of a company doesn't stay on watch, evidence of discrimination may soon develop. Companies and unions, for that matter, should look for patterns of discrimination rather than simply individual violations.

In most employment situations, equal employment opportunity can be made viable if management makes a firm commitment to implement nondiscriminatory policies. An unequivocal management policy of employment equality, adhered to firmly, will gain the acceptance of the overwhelming majority of employees. To be effective, policies for Negro employment and promotion should be set and followed through by the chief executive. Management objectives must be emphatically and clearly made known to all levels of the firm so that from the policy standpoint, all employees understand that discrimination is not acceptable, and implement the company's nondiscrimination policy in their daily activities. Placement of the already qualified minority group employee generally is no problem. Any resistance on the part of other employees usually can be handled by communication and a firm stand by management.

Perceptions of top executives in both large corporations and small and medium-sized firms concerning the proper role of the head of a business were highly congruent. Table 29 presents the reactions of the smaller companies and indicates that most executives, 45 per cent of the total sample basis, prefer to set the tone and create the proper climate for employment equality, with approximately 3 of 10 contending that they must not only make the policy but see that it is carried out, and 2 of 10 merely stressing community leadership, as an adequate contribution in the battle to overcome employment discrimination. The pattern of responses in the four urban centers followed the sample totals quite closely. The comparable percentages for the larger companies had been 43, 33, and 23, respectively.

Setting the tone and creating a proper climate and exercising community leadership are helpful but comparatively passive activities in contrast to an affirmative action program which starts at the top of a company and is communicated to all levels of management for effective implementation. Over the long term, there has to be total commitment and involvement by all of management. There is no assurance that subordinates will follow through on a day-to-day basis and conform to orders sent through the chain of command unless the chief executive determines that performance conforms to policy pronouncements.

PARTICIPATION IN COMMUNITY ACTION PROGRAMS

Community action programs sponsored by private enterprise can be a practical contribution by the business sector toward the alleviation of minority group employment problems. Ninety-five per cent of the corporations had shown an unequivocal or conditional willingness to participate in such efforts. However, the smaller firms, as Table 30 indicates, were a good deal more negative toward programs of this type, with 2 of 3 demonstrating either a clear-cut or conditional interest. However, 1 of 4 employers were categorically opposed to involvement, in contrast to only one large firm. Once again, there was considerable uniformity on an intercity basis, with only the Los Angeles firms departing somewhat from the general consensus, with substantially fewer employers desirous of unconditional participation and more attaching strings to their involvement. No obvious reason for this more conservative attitude is apparent. Only two firms stated that they had already participated in these programs and were willing to do so again without conditions. Several employers were willing but only "within the framework of company needs and employee capability." Others maintained that they were too small to contribute in this capacity while a few businesses would participate "only if the group-sponsored applicants were truly qualified." The latter seemed to overlook the fact that these programs were aimed at assisting the unqualified, hard-core, or unemployable individual.

A Houston executive volunteered that his firm would participate but had never been exposed to such programs nor educated in their function. Possibly, the small or medium-sized businessman is not as publicity conscious and feels less need than the corporate executive to project a favorable image by participation in community-action efforts. Comments also emphasized the lack of adequate resources or time in the opportunity cost sense for small firms to offer their services.

PREVALENCE AND IMPLEMENTATION OF EQUAL OPPORTUNITY POLICIES

Against this backdrop of general attitudes toward Negro employment problems, the respondents were asked to evaluate their individual firm's minority employment problems as being "major," "minor," "somewhere in between," or "major in some areas, minor in others." In the earlier survey, more than 4 out of 10 employers had considered Negro hiring to be either a major problem generally or in some areas. In marked contrast as shown in Table 31, only 20 per cent of the small and medium-sized firms concurred in this appraisal. Moreover, 7 of 10 companies maintained that the problem was of minor scope compared to only 3 of 10 large corporations who were willing to analyze it in similar terms.

Several possible explanations can be advanced for these different interpretations. First, although a substantial number of the smaller employers indicated some difficulty in finding qualified Negro personnel, their smaller-scale operations would normally result in fewer manpower shortages than those occasioned by the labor requirements of large assembly-line operations where literally hundreds of unskilled and semiskilled workers might be needed at any point in time to satisfy production schedules.

Second, an employer may view the matter of Negro employment as a minor problem either because he had little difficulty in hiring Negroes or because few ever initiate job requests. If many file job applications but are rejected for failing to meet hiring standards, the firm may consider minority group employment to be a major problem area.

Third, management may not perceive that employed Negroes have employment problems while they are gainfully employed, no matter how undesirable their jobs are relative to actual or potential skill levels, which is another way of describing underemployment. These possible interpretations are all based on pragmatic, economic, employment parameters. However, a final assessment which may be just as significant would depend on an employer's overall appraisal of national employment figures, the nature of which would influence his own firm's situation. On the one hand, if Negro employment problems were considered to be of sizeable proportions in the economy, then plausibly, the employer might evince concern when and if his equal employment policy foundered, whether from a dearth of job applicants or because jobseekers were found to be unemployable due to educational or skill deficiencies or both. On the other hand, if an employer felt that minority employment problems were exaggerated or overemphasized, his efforts to implement equal employment opportunity policies might be somewhat less than zealous.

Responses from the four cities were quite uniform, thereby discounting the influence of region as a significant variable. Although slightly more Houston firms rated the problem as minor, which could have been anticipated, at least 2 of 3 of the other employers responded with similar sentiments. Fewer than 10 per cent of the firms in each city indicated a major concern, with Detroit somewhat surprisingly possessing the lowest percentage.

In addition, Table 32 indicates that the employment size of the firm, whether medium-sized or small, was of little import in influencing the nature of the comments, as no clear-cut trend was discernible.

Table 33 confirms the presence of equal opportunity employment policies in the great majority of firms in three of the urban centers with Houston companies lagging somewhat behind the others. The South generally had not voluntarily accepted the notion of racial employment equality before Title VII of the Civil Rights Act of 1964, effective July 1, 1965, banned all types of employment discrimination.

In the earlier study, all of the large corporations had adopted equal employment opportunity policies. It is conceivable that some smaller employers are still ignorant of the Title VII requirements.

In the corporation survey, 43 per cent of the firms reported less than complete effectiveness in implementing equal employment opportunity policies; 49 per cent said their programs were effective; not one employer indicated ineffective implementation. However, responses from the small and medium-sized firms depict a different pattern: 44 per cent stressed effective action; 33 per cent indicated less than complete implementation; but 12 per cent said their policies were being ineffectively implemented. An intercity comparison from the figures in Table 34 indicates generally uniform percentages, again discounting the influence of geographical differences.

Although a few employers in each city stated that they had little difficulty in hiring qualified Negroes, the main problem areas that were emphasized by most firms were the following: (1) Companies were unable to find qualified individuals for management, sales, clerical or skilled craft positions. (2) There is a certain amount of prejudice toward working with Negroes. (3) Negroes were not motivated to apply for job vacancies. (4)

Entrance barriers established by unions hampered management hiring efforts. (5) Smaller firms are financially unable to initiate recruitment and training programs for unqualified jobseekers, many of whom are functional illiterates.

Houston Representative comments included the following observations:

"We have about 120 employees. Much of our work is material handling requiring unskilled and semiskilled labor. About 65 of our men are Negro — mostly operating but some clerical and some supervisory, including supervisors over whites. We have complete integration and use the best man for the job regardless of color."

"Our company has no published equal opportunity employment policy. We do hire the first qualified applicant for any job open. We do so without consideration of race. This statement is true only for our warehouse and shop. We attempt to avoid race conflict within our office by excluding Negro employees. Our present employees lack the sophistication and nonprejudicial attitude to work with Negroes. Their presence would be violently disturbing within our office. This is unfortunate, but true."

"We have much to learn in order to do the best job in the employment of blacks in our office. In the factory, it has been no problem for 23 years."

"It is difficult to eliminate prejudice by subordinates in applying the policy."

"All they need is the *desire to work!*"

Los Angeles   Firms furnished the following opinions:

"Negroes very seldom apply."

"We have tried to hire minorities — Chicanos, etc., but feel that it is more a failure on their part. One man off training school left in a month, as he wanted more pay — a shop man getting $2.35 an hour."

"We can't seem to find qualified help even though we are looking very hard."

"It is difficult to find qualified applicants for a firm without a true effective training program."

"We hire qualified Negroes — not the 'hard core' in the majority of cases."

"We cannot find qualified middle management or blue-collar foremen or office girls among Negroes. So we do not have any in these jobs."

"The biggest problem is language proficiency."

"We probably give preference to the promising Negro applicant."

"We are in an area of Mexican-Americans but employ 75 per cent of all Negroes that apply."

Detroit   Small and medium-sized businesses had the following comments:

"Our program is ineffective because our work is highly skilled. Most openings are for skilled people."

"Approximately 25 per cent of our hourly personnel is Negro, but it is very difficult to obtain qualified black people for office functions."

"Where applicants have equal ability, there is equal opportunity."

"We now have a Negro in complete charge of our warehouse; we are very happy."

"It is effective in mechanics and retail sales. It is ineffective in lesser jobs like porters, car washers, lubricating."

"We are not large enough to incur additional expenses for training and related training items."

"The number of Negro applicants in a creative field is limited."

Baltimore   Owners of firms provided some of the most valuable in-depth remarks:

"Our plant has been open and a Fair Civil Rights platform established years before the Act was passed. If you expect to improve conditions, you should commence with the labor unions in Baltimore who have placed a group of 'unwritten' restrictions against Negroes, especially in the trade groups."

"Unions, they demand qualified highly-skilled people, linotype operators, compositors, etc."

"I sincerely believe in equal opportunity for all; but I also believe a person must be able to command the job and salary through his skill, knowledge, and ability and not by demand and cries of discrimination. My experience during my 23 years in business where we hired black, white, and oriental was that the Negro seldom wanted a job or responsibility and all too frequently suffered from racial inferiority. I believe they should be trained, educated and reassured that they are the equal of anyone, and it is up to the individual to prove it."

"I own and operate three commercial printing plants. After 3½ years of operating a printing plant where Negroes were given more than an equal opportunity, I have been forced to close and move this operation. The Negro leaders failed to lead, and Negro followers refused to follow. It resulted in $150,000 in losses, damaged machinery, stolen property, lost clients, added costs for repairs and new security guards. They further brought in the union which costs us many thousands of dollars. My experience has caused me to move the plant and start over again staffing. Ten or 15 per cent will be my maximum."

At the present time, the Negro has a tremendous educational and cultural gap to bridge. We attempted to place more Negroes in production, but their reading skills were at such low levels that we had to abandon our plans. Until the schools raise this particular skill to a comparable level, I think that the Negro will not be able to fit into the printing industry properly. Perhaps, the next generation will acquire this skill. The mere fact that schools have opened their doors to them is not enough. The Negro will have to work extremely hard to just catch up. At the present time though, the Negro resents the fact that they need this extra effort. Regardless of the reason for the gap, the fact is that a gap exists. We do not hesitate to hire qualified Negro personnel."

"Shop men object to working with colored."

"We have found no skilled craftsmen in the Negro labor market. We have been looking for over eight years."

"We feel that much could be done if the labor unions were forced to comply with the law for the entrance of Negroes who are qualified. On the other hand, we do not feel it a good policy to insist that racists and militants be forced on any organization."

The attitudes and policies of small and medium-sized employers in the inner city toward hiring the hard-core unemployed are especially important because the chronically jobless residents are usually not located convenient to the available jobs and city transportation does not run into surrounding areas where industry is located.

The distance and difficulty of reaching certain jobs from Negro residential areas may impose costs on Negroes high enough to discourage them from seeking employment there. The automobile population in cities is increasing even more rapidly than the human population; at the same time, transportation aid for highways does not benefit the urban poor. The Department of Transportation estimates that while nearly all families with incomes in excess of $10,000 have a car, less than half those with incomes under $3,000 own a car.[1]

The Los Angeles employer who stated, "Our policy has been ineffective because there are no Negro residential areas near our place of business," demonstrated that demographic shifts are working against poor, urban Negroes. Industries are increasingly moving to the suburbs beyond the service of public transportation. Jobs are moving out of reach of the slum Negro even if he has the training. Distance and travel cost shut most slum dwellers out of the fastest growing job market. Even within the city, plants are often many miles distant from the slum areas, and transportation is costly and time consuming. Transportation to the suburbs is prohibitive at the low wages most slum residents can command. Most metropolitan centers have this problem to varying degrees, but Los Angeles is a major city where transportation problems are acute. Since World War II, important industrial centers have sprung up outside of central Los Angeles whereas previously most industry in the metropolitan area was within the city. Los

Angeles is a horizontal city, and it is huge. Most industrial jobs are ten to twenty miles from the black ghettos. City residents own 3,000,000 cars but 31 per cent of the black families don't have cars to take them to work. It costs anywhere from 50 cents to $1.78 to make a roundtrip between central Los Angeles and the nearest industrialized areas. On trips to more outlying points, costs are much higher and service less frequent. Within the south-central area, Watts, very, very few jobs are available. Private transportation is a necessity if Watts residents are to find jobs. Thirty per cent of the households in this area do not possess automobiles. A new bus line was opened in July, 1966 connecting Watts with the industrial and commercial areas. Within two months, the line was handling over 10,000 passengers a week, and fares had been substantially reduced. Shortly after the line was opened, a passenger count showed that the majority were either going to work or looking for work.[2]

EVALUATION OF NEGRO WORK PERFORMANCE

Negro employees who are clustered in unskilled classifications have special problems of work adjustment since their employment often means substandard wages, great instability and uncertainty of tenure, extremely low status in the eyes of employer and employees, little or no chance for meaningful advancement, and unpleasant working conditions. Therefore, the success or failure of the disadvantaged worker is contingent upon the presence or absence of special provision for him within the company. The placement of a disadvantaged person into a job is only a beginning. Disadvantaged workers modify their behavior, become cooperative and motivated to work, to the degree that representatives of companies adapt their behavior to become actively concerned and involved with the workers. The commitment of an employer to the culturally different person he employs must compensate for the general lack of initially expressed commitment on the part of the new worker. This worker may become an excellent worker, the best worker, but initially his loyalty and abilities are held in a self-defensive abeyance. The translation of the employer's commitment into flexible company practices that are tangible and that are recognizable responses to the special needs of the disadvantaged worker will create favorable changes in the behavior of the worker. Evaluation of Negroes as workers by urban employers emphasize some of the handicaps the disadvantaged individual brings with him to the job.

Baltimore   Firms offered the following appraisals:
    "I have tried to train several Negroes to be pressmen in our engraved stationery department. All have failed miserably and all came from the local

Concentrated Employment Program. (Concentrated Employment Program areas are target poverty areas in which the Department of Labor has combined separate manpower programs in order to concentrate the effects of these programs in specific neighborhoods.) Their attendance was good, but they lacked any kind of mechanical ability. CEP told me all had good mechanical ability and were able to work well with their hands. Programs such as CEP should accurately test the job seekers to determine what abilities the applicant has. Small companies can't afford to waste time and money finding these things out."

"Those who make the grade are good."

"Poor workers! We deal in custom work; we cannot tolerate unskilled labor."

"I will hire any man on his contribution only; unfortunately, the Negroes we hire don't show up, are drunk, are often belligerent, are undependable."

"We have found that workers generally now are not what they were 5 to 10 years ago. No new help is willing to really work, regardless what pay rates are."

"It has been our experience that when we do hire some on a trial basis, they either do not work out or fail to return after a few days. The girls we have in our shop do their jobs well, and have been with us for many years."

Los Angeles   These remarks were volunteered by executives:

"Our firm works 3 shifts 24 hours per day day 7 days per week. We have no layoffs or slow periods and plenty of overtime. Our other minority group in Southern California is Mexican-American. We have equal opportunity for all. And can only hire and keep about one out of 25 Negroes hired compared to one out of 5 Mexican-Americans. Because of plenty of steady work, there is, we feel, a good opportunity for steady employment and advancement. Our experience is that the Negro worker will not stay even though skill is not a high requirement. A case of lack of will, motivation to work as compared to other employees. The exceptions usually are female employees. This has caused some problems with other workers that we give more chances to the Negroes than the other workers trying to comply with equal employment opportunity. However, like all races, a good one is very good and loyal. Here is a case of plenty of opportunity and still poor results. Education and motivation, we feel, is the answer."

"Our one is very good (of 36 employees)."

"Average; but when they're bad, they're very bad."

"Good workers, female. Average to poor workers, male."

Detroit   Businessmen added these statements:

"Average workers but so poorly equipped mentally and educationally."

"Some good, some bad — just like whites."
"Average to poor workers; few are really good workers.".
"Either very good or very poor."
"Poor — ones working here for 6 months; then average."

Houston   Replies were quite categorical:
"Some are exceptional, others are below average."
"None any good."
"Good workers or worthless!"

The smaller employers had uniformly less favorable comments concerning Negro employees than the large companies, where 2 of 3 employers had rated Negroes as average workers, while 1 of 4 considered them to be good, and only 1 of 12 rated them as average-to-poor or poor. In contrast, fewer than 1 of 5 small businesses rated them in the "good" category, while 2 of 5 contended they were average-to-poor or poor employment risks. Slightly more than 1 of 3 firms evaluated their work performance as average. Table 35 indicates that Houston and Baltimore firms' assessments were more negative than the sample averages and Los Angeles and Detroit ratings. This may be due to lower educational and skill levels in the Southern cities.

It is particularly important to avoid placing disadvantaged minority persons in "dead-end" jobs that offer no advancement opportunities. Such persons have seen members of their group mired in this type of job all their lives, and they have little motivation to stay at work once they are so placed. The job-holding ability of gang members, school dropouts, and the underprepared is generally poor in relation to the regular workforce. Many such people lack staying power in training programs, preferring a job now with money to spend now. Their expectations are often unrealistic in terms of their backgrounds. Merely creating jobs will not correct this; the creation process without a job retention effort ends in more failure for both the individual and the employer. What may be understandable behavior to the sociologist is laziness and lack of responsibility to the employer; he cannot condone it.[3]

Training the hard-core unemployed, even for factory work, is more difficult than imagined, and there are no overnight solutions. It can involve teaching a man how to catch the correct bus, or how to get up in the morning, or getting him glasses so he may learn enough reading for simple jobs. These people have to be taught the letters that spell common colors so they can read the instruction cards that tell them to put a blue or green steering wheel on a car as it comes down the assembly line. They must learn simple addition so that they can count boxes of parts they take off a supplier's truck. Some sign an "X" for their names. Employers have had to overcome fear and resentment, hostility and a history of failure.[4]

Several large corporate employers had particularly discouraging experiences with the ghetto job applicant. Some of Chrysler Corporation's applicants signed on for job training, then never showed up. Others who did report were notoriously late. As Chrysler registered those who did report, it found that many of them had never been counted in a census, had no Social Security number, had never registered to vote, and belonged to no organizations of any kind. In most of the accepted senses, they really did not exist. Many of the hard-core unemployed are so lacking in education that they even have to be taught how to learn. In their homes, there is little tradition of work, education, family stability, community responsibility, or individual achievement. A Honeywell interviewer tells the story of offering a young, disadvanted youth a job, and explaining that the shift started at 8 A.M. The applicant replied, without a trace of sarcasm or rancor, "I don't get up that early." and out the door he went.[5] Therefore, not only the skills but the attitudes of workers, few of whom are high school graduates, require hours of attention. Many have never held full-time jobs before. They do not conform readily to work habits such as punching time clocks and showing up on Monday morning.

Smaller firms, those that place a high premium on education or skill and those where appearance and conduct are important, feel the need to have the applicants "processed" before putting them on the job. Comportment, dress, and grooming are problems to some, but the most disconcerting tends to be the language of the inner-city ghetto. Many employers regard the language differences of minority group workers as barriers to promotion since they cannot communicate effectively, and many employers have negative attitudes regarding the abilities and ambitions of low-skill workers, attitudes often based upon contact with seemingly apathetic, indifferent workers who have resigned themselves to a lifetime of poverty.

As to eight items of specific job performance, the earlier study indicated that ". . . Negro employees compared quite favorably with others on the first six items (reporting for work on time, regularity of attendance, quantity of work produced, quality of work produced, getting along with others, and honesty) in that at least 8 of 10 firms rated Negroes equal to whites. Fifty-one per cent appraised Negro promotability potential as the same as whites, and 6 of 10 employers rated them equal with other workers in the willingness to assume responsibility." As Table 36 demonstrates, the smaller firms, notably those in Houston and Baltimore, were decidedly less positive on the same six items, and with respect to promotability and willingness to assume responsibility, white employees were rated considerably better.

Once again, additional comments emphasized the negative aspects of Negro work habits.

Baltimore   Representative remarks mentioned the following inadequacies:

"My experience during my twenty-three years in business where we hired black, white, and oriental was that the Negro seldom wanted a job or responsibility and all too frequently suffered from racial inferiority."

"Frequently, I found that Negroes, when offered jobs of responsibility, did not want to assume responsibility."

"Our basic problem with the Negro worker is that he is prone to absenteeism. After a week or several weeks, he usually wanders off and appears no more."

"We have had extremely poor experience with Job Corps trainees in duplicating and printing fields. They have had very poor training."

"Promotion has not yet been possible; it is too early in training."

"We have, for many years, employed Negro typists and clerical workers. We have been unable to experience any company loyalty from any Negro we have employed, nor have we been able to promote a Negro to a supervisory job, although we tried to train one for it, rather than employ a supervisor from the outside."

Houston   Several small firms added:

"My own evaluation is that Negroes, in general, have been a mild disappointment as employees due to their general irregular habits and heavy absenteeism. However, we have notable exceptions among our employees."

"Our basic problem is turnover."

Los Angeles   More criticisms were offered by Los Angeles companies:

"He sometimes has a chip on his shoulder as to race."

"Others better; he is limited — started work at 12."

"He is responsible up to his capabilities."

"They are generally unable to communicate. Need better use of oral and written language."

"They are generally not used to leadership role."

"Our greatest complaint with our Negro employees is that they have no responsibility to their job. We find that putting in a full week's work by the majority is quite rare."

"They get along with others the same as whites, except for an occasional incorrigible."

"Our principal problem has been hostility."

"I could write a 'book', but I have a job to do. In office field, Negro employees have been mediocre to fair, very complaining 'chip on shoulder', though paid equally for equal work. Our Negro salesman has done a fine job. In warehouse and chemical plant, Negro personnel employed in all areas do equally as well as 'non'. I think these surveys calling attention to differences in people border on the ridiculous as we all should work together regardless of color, religion or ethnic differences."

"While we realize that one or two incidents can hardly be important, we got the impression that some of the Negroes who were dependable in 'lower-pay' work grew less dependable when they were promoted to jobs that paid better. It seemed that the higher pay allowed them to take time off and still earn as much as they did for full-time work at the lower rate."

One employer recommended a highly novel approach: "The big stopper is giving blacks positions from which they can gain pride. But small businessmen can't afford the luxury of taking chances and hoping the man will shape up. Subsidize MANAGERS! Give the small businessman $12-15,000 (tax, cash, rebate, what have you!) to promote his most promising black to supervisor or manager. Don't let him know he's being subsidized. Let him act like a manager, absorb some pride and self-confidence. If he succeeds, the whole morale of the shop would be transformed. Carry him for 6 months if necessary, and see if he can't grow into the job. If necessary, underwrite the cost of the boo-boo's. Do anything to get these people some pride in their position, people to emulate, a stake in the game. The Muslims and Panthers are only attempts to gain pride. We must beat them to the punch!"

Detroit   Similar problem areas were stressed:

"Our policy is open; however, many Negroes do not pursue promotion outside of areas which are predominantly Negro."

"It depends on the individual. Some have the willingness to assume responsibility, some don't. I would say the Negro is beginning to be better."

"Uneducated — drink too much to be very honest. They still act like animals in many instances."

The chip-on-the-shoulder attitude, if it does exist, may represent a natural reaction to what is perceived as a hostile atmosphere. The claim of laziness and other faults may reflect either stereotypes on the part of management or the fact that in the Negro culture there is no tradition that hard work pays off. Often, supervisors seem to care little about constructively guiding new employees who have hard-core unemployed backgrounds. Sensitivity training is one method of giving them insight into the lives of the poor. The hoped-for result is that they then will participate in helping the disadvantaged become productive employees.

Problems of work adjustment are not unique to the largest minority group in the United States. Eisenstadt described employment experiences of Oriental-Jewish immigrants (from North Africa and Asia) in Israel and certain parallels with the American experience can easily be drawn:

... Another typical situation was the following. Some young Oriental Jews would be employed in a modern workshop or factory. They did not continue in their jobs, but changed them quite frequently, usually complaining of "unfair" treatment and the management's lack of interest in them and their work. Sometimes they sought employment with an acquaintance or relative, where conditions might be worse, and where, because of this, they did not remain. Quite often, they changed jobs to get slightly higher pay, without regard to stability or prospects for the future. They were not interested in vocational courses or opportunities of advancement; their most important inducement was the amount of money received daily or weekly — an amount which increased their temporary spending power and enhanced their prestige in the family and among their circle of friends.[6]

Patterson recounts the reactions of British managers toward West Indian immigrants employed as railroad workers; again demonstrating that minority groups in other countries have employment idiosyncracies not unlike the American Negro:

The management's general experience of colored workers was that the majority of recruits had little initiative or sense of responsibility and that they did not develop these traits with time. They had shown themselves slow workers (possibly as a consequence of climatic differences), and this slowness emerged most noticeably in the few all-colored gangs. ... Their turnover was not particularly high, but they were thought to make a lot of fuss about minor illness and to absent themselves unnecessarily. Most seemed to expect too much at the outset and showed little willingness to "work their passage to acceptance". ...[7]

For the many men in slums who are qualified only as laborers, the employment outlook is bleak. Employment in such jobs is declining relative to total employment in the United States. Opportunities in other blue-collar jobs are also growing much less rapidly than white-collar employment. Between 1947 and 1967, for example, total employment in seven large central cities rose by only 50,000, while employment in the metropolitan rings surrounding those same cities increased by 900,000. The jobs available to slum residents have been changing in response both to changing occupational patterns, to the disadvantage of semiskilled and unskilled workers, and to shifts in the location of industry. Between 1954 and 1965, almost two-thirds of all new industrial buildings (measured by valuation) and a little over half of all new stores were constructed outside the nation's central cities. In some areas, the proportions considerably exceeded even these high national averages: in Los Angeles 85 per cent of the new industrial buildings and 63 per cent of the stores. The central city is becoming more and more the working place of office workers, largely white people, who commute from the suburbs, while the shortage of unskilled jobs in or even near the slum areas increases year after year.[8]

THE JOBS EXPERIENCE

The federal government's JOBS program (the intials stand for *J*ob *O*pportunities in the *B*usiness *S*ector) subsidizes a nationwide campaign by businessmen to hire the hard-core unemployed, but has produced only about one-fourth of the jobs hoped for, according to government figures. Many corporations have failed to meet the hiring and training targets of their federal reimbursement contracts. In addition, there has been a 45 per cent turnover rate among the trainees. The contract requires not only on-the-job training, for which the government normally pays reimbursement of $20 to $60 a week per trainee, but a period of initial, full-time orientation, which in many cases is the trainee's first introduction to work procedures of any kind. The government reimburses the contract holder for the difference between what it would cost to hire and train an ordinary employee and the cost of hiring, training, and retaining a hard-core JOBS worker. Many of the 3,300,000 American businesses which employ fewer than 50 persons are being encouraged to enter into training contracts with the Department of Labor under the JOBS program. Such contracts are a financial necessity for many smaller companies and enable even the largest to make the full commitment to resources and management skills needed for a fully-successful program to hire, train and retain the disadvantaged. The JOBS program expanded in 1969 from 50 to 131 cities, with more than 21,000 companies participating in the effort.[9] However, small employers frequently shy away from the idea of signing a government contract for fear the government will dictate hiring and firing policies. There is a real financial problem even for those who sign. Few small businesses can add to their payrolls trainees who will not be productive for at least two months. Also required where needed are basic or remedial reading, writing, arithmetic and communications skills.[10]

The National Alliance of Businessmen is attempting to broaden its base of finding jobs for the hard-core unemployed to service industries and small business. Previously, the Alliance had concentrated primarily on heavy industry, such as the automobile companies. There are 26,000 businesses in the United States with 50 or more employees, but as indicated earlier, 3,300,000 firms have 50 or less employees. The real strength and thrust of this program requires that small businesses be included.[11] The NAB in November, 1969 had 18,500 member companies and had placed more than 200,000 ghetto residents in jobs, and is aiming for 614,000 placements by

June 1971. However, large companies still dominate the hiring, partly because many small and medium-sized companies are reluctant to commit themselves.[12] The obligation incumbent upon small and medium-sized employers would not be an especially onerous one. Estimates are that a "basic breakthrough toward the elimination of massive unemployment" would be achieved if the nation's small businesses (under 50 employees) would commit themselves to train only *two hard-core unemployed for permanent jobs* (author's italics).[13]

TABLE 29.   Perception of Role of Company President in Promoting Equal Employment Opportunity at Firm Level, by City.

	Sample Totals		Baltimore		Los Angeles		Detroit		Houston	
	No.	*%*	*No.*	*%*	*No.*	*%*	*No.*	*%*	*No.*	*%*
He sets tone and creates proper climate	143	45.0	45	40.5	43	45.7	33	44.0	22	45.8
He makes and executes the policy	87	27.4	35	31.5	27	28.7	23	30.7	12	25.0
He exercises community leadership	63	19.8	19	17.1	16	17.0	16	21.3	12	25.0
No response	25	7.8	12	10.9	8	8.6	3	4.0	2	4.2

Source: Negro Employment Questionnaire.

TABLE 30.   Willingness of Firms to Participate in Community Action Programs Sponsored by Private Enterprise, by City.

	Sample Totals		Baltimore		Los Angeles		Detroit		Houston	
	No.	%	No.	%	No.	%	No.	%	No.	%
Yes	56	24.6	21	26.6	10	16.1	17	30.9	8	25.0
No	61	26.8	19	24.1	16	25.8	17	30.0	9	28.1
Under certain conditions	96	42.1	27	34.1	34	58.8	21	38.2	14	43.7
No response	15	6.5	12	15.2	2	3.3	0	0.0	1	3.1

Source: Negro Employment Questionnaire.

TABLE 31.   Perception of Seriousness of Negro Employment Problem in Individual Firms, by City.

City	Major		Minor		Somewhere in between		Major in Some; Minor in Others		No Response	
	No.	%	No.	%	No.	%	No.	%	No.	%
Houston	1	3.1	25	78.1	1	3.1	4	12.6	1	3.1
Baltimore	7	8.9	52	65.8	3	3.8	14	17.7	3	3.8
Detroit	1	1.9	36	66.7	10	18.5	7	12.9	0	0.0
Los Angeles	5	8.2	43	70.5	5	8.2	7	11.5	1	1.6
Sample Totals	14	6.2	156	69.0	19	8.4	32	14.2	5	2.2

Source: Negro Employment Questionnaire.

TABLE 32. Perception of Seriousness of Negro Employment Problem in Individual Firms, by City and by Employment Size of Firms.

City and Employment Size of Firms	Major		Minor		Somewhere in between		Major in Some; Minor in Others		No Response	
	No.	%	No.	%	No.	%	No.	%	No.	%
Houston										
Under 50	0	0.0	9	69.2	1	7.7	2	15.4	1	7.7
Over 50	1	5.3	16	84.2	0	0.0	2	10.5	0	0.0
Baltimore										
Under 50	5	12.3	38	63.3	3	5.0	12	20.0	1	3.3
Over 50	2	10.5	14	73.7	0	0.0	2	10.5	1	5.3
Detroit										
Under 50	0	0.0	21	77.8	2	7.4	4	14.8	0	0.0
Over 50	1	3.8	15	57.7	8	30.8	1	3.8	0	0.0
Los Angeles										
Under 50	1	5.6	13	72.2	1	16.7	1	5.6	1	5.6
Over 50	4	9.3	30	69.8	2	4.7	6	14.0	1	3.2

Source: Negro Employment Questionnaire.

TABLE 33.   Prevalence of Equal Employment Opportunity Policies at Firm Level, by City.

	Sample Totals		Baltimore		Los Angeles		Detroit		Houston	
	No.	%	No.	%	No.	%	No.	%	No.	%
Yes	212	93.0	75	94.4	60	96.8	52	94.5	25	78.1
No	15	6.6	3	3.8	2	3.2	3	5.5	7	21.9
No response	1	0.4	1	1.8	0	0.0	0	0.0	0	0.0

Source: Negro Employment Questionnaire.

TABLE 34.   Degree of Implementation of Equal Employment Opportunity Policies at Firm Level, by City.

	Sample Totals		Baltimore		Los Angeles		Detroit		Houston	
	No.	%	No.	%	No.	%	No.	%	No.	%
Effectively	101	43.9	33	41.8	29	46.8	24	42.2	15	46.9
Varies	76	33.0	24	30.4	24	38.7	17	29.8	11	34.4
Ineffectively	27	11.7	8	10.1	6	9.7	8	14.0	5	15.6
No response	26	11.4	14	17.7	3	4.8	8	14.0	1	3.1

Source: Negro Employment Questionnaire.

TABLE 35.   Evaluation of Negroes as Workers at Firm Level, by City.

	Sample Totals		Baltimore		Los Angeles		Detroit		Houston	
	No.	%	No.	%	No.	%	No.	%	No.	%
Good workers	44	18.0	14	17.3	12	18.2	13	21.0	5	14.7
Average workers	96	39.5	31	38.3	28	42.4	24	38.7	13	38.1
Average-to-poor workers	67	27.6	21	25.9	22	33.3	16	25.8	8	23.5
Poor workers	32	13.2	14	17.3	4	6.1	7	11.3	7	20.6
No response	4	1.6	1	1.2	0	0.0	2	3.2	1	3.1

Source: Negro Employment Questionnaire.

TABLE 36.   Comparison of Negro Employees with Other Employees by Work Characteristics at Firm Level, by City.

	Same		Others Better		Negroes Better		No Response	
	No.	%	No.	%	No.	%	No.	%
Baltimore								
Reporting for work on time	40	50.6	30	38.0	2	2.5	7	8.9
Regularity of attendance	33	41.8	37	46.8	2	2.5	7	8.9
Quantity of work done	37	46.8	31	39.2	1	1.3	10	12.7
Quality of work done	39	49.4	29	36.7	1	1.3	10	12.7
Getting along with others	59	74.7	12	15.2	0	0.0	8	10.1
Honesty	57	72.2	13	16.5	0	0.0	9	11.3
Promotability	30	38.0	37	46.8	0	0.0	12	15.2
Willingness to assume responsibility	24	30.4	44	55.7	1	1.3	10	12.7
Houston								
Reporting for work on time	21	65.6	9	28.1	0	0.0	2	6.3
Regularity of attendance	14	43.7	16	50.0	0	0.0	2	6.3
Quantity of work done	16	50.0	12	37.5	2	6.3	2	6.3
Quality of work done	14	43.7	16	50.0	0	0.0	2	6.3
Getting along with others	22	68.7	4	12.5	3	9.4	3	9.4
Honesty	18	54.5	12	36.4	0	0.0	3	9.1
Promotability	8	25.8	21	67.7	0	0.0	2	6.5
Willingness to assume responsibility	7	21.9	23	71.8	0	0.0	2	6.3
Detroit								
Reporting for work on time	38	69.1	13	23.6	1	1.8	3	5.5
Regularity of attendance	33	60.0	18	32.7	1	1.8	3	5.5
Quantity of work done	38	59.1	12	21.8	1	1.8	4	7.3
Quality of work done	37	64.9	15	26.3	0	0.0	5	8.8
Getting along with others	42	76.4	9	16.3	1	1.8	3	5.5
Honesty	48	87.3	4	7.2	0	0.0	3	5.5
Promotability	31	55.4	22	39.3	0	0.0	3	5.3
Willingness to assume responsibility	25	45.5	25	45.5	2	3.6	3	5.4
Los Angeles								
Reporting for work on time	44	69.8	15	23.8	1	1.6	3	4.8
Regularity of attendance	34	54.0	24	38.1	1	1.6	4	6.3
Quantity of work done	45	71.4	13	20.6	1	1.6	4	6.4
Quality of work done	43	68.3	16	25.4	1	1.6	3	4.7
Getting along with others	43	69.4	14	22.6	1	1.6	4	6.4
Honesty	48	78.7	5	8.2	1	1.6	7	11.5
Promotability	30	49.2	25	41.0	1	1.6	5	8.2
Willingness to assume responsibility	22	34.9	35	55.6	1	1.6	5	7.9

Table 36 continued

	Same		Others Better		Negroes Better		No Response	
	No.	%	No.	%	No.	%	No.	%
Sample Totals								
Reporting for work on time	143	62.4	67	29.3	4	1.7	15	6.3
Regularity of attendance	114	49.8	95	41.5	4	1.7	16	7.0
Quantity of work done	136	62.1	68	31.1	5	2.3	10	4.5
Quality of work done	133	57.6	76	32.9	2	0.8	20	8.9
Getting along with others	166	73.8	39	17.3	5	2.2	15	6.7
Honesty	171	76.0	34	15.1	1	0.4	19	8.5
Promotability	99	43.6	105	46.3	1	0.4	22	9.7
Willingness to assume responsibility	78	34.1	127	55.5	4	1.7	20	8.7

Source: Negro Employment Questionnaire.

REFERENCES

1. Jones, William H. "U.S. Begins Facing Up to Auto's Impact." *The Washington Post,* January 23, 1970, p. D-1.

2. *Manpower Report, op. cit.,* pp. 87-88.

3. "Realities and Opportunities in the Development of Jobs." *Business and Society,* Spring, 1968, p. 25.

4. "Jobless Training Begins with ABC's." *The New York Times,* June 16, 1968, p. 35.

5. "The War That Business Must Win." *Business Week,* November 1, 1969, p. 67.

6. Eisenstadt, S. N. *The Absorption of Immigrants.* London: Routledge & Kegan Paul Ltd., 1954, p. 99.

7. Patterson, Sheila. *Dark Strangers,* A Sociological Study of the Absorption of a Recent West Indian Migrant Group in Brixton, South London. London: Tavistock Publications, 1963, p. 92.

8. *Manpower Report of the President — 1967.* Washington, D.C.: U.S. Government Printing Office, April, 1967, pp. 81-82, 87.

9. "Job Finding Agency Reports to Business." *The Washington Post,* Dec. 22, 1969, p. E-7.

10. Green, Sterling F. "U.S. Finds Lag in Drive for Slum Jobs." *The Washington Post,* Sept. 22, 1969, p. A-6.

11. "Businessmen's Alliance Is Broadening Its Base of Finding More Jobs." *The Wall Street Journal,* Dec. 3, 1969, p. 26.

12. "The War That Business Must Win." *Business Week,* November 1, 1969, p. 65.

13. Cushing, William G. "Slowdown Won't Affect JOBS Goal, Says NAB." *The Washington Post,* December 8, 1969, p. D-10.

Chapter 4
Labor and Management Participation in Remedial Programs

EVIDENCE OF UNION EMPLOYMENT DISCRIMINATION

Labor unions, as well as the business community, have come in for their share of criticism with regard to their record in creating employment opportunities for minorities. In particular, several Baltimore businessmen in responding to questions about the factors which obstruct total implementation of equal employment opportunity policies cited union policies in the following words:

"We feel that much could be done if the labor unions were forced to comply with the law for the entrance of Negroes who are qualified."

"Our policy is ineffective because unions demand qualified highly skilled people: linotype operators, compositors, etc."

"Our plant has been open, and a Fair Civil Rights platform established years before the Act was passed. If you expect to improve conditions, you should commence with the labor unions in Baltimore who have placed a group of 'unwritten' restrictions against Negroes, especially in the trade groups."

Specifically, seven union policies or practices or both have been singled out as examples of employment discrimination. They include:

1. The refusal of all but a few of the eighteen building-trades unions to open up their ranks to qualified Negroes; most of the highly-paid skilled construction jobs are held by whites.

2. Industrial-union seniority systems that relegate Negroes to menial jobs. In many plants the senior Negro employees have less desirable jobs than the most junior white worker.

3. The systematic exclusion of Negroes from apprenticeship programs (mostly in the building trades); only 3 per cent of registered apprentices are black.

4. Failure to eliminate local unions that are segregated by race. There are over 150 all-Negro locals affiliated with the AFL-CIO.

5. The use of hiring halls and referral systems to prevent qualified nonunion Negroes from bidding for jobs.

6. The deliberate exclusion of Negroes from unions in some industries.

7. Union attempts to evade federal law by accepting a token number of Negroes.[1]

The most blatant instances of racial discrimination in unions occur in the highly-paid skilled building trades. Skilled craftsmen such as electricians, plumbers, sheet metal workers and carpenters enjoy the highest hourly wage rates in the nation. Many Negroes do hold jobs in these trades, but very few work on lucrative construction projects for a simple reason. Union membership is a requisite for employment on construction projects. A two- to five-year apprenticeship program is the eligibility requirement for union membership. Apprenticeship memberships in the building trades are extremely hard to obtain; for blacks, they are almost impossible to secure.

Spokesmen for construction unions insist that Negroes are not barred, but that most are incapable of qualifying for membership. This explanation, however, is questionable. O'Hanlon has said, "A number of Negroes more highly qualified than George Meany himself (who holds a plumber's card) have been denied membership in unions."[2] An example of discrimination which is often cited is the case of one Anderson L. Dobbins, a college graduate who majored in trade education and minored in electricity. He easily passed a union membership test in 1955 and applied to IBEW Local 212 in Cincinnati for membership. His application was rejected then, as it was subsequently in 1958, 1964, and 1965. Despite much legal maneuvering and government pressure, Dobbins is still not a union member. This is not an isolated case, but a typical craft union situation. It takes little perception to realize that this continuing discrimination is crippling one of the best hopes for easing the plight of the ghetto dweller, since construction work represents by far the most promising opportunity for poorly-educated blacks to earn high wages. Employment of more Negroes would also ease the needless labor shortages that have sent building costs soaring.[3]

Any attack upon union policies must go further than elimination of racial discrimination alone. It must include reform of the entire system of apprenticeships and entrance restrictions. The fact is that the trouble in the building trades is not simply bigotry toward Negroes; rather it is nepotism — keeping all outsiders out of the unions.[4]

A 1965 survey of five unions (Plumbers, Electricians, Ironworkers, Carpenters and Sheet Metal Workers) showed that of 5,908 apprentices in selected Northern areas, only 133 were Negroes.[5] In 1969, after two years and nearly $4 million in federal funds to help train Negro and other minority-group apprentices, the once nearly all-white construction unions still included only about 4 per cent Negroes: 5,280 of 132,000 total apprentices. Federal statistics indicated that the 4 per cent Negro representation in the building trades is about the same or a little better than apprenticeship openings in the metal, manufacturing, public utilities, mining and transportation industries and trade and service jobs. Figures are lacking on the number of top-paid Negro journeymen among the nation's 3.5 million union construction workers, but since apprenticeship is the main route to jobs, the figures are believed an accurate indication of how rapidly unions are admitting Negroes. Federal reports through the first half of 1969 showed that the two highest paid construction trades then (plumbers averaging $6.20 an hour and electricians, $6.10) still counted only 2 per cent Negro apprentices. Government figures did not include the AFL-CIO's Laborers' Union which had about 25 per cent Negroes and nearly 50 per cent minority groups among its 500,000 members, averaging $4.26 an hour, compared to an average $5.59 hourly-wage for construction union journeymen. In addition to the building trades apprenticeships, the 1969 statistics included these estimates for other industry job training apprenticeships:

1. Metal manufacturing: A total of 57,600 apprenticeships of which 3 per cent, or 1,728 are Negro.
2. Other manufacturing: A total of 14,400 of which 3.2 per cent, or 460, are Negro.
3. Public utilities and other transportation: A total of 7,200, of which 3.9 per cent, or 280, are Negro.
4. Miscellaneous trade and services: A total of 24,000 of which 5.8 per cent, or 1,392, are Negro.
5. Mining: A total of 2,000 of which 5.1 per cent, or 102, are Negro.

The figures cover only those apprenticeship programs registered with federal or state governments and do not exhaust all areas of job training partially or totally controlled by unions.[6]

A recent report by the Equal Employment Opportunity Commission showed that blacks averaged 7.4 per cent of all jobs in the construction industry — with their ratio varying from virtually none in the Asbestos Workers to a high of 29.2 per cent among low-skilled laborers. Minority membership in the latter group exaggerates the position of blacks in the building trades. EEOC studies demonstrate that almost three out of four Negroes in the construction industry are laborers. In general construction, blacks make up 3.2 per cent of the work force; in the higher skilled mechanical trades, only about 1.4 per cent. Only 1.6 per cent of union carpenters are blacks; among electricians, the figure is 0.6 per cent; among plumbers, 0.2 per cent. Lengthy apprenticeship programs and outmoded qualifying examinations also make it difficult for blacks to become journeymen workers. Under union-imposed standards, it takes four years or 8,000 hours to train a carpenter; by contrast, an air-traffic controller receives 1½ years of training.[7]

In order that the same kind of comprehensive employment profile might be available concerning labor organizations as well as employers, the Equal Employment Opportunity Commission in fiscal year 1968 implemented its plans to collect data on minority representation in unions and joint labor-management apprenticeship programs. Apprentice Information Report EEO-2 was mailed to some 7,000 joint labor-management apprenticeship committees, and Local Union Equal Employment Opportunity Report EEO-3 was mailed to 5,000 local unions. A preliminary analysis of the apprenticeship programs in the three states that have the largest number of apprenticeships found low participation by Negroes in apprenticeship programs. Among 23,497 reported apprentices in California, New York, and Michigan, only 4.0 per cent were black. Form EEO-3, filed annually by local unions, is a companion report covering minority group participation in labor unions (by unions with 25 or more members). The form is filed by "referral unions," those which operate hiring halls or an equivalent service, and contains statistical breakdowns by minority group of total membership, applicants for membership, referrals, and applicants for referral. Unions are also required to report steps they have taken to promote equal employment opportunity.[8]

Tables 37 through 44 describe black membership figures in Baltimore, Detroit, Houston and Los Angeles referral unions for 1967 and 1968. Negroes seem to have made some progress in gaining entry into the General Construction Trades unions. However, their percentages in the highly skilled Mechanical Trades organizations still remain miniscule. A percentage range of from 0.0 per cent in Houston to 1.4 per cent in Detroit in 1968 means that literally only a handful of blacks can be found among boilermakers, electrical workers, elevator constructors, iron workers, plumbers, and sheet metal workers in the four sample cities.

"AFFIRMATIVE ACTION" REQUIREMENTS

On September 24, 1965, President Johnson signed Executive Order 11246 (amended in 1967 by Executive Order 11375 to include sex and made explicit in regulations adopted in 1968) in which he directed that Federal contracts and federally-assisted construction contracts include specific provisions that would obligate the contractor and his subcontractors not to discriminate in employment because of race, color, religion, sex or national origin. The administration of this portion of the Order was made the responsibility of the Secretary of Labor who shall "adopt such rules and regulations and issue such orders as he deems necessary and appropriate to achieve the purposes thereof."[9] Among the provisions set forth by the Order are the obligation that the contractor will take "affirmative action to ensure that applicants are employed, and that employees are treated during the employment without regard to their race, color, religion, sex, or national origin."[10] The Office of Federal Contract Compliance was created in 1965 to investigate discriminatory practices among federal contractors. Its jurisdiction includes not only policies and practices affecting employment, but those affecting promotion, transfer, rates of pay and termination. Generally speaking, all Federal contractors are supposed to have been taking affirmative action to hire minorities since 1965. If a company fails to broaden its recruitment base and increase the flow of minority applicants, it will have violated the executive order. Employers cannot defend their hiring practices simply by arguing that few minority workers are employed because few apply for jobs. Corporations doing $50,000 worth of business annually with the government and employing more than 50 people are subject to an annual review of the religious and racial distribution of their employees.[11]

The "affirmative action" program which a contractor must establish and submit to the Secretary of Labor must include identification and analysis of the inherent problems in minority employment coupled with an evaluation of opportunities for minority group personnel utilization. Further, the contractor's program is to include specific steps to guarantee equal employment opportunity geared to the problems and needs of the minority workers, which will recognize deficiencies when they exist and establish specific goals and timetables for prompt and full achievement of equal employment opportunity. To accomplish these objectives, the employer must devise a "program of action." The "Affirmative Action Program" as it is called, is a set of principles that are tailored to suit the particular set of circumstances of the project, the contractor, the local labor market, and the locality and is designed to demonstrate that the management of the company intends to and will exert positive efforts to assume equal employment opportunity. The formulation of such a program would include some or all of the following measures. First, an Equal Employment Opportunity Policy would be established, and made known to all employees, subcontractors, and sources of employees, with efforts being made to assure the cooperation of those involved. Secondly, an Equal Employment Opportunity Officer would be appointed from top management to coordinate, assist, and advise on the implementation of the policy. Further, nondiscriminatory recruiting practices would be initiated such as: (1) placing employment advertisements in newspapers which serve minority areas; (2) recruiting through schools which have significant minority enrollments; (3) encouraging referral of qualified minority workers by civic leaders and human relations organizations; (4) encouraging referrals of minority workers by present employers; and (5) informing all sources of employees that the company is seeking qualified minority group members for supervisor, journeymen and office positions. Next, assure nondiscriminatory hiring by instructing those making hiring decisions to consider all applicants regardless of race, work with unions to develop programs to assure equal opportunities for all minorities in construction trades, include an effective, nondiscrimination clause in new or renegotiated union agreements, use as many apprentices, part-time trainees, and summer employees from minority groups as the work needs and union agreements will permit.

Within the scope of cooperation with unions, contractors view certain basic factors as contributing to minority discrimination in construction. These are the hiring halls, complex seniority systems and union referral arrangements, which are allowed by Section 8(f) of the Taft-Hartley Act, which states:

> It shall not be an unfair labor practice under Subsections (a) and (b) of this section for an employer engaged primarily in the building and construction industry to make an agreement covering employees engaged (or who will be engaged) in the building and construction industry with a labor organization of which building and construction employees are members (not established, maintained, or assisted by any action defined in Section 8(a) of this Act as an unfair labor practice) because (1) The majority status of such labor organization has not been established under the provisions of Section 9 of this Act prior to the making of such agreement, or (2) Such agreement requires as a condition of employment, membership in such labor organization after the seventh day following the beginning of such employment or the effective date of the agreement, whichever is later, or (3) Such agreement requires the employer to notify such labor organization of opportunities for employment with such employer, or gives such labor organization an opportunity to refer qualified applicants for such employment, or (4) Such agreement specifies minimum training or experience qualifications for employment or provides for priority in opportunities for employment based upon length of service with such employer, in the industry or in the particular geographical area. . . ."

The problems posed by the hiring hall and other arrangements utilized by construction unions are apparent on federally funded projects where the executive orders holding the contractor alone responsible for discrimination and sanctions are applied only to the employer despite patent discrimination by the construction unions. For this reason, contractors would like to exclude hiring halls and related provisions from bargaining but are unable to do so under the law delineating them as mandatory bargaining subjects. Contractors find themselves whipsawed by the executive orders which forbid discriminatory employment practices and the National Labor

Relations Board ruling that refusal to bargain with unions who do discriminate is an unfair labor practice on the part of management. To overcome this dilemma, The Associated General Contractors of America have proposed that Congress take the following two steps: (1) Hold building trade unions solely responsible for unlawful discrimination, racial and otherwise, that occurs as a result of their operation of hiring halls, and similar referral arrangement, and (2) consider hiring halls and related arrangements a permissive rather than a mandatory subject of bargaining.[12]

Contractors should also be encouraged to make maximum use of apprentice and other training to help equalize opportunity for minority persons by sponsoring and assisting youths in entering pre-apprenticeship and apprenticeship programs, encouraging minority members to improve their job skills and job potential through training and education, actively participating in joint apprenticeship committees and the establishing of training and educational programs for older minority workers, and working with civic, labor and contractors' associations to conduct an open-admission training resource for the construction trades in the area.

Employers should also pursue policies and practices which will eliminate racial discrimination in matters of placement, promotion, compensatory pay, compensation and working conditions. In addition, where demotion, layoff, or termination of employees is being considered, advance clearance of such action by the firm's Equal Employment Opportunity Officer would be required. Minority subcontractors should also be encouraged to bid for work, while minority craftsmen desirous of becoming subcontractors should be counseled and assisted by management.

THE PHILADELPHIA PLAN

In other industries, the government can act against individual employers who practice racial discrimination in employment by treating such acts as violations of Title VII of the Civil Rights Act of 1964. However, because of the special problems of the construction industry, with its casual employment and hiring through unions, a different approach was taken. To implement Executive Order 11245 further, on June 27, 1969 Secretary of Labor George P. Shultz ordered the "Revised Philadelphia Plan for Compliance with Equal Employment Opportunity Requirements" to take effect. This order, or "Philadelphia Plan," as it is called, provided that no Federal or Federally-assisted construction contracts in excess of $500,000 be awarded in the Philadelphia area unless the bidder submitted an acceptable affirmative action program including specific goals of minority manpower utilization standards set forth in the invitation and specifications for bid. The plan to be submitted included the following trades: iron workers, plumbers, pipefitters, steamfitters, sheet metal workers, electrical workers, roofers and waterproofers, and elevator constructor workers. The roofers and waterproofers were later exempted.[13] The new plan overcame the objections of the Head of the General Accounting Office, Comptroller General Elmer B. Staats, who had ruled the Philadelphia Pre-Award Plan illegal, since it set specific racial hiring quotas in violation of the Civil Rights Act of 1964.

To justify the implementation of this plan, the government cited findings from the following surveys: (1) The Commission on Human Relations in Philadelphia found that unions in five trades (plumbers, steamfitters, electrical workers, sheet metal workers, and roofers) were discriminatory in their employment practices. (2) Marshall and Briggs, authors of *Negro Participation in Apprenticeship Programs,* stated that the 1964 Philadelphia Local AFL-CIO Human Relations Committee had made public the fact that no Negro apprentices were found in any of the building trades in that city. (3) At the end of 1967, less than 0.5 per cent of the membership of the unions in the aforementioned trades were Negroes.[14] It was also found that the unions failed to refer Negroes for employment, which resulted in priorities in referrals being granted to union members and to persons who had previously worked under union contracts.[15]

To help present its case before a public hearing in August, 1969 in Philadelphia, the government conducted its own survey which revealed the following results in the Philadelphia area:

1. *Iron Workers:* Total union membership was 850; 12 are from a minority group (1.4%).
2. *Steamfitters:* Total union membership was 2,308, 13 of whom or 0.65% were representatives of the minority group.
3. *Sheetmetal Workers:* Total union membership, 1,688; 17 or 1% were minority group representatives.
4. *Electricians:* Total union membership, 2,274; 40 or 1.7% of whom belonged to a minority group.
5. *Elevator construction workers:* Total union membership, 562; 3 or 0.54% were nonwhites.
6. *Plumbers and Pipefitters:* Total union membership, 2,335; 12 or 0.51% of whom are minority group representatives.[16]

This particular survey further identified the pool of labor available from minorities: (1) In the first half of 1969, in the Philadelphia area, nonwhite unemployment rates were double that of the labor force as a whole, or approximately 21,000 persons. There were between 1,200 and 1,400 nonwhites who are craftsmen and available for employment. (2) There were 7,500 minority group individuals in the Laborers Union who were working side by side with journeymen in the construction trade. Many worked as journeymen helpers and could, therefore, be easily trained in the crafts. (3) Between 5,000 and 8,000 prospective minority craftsmen would be prepared to accept training provided that jobs in the construction crafts were to be guaranteed upon completion of such training. (4) The following minority group workers were qualified for the trades mentioned in the Plan, but were unemployed:

Trade	*Number Available*
Ironworkers	302
Plumbers, pipefitters and steamfitters	797
Sheet metal workers	250
Electrical workers	745

(5) A survey conducted by the Office of Federal Contract Compliance indicated that the following minority persons were either employed in a trade or would complete their training in 1970:[17]

Trade	*Number Available*
Ironworkers	75
Plumbers, pipefitters	500
Steamfitters	300
Sheet metal workers	375
Electrical workers	525
Elevator constructors	43

Specific goals or ranges (not quotas) for minority manpower utilization are spelled out in Table 45. The ranges are expressed in manhours to be worked on a project by minority workers and should be uniform during the length of the project.[18] The contractor is to include in his affirmative action program the goals for minority utilization in the specified trade areas, which are to at least fall within a set of standard ranges of minority manpower utilization established on the basis of specific criteria. These include the current extent of minority participation in the trade, the availability of minority group applicants for employment in such trades, the need for training programs in the area or the need to assure demand for those persons in or from such existing programs or both, and finally, the impact of the program upon the existing labor force.[19]

The implementation of the Philadelphia Plan is designed to be accomplished with a minimum of disruption of the existing labor force. It was hoped that denying a contractor the opportunity to bid for Federally funded projects with the resultant loss of employment opportunities for union members would encourage unions to implement programs to assure contractor compliance, including direct recruitment in the black community, use of a "first-come-first-served" referral arrangement, and relaxation of exclusive hiring hall arrangements to facilitate recruitment of minority group members by the contractor. The ranges set by the OFCC are within the normal attrition rates, thereby easing the fears of displacement of white workers. The goals established are not quotas the contractor must achieve to be in compliance. The contractor will be under surveillance to determine if he is meeting these goals through the Office of Federal Contract Compliance Area Coordinator. As long as the goals set are reached, he will have no problems; but if they are not reached, an employer could lose a project and forfeit consideration for future contracts as a "responsible prospective contractor." However, if the contractor cannot meet the goals set but has used "good faith" in efforts to employ minority group workers, his status will not be harmed.[20]

The Plan also applies to all subcontractors involved in applicable projects. The subcontractor must comply with all its provisions in the same manner as the contractor. Failure to do so will result in his loss of "responsible prospective contractor" status, in addition to project disqualification. As long as the subcontractor used "good faith" as specified, he will be covered. The contractor, moreover, is not held responsible for the acts of the subcontractor.

Unions, when acting as hiring halls and having full control of manpower recruitment through a union shop should make every effort to help the contractor meet his requirements, but are not compelled so to act. Also, it is no excuse for the contractor if he fails to meet his requirements because of lack of cooperation from the unions. The contractor under Title VI, Sec. 703 (c)(3) of the Civil Rights Act of 1964 has legal remedy to force compliance upon a union.[21]

The "good faith" provision is spelled out in detail and has some interesting requirements which the contractor is expected to meet.[22]

(a) The OFCC Area Coordinator will maintain a list of community organizations which have agreed to assist any contractor in achieving his goal of minority manpower utilization by referring minority workers for employment in specified trades. A contractor who has not met his goals may exhibit evidence that he has notified such community organizations of opportunities for employment with him on the project for which he submitted such goals as well as evidence of their response.

(b) Any contractor who has not met his goal may show that he has maintained a file in which he has recorded the name and address of each minority worker referred to him and specifically what action was taken with respect to each such referred worker. If such worker was not sent to the union hiring hall for referral or if such worker was not employed by the contractor, the contractor's file should document this and the reasons therefore.

(c) A contractor should promptly notify the OFCC Area Coordinator in order for him to take appropriate action whenever the union with whom the contractor has a collective bargaining agreement has not referred to the contractor a minority worker sent by the contractor or the contractor has other information that the union referral process has impeded him in his efforts to meet his goal.

Although the minority manpower utilization percentages are spelled out in definite terms with a set procedure, the contractor still has an escape option. He may request an exemption from the Plan by writing to the Director, Office of Federal Contract Compliance, at the U.S. Department of Labor, with justifications for noncompliance.[23]

In addition, a contractor may find that the Plan will not apply to him "when the head of the contracting or administering agency determines that such a contract is essential to the national security and that its award without following such procedures is necessary to the national security."[24] In fact, the powerful Armed Services Committee of the House of Representatives is already challenging these hiring goals as detrimental to defense production. Defense contracts constitute two-thirds of all federal contract work, and many — especially the shipyard contracts which the OFCC is investigating for noncompliance — are held by Southern companies. Twenty-seven show-cause orders have been issued against defense contractors on projects ranging from construction of a nuclear aircraft carrier to minor subcontracting work. These orders instruct the contractor to show cause why their contracts should not be cancelled for failure to comply with minority hiring requirements. A government setback would weaken the campaign against holdout defense contractors and undermine OFCC efforts that depend on less precisely defined legal powers, such as the Philadelphia Plan. If the government is forced to back down where its position is strongest, the OFCC and related agencies will find it extremely difficult to enforce their rulings in other less sensitive industries. If the special subcommittee's investigation concludes that equal employment policy is holding up defense contract delivery, which is anticipated, the committee chairman could move to invoke existing law on national security to waive hiring requirements on defense contracts. Then, if the Secretary of Defense decided to invoke national security, his decision could not be appealed.[25]

In February 1970, the federal government announced that it would impose "Philadelphia-type" plans for those local communities which were unable to develop on their own initiative acceptable area-wide agreements. Nineteen major cities were named where the government will enforce minority group employment on federal construction projects unless contractors come up with voluntary plans well within a year's time. The 19 cities listed by the Labor Department were Atlanta, Boston, Buffalo, Cincinnati, Denver, Detroit, Houston, Indianapolis, Kansas City, Los Angeles, Miami, Milwaukee, Newark, New Orleans, New York, Pittsburgh, San Francisco, Seattle and St. Louis. The Office of Federal Contract Compliance indicated it would designate as priority cities Boston, Detroit, Atlanta, Los Angeles, Seattle,, and Newark. The criteria used in selecting the 19 cities were the labor supply, availability of minority craftsmen, number of minorities, volume of federal construction and minority representation in critical trades.[29]

OPPOSITION TO THE PHILADELPHIA PLAN

There has been intense opposition to the Philadelphia Plan concept from both contractors and construction unions. The latter oppose the plan, contending it establishes hiring quotas in violation of the 1964 Civil Rights Act, and is unworkable and inequitable. Contractors complain that the plan's requirements place them in an impossible position. They contend that they would be required to hire blacks who are not available and who would not be usable or acceptable to unions if they were. As an additional irritant, civil rights group have protested that the plan does not assure enough minority jobs and depends on voluntary compliance.[27]

Organized labor, moreover, based its opposition to the plan on the fear that apprenticeships, seniority, and other jealously guarded programs would be undermined by its application. Instead of accepting the new governmental policy, the construction unions undertook a defense of their record in promoting minority group employment. The Building and Construction Trades Department (AFL-CIO) pointed to a resolution which had been passed at their 1967 convention stating that it "endorses generally the principle of affirmative action to assist Negroes and other minority group persons in finding suitable employment and improving their economic and social status.[28] Then at their fifty-fifth convention in Atlantic City, New Jersey on September 22, 1969, a Statement of Policy in Equal Employment Opportunity was issued, stressing that the Building and Construction Trades and their affiliates had not adopted a passive nondiscriminatory approach. The 1969 resolution called for a three-part program: (1) to accelerate and expand the outreach programs in apprenticeship, (2) to ask all local unions in the building trades to take minority journeymen onto the rolls, (3) to explore new learning programs for minority workers who do not qualify as either apprentices or journeymen but may have had construction experience.[29]

The major building trade efforts involve the Apprenticeship Outreach programs which have already been established as a result of grants from the Department of Labor to help finance the training of minority groups so that they can enter the crafts through apprenticeship programs.[30] These programs involve recruitment and pre-apprenticeship training for minority young people sponsored by the Urban League, the Workers Defense League and the Building Trade Councils cooperating nationally with the Labor Department. Outreach originated as a result of the efforts of the Workers Defense League of New York City, a human rights group, which came to the assistance of Sheet Metal Local 28, after the U.S. Supreme Court in 1965 ruled that the union, which in its 76-year history had not allowed a Negro to be an apprentice of journeyman, was guilty of racial discrimination. The union was ordered to "open its apprenticeship classes to all applicants with selection to be made on an objective basis."[31] To conform to the court's decree, the union established an admission examination (with the help of New York University) for all applicants. The Workers Defense League then contacted all interested minority groups and helped train applicants for this examination. The first test was given to 340 applicants vying for 65 apprenticeship openings, with only one person successfully qualifying. The government then intervened and established an Outreach Fund in 1967. From very modest beginnings, results improved so that by 1969, 20 per cent of the union's membership was composed of minority members. Outreach has now been extended to sixteen other states, and as of January 1970, had a total of 5,048 apprentices indentured into the building trades in 63 programs. There were 163 new indentures during January 1970 with the majority entering the bricklayer, carpenter, electrician, painters, pipefitters, and sheet metal trades and crafts.[32] Because of the systematic approach of the Outreach programs, the construction unions do not believe it is necessary for the government to force quota systems into contracts when effective programs are already in operation.

Furthermore, at their 1969 convention, the Building and Construction Trades Department provided additional statistics of minority group participation in seven craft unions, which the government had failed to reveal in launching the Philadelphia Plan. They reveal the following:

Trade	Minority Membership Percentage
Boilermakers	20%
Carpenters	20%
Cement masons	37%
Lathers	20%
Operating engineers	10%
Painters	10%
Reinforced rod setters	30%

These are trades also located in the controversial Philadelphia area. When added together (excluding the Laborers), the total percentage of minority groups in the construction trades amounts to 12%, according to organized labor.[33]

In further support of the building trades policies, a Civil Rights Resolution was adopted by the Eighth AFL-CIO Convention in October, 1969. In essence, the federation adopted the construction union policies, but also included the recommendation that all unions should make "vigorous efforts" to expand opportunities for minority groups in more skilled jobs throughout the nation, and especially in and around areas with heavy concentrations of minority groups.[34]

In addition to the union defenses against alleged exclusionary employment practices, the question of the legality of the Philadelphia Plan also presented itself. In support of the program, Assistant Attorney General Jerris Leonard of the Civil Rights Division of the Justice Department stated that "We have reviewed the proposed plan. We find it to be consistent with the Executive Order, the regulations issued pursuant thereto, and with the Civil Rights Act of 1964."[35] In December 1969, the Senate attached a rider (Section 904) to a Senate supplemental appropriations bill which provided "that no funds that are appropriated to any federal agency be spent by any federal agency where the Comptroller General rules that the conditions of the contract would be in violation of any federal law."[36] At this time, the Comptroller General who oversees all Federal contracts, offered the opinion that the plan was illegal. He based his position on the premise that the inclusion of minority manpower percentages forces an employer to notice if the employee is black or of some color, thereby taking race into account in violation of the Civil Rights Act. On the other hand, the Attorney General indicated disagreement with the Comptroller General's opinion and ruled the plan completely legal.[37] With Section 904 (referred to as the Philadelphia Plan) before the House as a rider, AFL-CIO and Construction Union lobbyists intensified their efforts to secure its passage, heartened by their success in getting the rider attached to the supplemental appropriations bill in the first place.[38] At the time of this legislative jockeying, the Federal budget for Fiscal Year 1969-1970 had not been approved. Federal agencies were dependent upon congressional appropriations bills for finances and predictably applied pressures to pass Section 904. The administration responded by (1) the President coming out in full support of the Philadelphia Plan and asking that the question of legality be decided in the courts,[39] and (2) Labor Secretary Shultz's request that a roll call vote be taken in the House when the bill was presented thereby labeling opposition congressmen as anti-civil rights in posture.[40] The government strategy was successful in that the rider was rejected on December 23, 1969.[41]

LABOR'S ALTERNATIVE — THE CHICAGO PLAN

In January 1970, organized labor continued its efforts to weaken the Philadelphia Plan when the AFL-CIO helped settle a bitter, seven-month jobs dispute between blacks and construction unions by working out an agreement between the Chicago and Cook County Building Trades Council, The Building Construction Employers Association of Chicago, Inc., and the Coalition for United Community Action, known as the "Chicago Plan." The agreement opened 4,000 jobs immediately to minority group applicants. If general business conditions permit expansion in the building trades, the number of workers from minorities will be increased within five years until the percentage in the industry locally will be proportionate to the 42 per cent in the population. Between 4% and 5% of skilled workers among the 90,000 Chicago construction workers are black, and unskilled workers swell the total to 12%. The new plan called for 1,000 black journeymen to be employed immediately and taken into craft unions, with 3,000 to be accepted in apprenticeship, pre-apprenticeship, and other training programs in 1970. Unlike the Philadelphia Plan, the one adopted January 12th in Chicago is voluntary. It sets no goals or quotas for minority group employment in specific crafts. It provides no penalties, and no craft is listed individually as needing to bring in more Negroes or other minorities. Another feature is a partial payment plan for initiation fees over a three-month period.[42] In contrast, however, the Chicago Plan has full support in that city, including city officials, minority groups, employers and unions that have bitterly denounced the Philadelphia Plan.

The agreement established two committees to implement the plan. First, the Administrative Committee consisting of Mayor Daley and two members for each of the parties involved is in charge of implementation and necessary funding. A majority of five is needed for approval of proposed actions. Second, the Operations Committee, consisting of two representatives from each of the three parties, is responsible for recruitment, counseling, teacher recruitment, staffing, motivation and retention, certification of journeymen status and the securing and maintenance of physical facilities. It will also be responsible for formulating particular programs appropriate to each craft. It cannot interfere with any collective bargaining arrangements or commitments of the union involved. Also, a unanimous vote is needed for program approval. The remaining points touch on training of the unqualified (Outreach Program), certification of qualified journeymen, and residency requirements. The programs usually require no prior tests or construction experience and involve on-the-job training. The duration of the Chicago Plan is six months; in other words, a trial period before full commitment.[43]

With assurances that the Nixon administration is "certainly not" backing away from its intensive drive to end discriminatory practices in the construction industry, a Labor Department official indicated that the government would be willing to withdraw the Philadelphia Plan if Philadelphia and other cities adopted plans "as good as the Chicago one seems on the surface." He stressed that preferably, each local community would work out a plan best suited to its own needs, but if it did not, the government would be forced to impose Philadelphia-type plans. He indicated that the Chicago Plan would be "closely monitored" by the government, "and if it is working, we are willing to withdraw our goal concepts."[44]

PROGRESS AND PROBLEMS UNDER THE VARIOUS PLANS

In November 1969, several months before the announcement of the Chicago Plan, five Seattle construction unions were charged with discrimination against Negroes when the government asked the U.S. district court in Seattle to enjoin the five unions "from failing and refusal to recruit, refer for employment and accept Negroes for membership on the same basis as white persons."[45] The complaint also asked an injunction to forbid the unions from engaging in any work stoppage designed to interfere with contractors' obligations on federally assisted construction projects. Named as defendants were the Ironworkers, Electrical Workers, Plumbers and Pipefitters, Sheet Metal Workers, and Operating Engineers union locals.[46]

A program similar to the Chicago Plan has been agreed upon in the Pittsburgh-Allegheny County area in Pennsylvania, which calls for introduction of 1,250 minority journeymen into unions over a four-year program which includes training provisions. Other trade councils in such urban centers are also beginning to work on similar plans. One such program is Project Build, Inc., in Washington, D.C. Its pre-apprentice training is designed primarily for innercity youths aged 17½ to 24 years who are school dropouts from disadvantaged backgrounds. The training amounts to a 24-week cycle of job orientation, counseling, math and English skill development, craft familiarization and work experience. Trainees in the program are paid the federal minimum wage which may be raised depending on individual progress. The second phase of Project Build's program is the Craftsmen Skill Refinement Training, the purpose of which is to prepare inadequately trained men or those who may have construction experience for qualification as journeymen. As well as training in the individual craft, the worker is refreshed in the essentials of blueprint reading, materials estimation, and the use of the latest equipment. Persons enrolled in this training are compensated by the project for the time lost from their regular employment. The next phase of the project involved on-the-job training in eighteen job skills in the building and construction trades. Trainees are recruited for employment by a local firm on new construction and renovation in innercity areas and are paid regular apprenticeship wage rates. Supportive services are the final stage in this program, the main purpose being to encourage and assist trainee graduates to stay on the job. This objective is accomplished by counseling and extensive follow-up programs.[47]

The Philadelphia Plan, as of June 1970, was tied up in the courts as the consequence of a suit filed in January 1970 by the Contractors Association of Eastern Pennsylvania, which alleged that the minority-group quota hiring requirement violated the 1964 Civil Rights Act and the Fifth Amendment.[45] The case is expected to wind up in the U.S. Supreme Court, with the distinct possibility that its quotas aspect will render it unconstitutional.

Other programs are doing no better, in part due to tight money and government spending cutbacks which have put a crimp in construction; and too few jobs are being created for the inexperienced, while building trades unemployment figures are substantial in many areas.

In Newark and Boston, where the plan was to be used, some hearings have been held, but actual programs appear far off. In Chicago and Pittsburgh, the plans worked out between the unions and contractors in an effort to keep the government out, and intended to put thousands of blacks into construction jobs at various levels — from starter jobs to trainees to journeymen — have made minimal progress. For example, in Chicago in August 1970, eight months after the plan was initiated, only 75 blacks were in training with the promise that another 75 would begin training at some unspecified future date. Joblessness among black youths, meanwhile, was conservatively estimated at 40 per cent, with thousands of young men roaming the streets of Chicago with nothing to do.[49] In Philadelphia, there is no estimate of how many minority group members, if any, have been hired. Only in Seattle is a plan working — and this formula developed with little federal involvement. The program grew from efforts to bring together federal contractors and unions, whose hiring halls impeded open hiring. Unions and employers agreed that there would have been more progress if the economic slowdown had not severely limited the number of available jobs. The plan is being implemented with the help of a nonprofit corporation, BUILD, set up and financed by the building unions, joint apprenticeship committees, and several nonconstruction unions.

In Washington, all future federal construction work was held up by a District of Columbia row over quotas for minority hiring on the city's new subway system. There black groups accused the government of presenting a false picture of minority employment in the area.[50]

In July 1970, representatives of unions, the building industry and minority organizations formally approved a "Los Angeles Plan" aimed at increasing the number of minority workers in the construction industry in that city. Basically, the plan requires the construction industry to have a percentage of minority workers equal to the percentage of minority group members in the community as a whole. It differs from the Philadelphia Plan because it applies to all construction and not just to federal projects. A special committee will set specific goals for each craft signing the document and a nonprofit corporation will be set up to seek and administer funds to achieve the goals within five years.[51]

Also in July 1970, the federal government indicated its dissatisfaction with the rate of progress. The Departments of Health, Education and Welfare and Housing and Urban Development announced a total of seven show-cause orders charging Philadelphia area contractors with failure to make good-faith efforts to hire sufficient numbers of blacks under that city's plan.[52] At the same time, Labor Secretary James D. Hodgson declared that more jobs for blacks would have to be found in the construction trades during the summer of 1970 or federal quotas would be enforced in 73 cities. The 73 metropolitan areas would be given time to develop voluntary job plans for construction work, but unless it was done soon, the government would move to impose racial hiring quotas as it has already done in Philadelphia and Washington. The 73 areas were added to 19 others targeted earlier. Most of the cities had asked the government for assistance in developing their own plans. Labor Department officials were to provide technical assistance to municipalities, minority groups, unions and contractors.[53] In each case, the hiring goal that will apply to federal contractors will be governed by the overall nonwhite percentage of the local labor market. The minimum level for most job categories would be 11 per cent, the nonwhite share of the national labor market. In some cities, however, blacks comprise 25 to 30 per cent of the total work force. In such instances, federal contractors would be told to apply a standard of nonwhite hiring that more closely approaches the local labor market picture. The main goal of federal contract enforcement is to equalize the earnings of black with white workers.[54]

"ORDER NUMBER 4"

In February 1970, the Office of Federal Contract Compliance issued Order No. 4, which covers nonconstruction contractors' bidding for Federal contracts, and described what constitutes an affirmative action, minority group hiring program. It requires that within 120 days from the beginning of a contract, each prime contractor or subcontractor with 50 or more employees and a contract of $50,000 or more must develop a written affirmative action compliance program for each of its establishments. This order was promulgated subsequent to a review of OFCC compliance surveys indicating that many contractors do not have affirmative action programs on file at the time an establishment is visited by a compliance investigator. If the contractor defaults on this obligation, the federal contracting officer will declare the contractor-bidder nonresponsible unless he can otherwise affirmatively determine that the contractor is able to comply with equal employment obligations. If a contractor-bidder is declared nonresponsible more than once for inability to comply with the equal employment opportunity clause in the contract, he will be declared ineligible for future contracts and subcontracts.[55]

An acceptable affirmative action program must include an analysis of areas within which the contractor is deficient in the utilization of minority groups, and further, goals and timetables to which the contractor's good faith efforts must be directed to correct the deficiencies, and thus to increase materially the utilization of minorities at all levels and in all segments of his work force where deficiencies exist.[56]

Contractors must also indicate that they have conducted a thorough analysis of all major job categories at a facility, with explanations if minorities are currently being underutilized in any one or more job categories. (Job "category" is defined as one or a group of jobs having similar content, wage rates and opportunities.) "Underutilization" is present if there are fewer minorities in a particular job category than would reasonably be expected by their availability. In determining whether minorities are being underutilized in any job category, the contractor is required to consider at least all of the following factors:

1. The minority population of the labor area surrounding the facility.

2. The size of the minority unemployment force in the labor area surrounding the facility.

3. The percentage of minority work force as compared with the total work force in the immediate labor area.

4. The general availability of minorities having requisite skills in the immediate labor area.

5. The availability of minorities having requisite skills in an area in which the contractor can reasonably recruit.

6. The availability of promotable minority employees within the contractor's organization.

7. The anticipated expansion, contraction and turnover of the work force.

8. The existence of training institutions capable of training minorities in the requisite skills.

9. The degree of training which the contractor is reasonably able to undertake as a means of making all job classes available to minorities.[57]

An employer is required to take "special corrective action" when his in-depth analysis of problem areas by organizational unit and job categories indicates the following:

1. The ratio of minority applicants recruited fails to approximate or equal the ratio of minorities in the population of each location.
2. Lateral or vertical movement or both of minority employees (promotions, etc.,) occurs at a lesser rate than that of nonminority employees.
3. The selection process eliminates a higher percentage of minorities than nonminorities.[58]

In other words, the regulations require a company doing business with the federal government to set its own hiring quotas subject to government approval — by division, department, location, and job classification — before it can secure a government contract.[59]

One reason suggested for the mandatory guidelines imposed for nonconstruction contractors is that they may have been partially intended to offset criticism that the Office of Federal Contract Compliance had singled out the construction industry with its implementation of the Philadelphia Plan. Another reason is that many Federal contractors have been asking for guidance on the requirements for satisfactory affirmative action programs.[60]

TABLE 37.   Total and Negro Membership in Referral Unions in the Baltimore Metropolitan Area, 1967.

	Membership in Referral Unit		
International Union/Trade[1]	*Total*	*Negro*	*% Negro*
All unions reporting in the Baltimore SMSA	12,464	2,246	18.0
Building Trades Unions	5,658	752	13.3
Mechanical Trades[2]	1,007	9	0.9
General Construction Trades[3]	4,651	743	16.0
Non-Building Trades Unions	6,806	1,494	22.0

[1] Each international union for which separate statistics are shown has at least three local unions.
[2] Mechanical Trades figures include data for Boilermakers, Electrical Workers, Elevator Constructors, and Plumbers.
[3] General Construction Trades figures include data for Bricklayers, Carpenters, Laborers, Operating Engineers, Painters, Plasterers, and Roofers.

Source: 1967 Local Union Report EEO-3, Washington, D.C.: Office of Research, Equal Employment Opportunity Commission.

TABLE 38.   Total and Negro Membership in Referral Unions in the Detroit Metropolitan Area, 1967.

		Membership in Referral Unit		
International Union/Trade[1]		*Total*	*Negro*	*% Negro*
All unions reporting in the Detroit SMSA	(38)	31,455	3,635	11.6
Building Trades Unions	(20)	23,663	3,289	14.0
Mechanical Trades[2]	(9)	13,389	71	0.5
General Construction Trades[3]	(11)	10,274	3,218	31.3
Bricklayers	(6)	7,132	916	12.8
Non-Building Trades Unions	(18)	7,792	346	4.4
Printing Pressmen	(3)	1,390	18	1.3

[1] Each international union for which separate statistics are shown has at least three local unions.
[2] Mechanical Trades figures include data for Boilermakers, Electrical Workers, Elevator Constructors, Iron Workers, Plumbers, and Sheet Metal Workers.
[3] General Construction Trades figures also include data for Painters, Plasterers, and Laborers.

Source: 1967 Local Union Report EEO-3, Washington, D.C.: Office of Research, Equal Employment Opportunity Commission.

TABLE 39.   Total and Negro Membership in Referral Unions in the Houston Metropolitan Area, 1967.

		Membership in Referral Unit		
International Union/Trade[1]		*Total*	*Negro*	*% Negro*
All unions reporting in the Houston SMSA	(24)	25,153	5,227	20.8
Building Trades Unions	(16)	22,159	4,003	18.1
Mechanical Trades[2]	(9)	7,966	6	0.1
Laborers	(3)	4,508	3,690	81.9
General Construction Trades[3]	(7)	9,685	307	3.2
Carpenters	(3)	7,582	30	0.4
Non-Building Trades Unions	(8)	2,994	1,224	40.9
Longshoremen	(5)	2,513	1,222	48.6

[1] Each international union for which separate statistics are shown has at least three local unions.

[2] Mechanical Trades figures include data for Boilermakers, Electrical Workers, Iron Workers, and Plumbers.

[3] General Construction Trades figures also include data for Painters, Plasterers, and Roofers.

Source: *1967 Local Union Report EEO-3*, Washington, D.C.: Office of Research, Equal Employment Opportunity Commission.

TABLE 40. Total and Negro Membership in Referral Unions in the Los Angeles Metropolitan Area, 1967.

International Union/Trade[1]		Membership in Referral Unit		
		Total	Negro	% Negro
All unions reporting in the Los Angeles SMSA	(122)	124,646	11,147	8.9
Building Trades Unions	(59)	45,865	3,741	8.2
Mechanical Trades[2]	(16)	19,150	101	0.5
Electrical Workers	(3)	2,280	23	1.0
Iron Workers	(3)	3,052	10	0.3
Plumbers	(7)	8,735	39	0.4
Laborers	(8)	7,468	1,775	23.8
General Construction Trades[3]	(35)	19,247	1,865	9.7
Lathers	(3)	743	39	5.2
Marble Polishers	(3)	1,740	259	14.9
Painters	(16)	10,017	562	5.6
Plasterers	(10)	5,041	992	19.7
Non-Building Trades Unions	(63)	78,781	7,406	9.4
Bakery & Confectionery Workers	(3)	3,375	353	10.5
Building Service Employees	(3)	1,893	404	21.3
Garment Workers	(3)	5,579	1,081	19.4
Hotel & Restaurant Employees	(11)	30,044	3,637	12.1
Meat Cutters	(7)	7,939	460	5.8
Stage-Motion Picture Operators	(16)	15,163	120	0.8

[1] Each international union for which separate statistics are shown has at least three local unions.

[2] Mechanical Trades figures also include data for Elevator Constructors and Sheet Metal Workers.

[3] General Construction figures also include data for Asbestos Workers, Bricklayers, and Roofers.

Source: *1967 Local Union Report EEO-3*, Washington, D.C.: Office of Research, Equal Employment Opportunity Commission.

TABLE 41.   Total and Negro Membership in Referral Unions in the Baltimore Standard Metropolitan Statistical Area (SMSA), 1968.

		Negro		
	Number	*Membership in Referral Unit*		
	Reporting	*Total*	*No.*	*%*
All Unions[1]	18	11,867	2,184	18.4
Building Trades	12	7,579	814	10.7
Mechanical Trades[2]	5	3,127	25	0.8
General Construction Trades[3]	7	4,452	789	17.7
Non-Building Trades	6	4,288	1,370	31.9

[1] For each trade for which separate statistics are shown, at least three local unions reported.
[2] Mechanical Trades include Boilermakers, Electrical Workers, Elevator Constructors, Iron Workers, Plumbers, and Sheet Metal Workers.
[3] General Construction Trades include Asbestos Workers, Bricklayers, Carpenters, Lathers, Marble Polishers, Operating Engineers, Painters, Plasterers, and Roofers.

Source: 1968 Local Union Report EEO-3, Washington, D.C.: Office of Research Equal Employment Opportunity Commission.

TABLE 42.   Total and Negro Membership in Referral Unions in the Detroit SMSA, 1968.

		Negro		
	Number	*Membership in Referral Unit*		
	Reporting	*Total*	*No.*	*%*
All Unions[1]	25	20,279	951	4.7
Building Trades	12	14,280	626	4.4
Mechanical Trades[2]	7	10,526	147	1.4
General Construction Trades[3]	5	3,754	476	12.8
Bricklayers	3	3,574	471	13.2
Non-Building Trades	13	5,999	325	5.4

[1] For each trade for which separate statistics are shown, at least three local unions reported.
[2] Mechanical Trades include Boilermakers, Electrical Workers, Elevator Constructors, Iron Workers, Plumbers, and Sheet Metal Workers.
[3] General Construction Trades include Asbestos Workers, Bricklayers, Carpenters, Lathers, Marble Polishers, Operating Engineers, Painters, Plasterers, and Roofers.

Source: 1968 Local Union Report EEO-3, Washington, D.C.: Office of Research Equal Employment Opportunity Commission.

TABLE 43.   Total and Negro Membership in Referral Unions in the Houston SMSA, 1968.

		Negro Membership in Referral Unit		
	Number Reporting	*Total*	*No.*	*%*
All Unions[1]	21	17,161	5,344	31.1
Building Trades	12	13,643	4,234	31.0
Mechanical Trades[2]	2	840	0	0.0
General Construction Trades[3]	10	12,803	4,234	33.1
Carpenters	3	4,716	34	0.7
Non-Building Trades	9	3,518	1,110	31.6
Longshoremen	5	2,508	999	39.8

[1] For each trade for which separate statistics are shown, at least three local unions reported.

[2] Mechanical Trades include Boilermakers, Electrical Workers, Elevator Constructors, Iron Workers, Plumbers, and Sheet Metal Workers.

[3] General Construction Trades include Asbestos Workers, Bricklayers, Carpenters, Lathers, Marble Polishers, Operating Engineers, Painters, Plasterers, and Roofers.

Source: 1968 Local Union Report EEO-3, Washington, D.C.: Office of Research Equal Employment Opportunity Commission.

TABLE 44.   Total and Negro Membership in Referral Unions in the Los Angeles SMSA, 1968.

	Number Reporting	Negro Membership in Referral Unit		
		Total	No.	%
All Unions[1]	110	156,078	10,668	6.8
Building Trades	52	61,388	2,736	4.5
Mechanical Trades[2]	13	20,116	95	0.5
Plumbers	7	8,579	40	0.5
Laborers	6	6,119	1,433	23.4
General Construction Trades[3]	33	35,153	1,208	3.4
Lathers	4	1,166	64	5.5
Painters	15	7,641	591	8.2
Plasterers	9	4,606	510	11.1
Non-Building Trades	58	94,690	7,932	8.4
Garment Workers	4	4,494	839	18.7
Hotel & Restaurant Employees	12	29,854	3,438	11.5
Meat Cutters	5	10,599	450	4.2
Seafarers	3	4,104	30	0.7
Stage Employees	12	12,071	131	1.1
Teamsters	5	5,385	542	10.1

[1] For each trade for which separate statistics are shown at least three local unions reported.
[2] Mechanical Trades include Boilermakers, Electrical Workers, Elevator Constructors, Iron Workers, Plumbers, and Sheet Metal Workers.
[3] General Construction Trades include Asbestos Workers, Bricklayers, Carpenters, Lathers, Marble Polishers, Operating Engineers, Painters, Plasterers, and Roofers.

Source: *1968 Local Union Report EEO-3*, Washington, D.C.: Office of Research Equal Employment Opportunity Commission.

TABLE 45.   Desired Minority Group Employment Percentages, 1970-1973, by Trade.

Trade	*1970*	*1971*	*1972*	*1973*
Ironworkers	5%–9%	11%–15%	16%–20%	22%–26%
Plumbers and pipefitters	5%–9%	10%–14%	15%–19%	20%–24%
Steamfitters	5%–8%	11%–15%	15%–19%	20%–24%
Sheet metal workers	4%–8%	9%–13%	14%–18%	19%–23%
Electrical workers	4%–8%	9%–13%	14%–18%	19%–23%
Elevator constructors	4%–8%	9%–13%	14%–18%	19%–23%

Source: Fletcher, Arthur H. (Assistant Secretary of Labor). *Order to Heads of All Agencies*, U. S. Department of Labor, Inter–Agency Memoranda, September 23, 1969.

REFERENCES

1. Thomas O'Hanlon, "The Case Against the Unions." *Fortune,* January, 1968, p. 170.
2. *Ibid.*
3. "Black Battleground." *Time,* Sept. 5, 1969, p. 78.
4. "Union Racial Policies and Practices." *Labor Law Journal,* May 1967, pp. 296-299.
5. Gannon, James P. "Building Trades Feel New Pressure to Admit Negroes as Apprentices." *The Wall Street Journal,* Oct. 16, 1967, p. 1.
6. Gilbride, Neil. "Minorities Gain in Skilled Crafts." *The Washington Post,* Sept. 22, 1969, pp. A-1, A-6.
7. "Integration Drive Fails to Overcome." *Business Week,* June 6, 1970, p. 48.
8. Equal Employment Opportunity Commission. *3rd Annual Report.* Washington, D.C.: U.S. Government Printing Office, 1969, p. 18.
9. *Executive Order 11246, Equal Employment Opportunity,* September 24, 1965. *In Code of Federal Regulations, Title 3 — The President — 1964 and 1965 Compilation.* Washington, D.C.: U.S. Government Printing Office, 1967, s.201, p. 340.
10. *Ibid.* s. 201, p. 340.
11. "Has Bias Locked up the Room at the Top?" *Business Week,* January 24, 1970, p. 38.
12. *Equal Employment Opportunities Enforcement Act, Hearings Before the Subcommittee on Labor of the Committee on Labor and Public Welfare on S. 2453.* U.S. Senate, 91st Congress, 1st Sess., August 11, 12, September, 10, 16, 1969. Washington, D.C.: U.S. Government Printing Office, 1969, p. 228 (statement by William E. Dunn, Executive Director, The Associated General Contractors of America).
13. Fletcher, Arthur H. (Assistant Secretary of Labor), *Memorandum to All Agencies.* U.S. Department of Labor, Inter-Agency Memoranda, June 27, 1969.
14. Fletcher, Arthur H. (Assistant Secretary of Labor). *Order to Heads of All Agencies.* U.S. Department of Labor, Inter-Agency Memoranda, September 23, 1969.
15. Fletcher, *Memorandum, op. cit.*
16. Fletcher, *Order, op. cit.*
17. Fletcher, *Order, Ibid.*
18. Fletcher, *Order, Ibid.*
19. Fletcher, Arthur A. "On Philadelphia Guidelines." *News,* U.S. Department of Labor, Bureau of Labor Statistics, September 23, 1968, pp. 2-3.
20. Fletcher, *Order, op. cit.*
21. Fletcher, *Memorandum, op. cit.*
22. Fletcher, *Order, op. cit.*
23. Fletcher, *Order, Ibid.*
24. Fletcher, *Order, Ibid.*
25. "Minority Hiring under New Attack." *Business Week,* June 13, 1970, p. 110.
26. "19 Cities Named for Hiring Plan." *The Washington Post,* February 10, 1970, p. A-2.
27. "Shultz Job Plan for Blacks Hits Snags." *Business Week,* November 15, 1969, p. 109.
28. Building and Construction Trade Department, AFL-CIO. *Statements of Policy on Equal Employment Opportunity.* Washington, D.C.: AFL-CIO, September 22, 1969, p. 1.
29. *Ibid.*
30. McGlotten, R. M. and Hardesty, D. G. "Outreach: Skills for Minority Youth." *AFL-CIO,* April, 1969, pp. 5-10.
31. *Ibid.*
32. U.S. Department of Labor. *Outreach Program Activity Summary Charts.* Washington, D.C.: U.S. Government Printing Office, January 1970, p. 1.
33. Building and Construction Trade Department, AFL-CIO. *Statements of Policy, op. cit.*

34. The Eighth Convention of the AFL-CIO. *Civil Rights, an Adopted Resolution.* Washington, D.C.: AFL-CIO, October 1969.

35. "Philadelphia Plan." *News,*   U.S. Department of Labor, Office of Information, September 23, 1969.

36. "White House Press Conference on Revised Philadelphia Plan Guidelines." *News,* U.S. Department of Labor, Office of Information, December 18, 1969.

37. *Ibid.*

38. "White House Press Conference," *op. cit.,* December 20, 1969.

39. *Ibid.*

40. *Ibid.*

41. "White House Press Conference," *op. cit.,* December 23, 1969.

42. Building and Construction Trades Department, AFL-CIO. *The Chicago Plan.* Washington, D.C.: AFL-CIO, January 12, 1970.

43. "The Philadelphia Plan for Negroes." *The National Observer,* January 19, 1970.

44. Bernstein, Harry. "U.S. Willing to Ease Minority Job Plan." *The Washington Post,* January 27, 1970, p. A-1.

45. "U.S. Files Bias Action Against Seattle Union." *The Washington Post,* November 1, 1969, p. A-2.

46. *Ibid.*

47. "Working in the White Man's World." *Time,* April 6, 1970, p. 92.

48. Meany, George (President of the AFL-CIO). Speech before the National Press Club, in *News,* U.S. Department of Labor, Office of Information, January 12, 1970.

49. Maynard, Robert C. "Chicago Blacks Split as Jobs Plan Lags." *The Washington Post,* August 10, 1970, p. A-1.

50. "Integration Drive Fails to Overcome," *op. cit.,* pp. 48, 52.

51. "Unions Back Minority Plan." *The Washington Post,* July 9, 1970, p. A-4.

52. Phillips, Kevin P. "Shift by White House on Rights Breeds Revolt of Conservatives." *The Washington Post,* July 17, 1970, p. A-17.

53. "Hodgson Issues Job Bias Warning." *The Washington Post,* July 10, 1970, p. A-2.

54. Stern, Laurence. "New Action Planned on Jobs for Negroes." *The Washington Post,* December 27, 1969, p. A-1.

55. Chapter 60. U.S. Department of Labor, Office of Federal Contract Compliance, Equal Employment Opportunity. *Federal Register,* Vol. 35, No. 25, February 5, 1970.

56. *Ibid.*

57. *Ibid.*

58. *Ibid.*

59. "The Unhappy Parent of New Hiring Rules." *Business Week,* January 24, 1970, p. 39.

60. "Hiring Order Drafted by Labor Department Covering Minorities." *The Wall Street Journal,* January 16, 1970, p. 15.

Chapter 5
"Black Capitalism"

CHARACTERISTICS OF BLACK BUSINESSES

The phrase "black capitalism" is of very recent vintage. In fact, before the 1968 presidential campaign it was virtually unknown. Then Richard Nixon declared, "It's no longer enough that white-owned enterprises employ greater numbers of Negroes, whether as laborers or as middle-management personnel. This is needed, yes — but it has to be accompanied by an expansion of black ownership, of black capitalism. We need more black employers, more black businesses." New jobs would be created for blacks and businesses set up inside ghetto areas through the assistance of the private sector, with little or no direct expenditure of federal funds.

At first glance, "black capitalism" would appear to be a meaningful approach in the effort to achieve a large increase in black ownership of businesses, as less than 1 per cent of all enterprises in the United States are owned by Negroes. Of the five million businesses, only forty-five thousand are Negro-owned.[1]

It may be helpful to designate four categories of enterprises: (1) small, individually-owned and operated retail businesses, commonly called "Ma and Pa" stores; (2) service and professional businesses; (3) franchise operations; and (4) middle-sized companies.

A study has shown that well over 80 per cent of black-owned businesses are in the services or retailing category; practically all these are small.[2] Another study estimates that the death rate of black-owned businesses probably exceeds the birthrate.[3] These and other studies conclude that small businesses will change the economy of the ghetto;[4,5] however, it has also been recognized that the multiplication of such small businesses may have a significant psycho-social effect upon residents of the ghetto.[6,7] A conclusion of these and other studies is that government, business, and ethnic organizations should strive to foster middle-sized, minority-owned companies which may have some economic impact on the ghetto.[8,9]

In the past, Negro business efforts have been limited, both in number and in scope. The Negro's lack of business experience and management skills, shortage of financial resources, and inability to raise capital or to rent space all combined to cause him to downgrade commercial enterprise. Instead, entry into the professions was stressed. Negro businesses that did develop have generally been confined to small operations in racially-restricted markets where segregation provided a crutch. They were mainly single proprietorships, many of them requiring the pooling of family labor to make them going concerns, and were heavily concentrated in fields in which free access was denied to Negro consumers elsewhere. Most common were beauty and barber shops, luncheonettes and restaurants, funeral parlors, and hotels. Negroes shied away from undertakings in which the Negro consumer dollar found ready acceptance in the open market, such as department, hardware, and furniture stores, and similar outlets. There are few Negro manufacturing firms, because considerable capital and existence of broad markets are requirements that are not easily met. The few enterprises that did develop were predominantly devoted to beauty products.

The following illustration is a case in point:[10]

Increasing numbers of black-owned liquor stores, clothing stores, day nurseries and consulting firms have contributed to a 16 per cent increase in the total number of businesses owned by Negroes in Washington. . . . The number of black-owned businesses comprises about 8.5 per cent of the 28,000 businesses of all types in the District of Columbia. . . . The report shows that almost 85 per cent of all black-owned enterprises fall into the service and retail categories. It listed 246 barber shops and 342 beauty shops, which together constitute nearly 25 per cent of the total 2,393 black-owned businesses . . . the black business categories showing the smallest growth since 1967 were wholesaling and manufacturing, which increased from a combined total of 53 to 66 firms. . . .

Although the city's population is increasingly black, there are no Negro-owned businesses in the downtown area. To succeed in the new environment, Negro businessmen will need greater technical know-how and financial counsel and backing.

American business is distinguished by constant change in products and methods. Some changes are introduced by old businesses, some by new. The entrepreneur's role is to initiate new businesses. He succeeds when he effectively satisfies unmet public needs or offers cheaper or better ways to satisfy needs. Each new business builds on those going before. This is why entrepreneurs initiating successful businesses usually utilize experience acquired in existing firms. But Negroes have been denied access to the entrepreneurial apprenticeship of experience in the management hierarchy of established big business. Negroes have not even known people with experience in that hierarchy. . . .[11]

Actually, the small self-employed businessman is becoming an anachronism.[12] Family-owned stores are being rapidly displaced by large chains which capitalize on large-scale economies (such as purchasing) to reduce costs. In the process, earnings of self-employed store owners have failed to keep pace with increases of salaried managers for large firms. Between 1958 and 1968, the median earnings of a self-employed businessman increased from $5,145 to $7,409, a rise of 44 per cent, but the pay of salaried managers jumped from $6,561 to $10,661, an increase of 62.5 per cent. Black-owned stores in ghetto areas face grave difficulties because they must serve inherently poor neighborhoods. Negroes with higher incomes appear to prefer living away from the central city.

EVALUATION OF FEDERAL EFFORTS TO PROMOTE "BLACK CAPITALISM"

The Nixon Administration's effort[13] to foster black capitalism has not yet resulted in the establishment of many Negro businesses. Critics have generally faulted the Administration for failing to provide a coordinated program of loans and other help to would-be black entrepreneurs. Actually, the difficulty may be much more fundamental. Recently, the nation's most prominent black economist contended that encouraging Negro-owned business in city ghettos is a mistaken strategy for promoting racial equality. Andrew Brimmer argued that black-owned businesses tend to be small, precariously financed: beauty parlors, food stores, and other personal-service or retail establishments catering to a poor market. Most of them owe their existence largely to residential segregation, said Brimmer. Negroes have dim prospects of founding businesses that can compete with white-owned establishments for a broader market, he said, and even in serving Negroes, they will have increasing trouble competing with national firms that are showing a new interest in the Negro consumer. "Self-employment is a rather rapidly declining factor in our modern economy," Brimmer said. "For the great majority of the Negro population, it offers a low and rather risky payoff." If many more Negro-owned businesses are formed, they "would certainly be more prone to failure than already established firms, and their failures would leave a lasting burden on the individuals starting these firms." Moreover, he argued, "the pursuit of black capitalism may retard the Negro's economic advancement" by distracting attention from programs that would really help blacks and by discouraging Negroes from "full participation in the national economy" What Negroes need is more jobs as salaried managers or as craftsmen for major companies, where they would have the capital resources of the national community behind them.

The new Minority Enterprise Small Business Investment Comapny program (MESBIC) designed to attract big corporate investment in minority companies is not meeting expectations, with only 11 of the 100 MESBICS expected to be in business by June 30, 1970 actually materializing. The program to secure franchises for minorities is divided between the Commerce Department and the Small Business Administration, with both agencies trying to persuade big franchisers to take on black businessmen. The rivalry between the two agencies appears to be hurting the black capitalism effort since only two hundred franchises were awarded to minority businessmen in the 1970-71 fiscal year. SBA loans to small business averaged approximately $61 million a month in 1970, about the same as in 1969. Critics charged that since the SBA has moved from lending its own money to simply guaranteeing bank loans, it should be possible to increase the flow. Agency spokesmen countered that in a period of tight money, keeping the loan rate from falling constituted a good performance. Actually, during the first five months of 1970, a one-third increase in the rate of loans awarded to minority businesses occurred, up from about $10 million monthly to an average of $13 million. Loans to Spanish-Americans doubled; loans to blacks increased 18 per cent. Approximately one-third of all SBA loans were being awarded to minorities.

According to Stephen Cotton,[14] ". . . While numerous critics of the idea have pointed out that setting up some Negroes in business will not cure the ghetto's ills, the proposal still has a considerable following that includes conservative bankers and leaders of the black establishment. There are indications that even some Southern congressmen figure that support for black capitalism is as good a way as any to pick up increasingly important black votes without offending white constituents."

EMPLOYER APPRAISALS OF "BLACK CAPITALISM"

Since Negroes would be aided by existing businesses in the ownership and management of inner city businesses, the respondents in the small and medium-sized firm survey were asked whether they favored or opposed proposals for "black capitalism." Table 46 shows their attitudes as roughly favoring the concept by a 2-to-1 margin on a total sample basis. Slightly fewer than twice as many firms in Los Angeles and Detroit furnished positive responses compared to those in opposition, while in Houston and Baltimore, slightly more than 2 employers favored "black capitalism" compared to each business which opposed this approach. Nearly 1 of 5 respondents was not willing to commit himself on the question. The responses can be interpreted in several possible ways. The more pessimistic appraisal would be that the small and medium-sized firms, assuming that most of the support and assistance will come from large corporations, can well afford to favor "black capitalism," while simultaneously pleading that a lack of funds and resources prevents them from making meaningful contributions. To a certain extent, this analysis has been borne out by developments. For example, in November 1969, eighteen corporations including General Motors, Prudential Insurance, and Phillips Petroleum had already committed themselves to set up Minority Enterprise Small Business Investment Companies (MESBIC's) to finance minority-group businesses. The corporations were to put up a minimum of $150,000 each with government providing matching funds on a two-to-one basis and guaranteeing up to $15 of bank loans for each dollar of initial capital. The respondents might also have favored the idea because keeping black businesses in the ghetto would get rid of the "Negro problem" by insuring economic apartheid. An optimistic evaluation would stress the point that the respondents were sincerely interested in participating in this effort regardless of geographic location.

No comparison can be made with the large firm survey since the same inquiry was not made at that time because "black capitalism" had not yet become part of our vocabulary in 1967.

Only two firms volunteered additional comments to explain why they favored "black capitalism." One executive indicated qualified approval when he stated that he would favor it if there were "no permanent government subsidy". Another indicated support if there were "proper supervision."

In contrast, a number of respondents stated their reasons for opposition. The comments indicated that the two basic reasons why businesses disliked "black capitalism" were either that it smacked of favoritism for blacks or that it would serve further to impede integration. The latter viewpoint often manifests a misconception on the part of the respondents to the effect that "black capitalism" would exclude white businesses from being established in the inner cities. This does not happen to be one of its objectives — rather, the program emphasizes the necessity for increasing the number of black entrepreneurs while not necessarily excluding white firms. Of course, as a fact of life, few white firms are willing to locate in ghetto areas because of recent urban disorders. The distinction, therefore, becomes academic.

A particularly articulate comment came from a Baltimore businessman who stated his reasons for opposing "black capitalism" in the following words:

> Black capitalism as well as white capitalism in this order should be considered as totally out of the question. The powers to be should first realize that a community that is made up entirely of a single race cannot survive. We need each other's support to survive as a healthy community, both economically and socially. If helping the Negro to establish his own business in his own community is good for the community, the type of business that would be useful, etc., and allow any other useful business to be established in the same community, then this is balance and justice at work. Otherwise it would only

present the same problems we are now facing, of prejudice and anarchy within the communities.

THE EFFICACY OF TAX CREDITS

A follow-up question concerning the opinions toward tax credits for firms who would train and employ Negroes provides a certain degree of substantiation and belief that firms favoring "black capitalism" were less than sincere. As Table 47 shows, a slightly higher percentage of firms rejected efforts to create black jobs than were in favor. Job creation is one of the objectives of "black capitalism." Houston firms were markedly more negative than employers in the other three cities, possibly due to generally lower skill levels among Southern Negroes, which in turn would require employers to allocate substantial resources for training purposes.

A variety of comments for and against tax incentives were expressed. One businessman who favored them considered that they were necessary subsidies similar to the benefits provided to World War II veterans. Another executive indicated support, but only if the tax write-offs were temporary. A Houston employer qualified his acceptance on the condition that tax incentives would also be utilized to provide equal opportunity for whites as well as blacks. A Detroit firm responded affirmatively, if "no pork barrel" was involved.

Those who were against the idea also voiced disparate opinions. Cost limitations were instrumental in persuading a Detroit respondent to answer in this fashion: "In our situation, we are unable to initiate our own programs because of cost; however, if the training costs (sending the man to proper schools available) were had, it would be fine. However, don't limit it to only one minority group."

Another Detroit entrepreneur was also opposed, if the program was restricted to a single minority. Along the same lines, a Houston employer disliked the concept, maintaining that "there is just as much a problem with the white poor people as there is the Negro. Both should be supported." Another Houston executive implied that Negroes lacked the necessary motivation when he cited as his reason for opposition, "Tax money is spent to train and educate willing people."

A Los Angeles respondent was quite succinct in stating, "Black, no; white, yes," while another Californian alleged that tax incentives were "actually more discrimination." Probably the most idealistic response of all came from another Los Angeles businessman who contended that "they should do it (train and employ Negroes) without tax credits."

In no uncertain terms, a Baltimore manager charged, "The first law of small business is to avoid the government; they are a bunch of goddamn ineffectual time wasters." Another Baltimorean maintained that tax incentives would be "discrimination against whites and people who won't get involved with government."

Several years ago, a study sponsored by the Commerce Department did try to estimate the impact and cost of a series of tax incentives proposed by the late Senator Robert F. Kennedy. The study estimated that over a ten-year period, the Kennedy incentives would develop 250,000 jobs in poverty areas. Since most of the jobs would be unskilled and low paying, they would generate only $770 million in annual wages, at a cost to the U.S. Treasury of $500 million. Investing that amount in upgrading jobs or reducing discrimination would almost certainly yield considerably larger gains to blacks in terms of jobs and income.

TABLE 46.   Attitude Toward "Black Capitalism," by City.

	Sample Totals		Baltimore		Los Angeles		Detroit		Houston	
	No.	%	No.	%	No.	%	No.	%	No.	%
In favor	113	49.6	39	48.1	29	47.5	28	50.9	17	54.8
Opposed	56	24.6	17	21.0	16	26.2	15	27.3	8	25.8
No opinion	48	21.0	18	22.2	14	23.0	10	18.2	6	19.4
No response	11	4.8	7	8.7	2	3.3	2	3.6	0	0.0

Source: Negro Employment Questionnaire.

TABLE 47.   Attitude Toward Tax Credits for Firms Who Would Train and Employ Negroes, by City.

	Sample Totals		Baltimore		Los Angeles		Detroit		Houston	
	No.	%	No.	%	No.	%	No.	%	No.	%
In favor	86	38.2	27	34.6	25	40.3	23	41.8	11	36.7
Opposed	96	42.7	32	41.0	25	40.3	24	43.6	15	50.0
No opinion	32	14.2	14	17.9	10	16.1	5	9.1	3	10.0
No response	11	4.9	5	6.5	2	3.3	3	5.5	1	3.3

Source: Negro Employment Questionnaire.

REFERENCES

1. McKersie, Robert B. "Vitalize Black Enterprise." *Harvard Business Review*, September-October, 1968, pp. 88-99.
2. *Survey of Business Ownership in Washington, D.C.* Washington, D.C.: Small Business Administration, 1969.
3. Kirchheimer, Joseph. *Economic Development and Negro Entrepreneurship.* Washington, D.C.: National Urban Coalition, 1969, unpublished.
4. Boland, William, Jr. *A Study of Afro-American Enterprises.* New York: Oppenheimer & Co., 1969, unpublished.
5. Mason, Anthony. *Black Capitalism, Rhetoric, and Reality.* New York: Equity Research Associates, 1969.
6. U.S. Riot Commission. *Report of the National Advisory Commission on Civil Disorders.* Washington, D.C.: Government Printing Office, 1968.
7. Unterman, Israel. "Black Capitalism: Can It Do the Job?" *Newsday,* January 25, 1969, p. 5.
8. Cross, Theodore L. *Black Capitalism.* New York: Atheneum, 1969.
9. Foley, Eugene P. *The Achieving Ghetto.* Washington, D.C.: The National Press, 1968.
10. "Negro Businesses Here Increase 16%." *The Washington Post,* February 23, 1970, p. B-2.
11. Batchelder, Alan B. "Economic Forces Serving the Ends of the Negro Protest." *The Annals* (American Academy of Political and Social Science), January 1965, p. 88.
12. Samuelson, Robert J. "Treasury Errors, Minority Capitalism Hit at Conclave." *The Washington Post,* December 30, 1969, p. D-5.
13. "Is Black Capitalism a Mistake?" *Time,* January 12, 1970, pp. 66-67.
14. Cotton, Stephen. "Capitalist Slow Down." *The New Republic,* September 27, 1969, p. 16.

Chapter 6
Government Legal Weapons Against Employment Discrimination

THE INVIDIOUS EFFECTS OF DISCRIMINATION

Racial discrimination creates in its victims an apathy or docility which inhibits them from asserting their rights against the perpetrator of the discrimination. This docility stems from a number of factors: fear, ignorance of rights, and a feeling of low self-esteem engendered by repeated second-class treatment because of race or national origin. Discrimination in employment is no different in this respect from discrimination in other spheres. In its historic decision in *Brown v. Board of Education of Topeka,* 347 U.S. 483, 494(1954), the Supreme Court stated: "... To separate Negroes from others of similar age and qualifications solely because of their race generates a feeling of inferiority as to their status in the community that may affect their hearts and minds in a way unlikely ever to be undone. . . ."

This docility has been recognized by union leaders, businessmen, government officials and psychologists. Thus, George Meany, President of the AFL-CIO, referred to the reluctance of Negro employees to file complaints under fair employment practices laws because of the fear of retaliation which accompanies racial discrimination.[1] Senate and House hearings on equal employment bills are laced with references to the degradation, disillusionment, lack of motivation, and lessening of incentive to improve which result from racial discrimination in employment.[2] The Civil Rights Commission has shown the debilitating effect of menial labor on Negroes and has pointed up the reluctance of those Negroes to ask for improvement.[3] Psychological studies have pointed out the psychologically debilitating effects of discrimination in general.[4] In particular, Dr. Kenneth B. Clark[5] has shown how discrimination-induced self-hatred in Negro inhabitants of slums, due in good part to discrimination in employment, creates a feeling of inferiority and lack of motivation to assert themselves to change their condition. In all this, discrimination in employment establishes or reinforces the effect of discrimination in other areas, an inhibition to act for change.

Racial discrimination also sets apart the white from the Negro and Latin American workers. The principle of "divide and conquer" is older than the history of labor relations in this country, but that does not lessen its application here. The white workers expend their energy against the Negroes, the latter resent the whites, and neither group sees that sometimes their interests might be better served by joint action against their common employer. Then white employees may suffer from upgrading the positions of Negroes, the employer's policy of discrimination inevitably sets group against group, thus frustrating the possibility of effective concerted action. This effect was noted by James B. Carey, then president of the International Union of Electrical, Radio and Machine Workers in his testimony before the House on the 1963 equal employment bills.[6]

There is little doubt of the enormous impact racial discrimination in employment has on the flow of commerce and on the allocation of economic resources in this country. It has always been unjustified, even before it was explicitly made illegal by Title VII of the Civil Rights Act of 1964. However, in 1957, the right of labor unions to bar Negroes from membership solely on racial grounds was upheld in a northern state that has a "Fair Employment Code." The Wisconsin State Supreme Court on April 9, 1957, in a 6-to-1 opinion, written by Justice Timothy Brown, upheld a lower court ruling in the case of two Negro bricklayers who were denied membership in a Milwaukee local of the Bricklayers Union. The following excerpt is taken from the Court's decision:[7]

Racial discrimination in employment, so far, is not declared to be illegal. It is pronounced undesirable and the announced public policy of the State is to encourage and foster employment without discrimination to the fullest extent practicable. It may be disadvantageous to an individual not to be chosen for membership in a voluntary association, but the courts hitherto have been powerless to compel the association to receive him.

STATE AND LOCAL PROGRAMS

The federal government is assuming primary jurisdiction in the battle against racial discrimination in employment because of the basic unreliability of state and local efforts. Some states have few or no provisions to deal effectively with employment discrimination, while others have surprisingly effective agencies. California, for example, increased apprenticeships 24.5 per cent in 1969 with the passage of a new law which the California Department of Industrial Relations credited with increasing apprenticeship opportunities for minority groups.[8]

Ohio, on the other hand, has its equal employment opportunity requirements tied up in litigation. A state judge restrained the State Director of Public Works from cancelling a $1.2 million contract for work at Ohio

State University for noncompliance. Subsequently, five individuals filed a federal court suit charging the state attorney general and the judge with efforts to circumvent the law.[9]

The problems that states have encountered can be exemplified by the experience of New York. The New York State Division on Human Rights has had reinforced powers in the form of cease and desist orders which are reviewable through the state courts. The Division's commissioner believes that his agency's success is predicated on these powers provided by law. However, others in the state are less sanguine toward state efforts. An independent study group, the Committee for Efficiency in Government, stated that Negroes and Puerto Ricans remain virtually excluded from construction jobs in New York, while more than 30,000 out-of-state workers commute to construction jobs in the state. The study group attributed the primary responsibility for this situation to the "politically motivated failure or refusal of state officials to enforce state public works and civil rights laws."[10]

Governor Rockefeller of New York announced on February 3, 1970 that he was lifting an eleven-month moratorium on state construction in the Buffalo area, including work on the Amherst campus for the State University of New York at Buffalo. He claimed that a satisfactory affirmative-action program had been worked out to provide recruiting, training, qualifying and employment of blacks and other minorities in the construction industry. Among the main points of the agreement are: (1) There will be a minimum of 10.6 per cent nonwhite employees in the total construction work force or approximately 2500 construction jobs. (2) Minority workers will enter as journeymen, journeymen trainees or as apprentices, and they will become union members. (3) The state will finance a preliminary training program to prepare minority workers for union-craft training programs or for immediate employment.[11]

In July 1970, a federal judge, acting on a suit filed two years earlier by the Justice Department, ordered the state of Alabama to halt racial discrimination in its hiring practices and offer state jobs to 62 Negroes who had been turned away earlier. Seven state departments were directed to change their hiring rules on the basis of "overwhelming" evidence that Negro applicants for clerical positions had been discriminated against. The jurist pointed out that the secretaries of the U.S. Departments of Defense, Labor, and Health, Edcuation and Welfare adopted regulations in January 1963 prohibiting racial discrimination in state agencies governed by Federal merit standards and requiring the states to adopt similar regulations. Alabama is the lone state which has refused to adopt such regulations. The discrimination consisted of denying appointments and interviews and preferring lower ranking white applicants. Negroes were often rejected even though their applications indicated them to be better qualified by training or experience than the favored white applicants. The seven departments were ordered to offer the 62 blacks the first available positions in a classification and at a rate of pay they would have been in but for discrimination; to appoint Negro applicants to positions other than custodial, domestics, laborer or laboratory aide, when such applicants were listed as certified eligible, unless higher ranking white applicants were appointed; and to refrain from appointing or offering a job to a lower ranking white applicant on a certificate in preference to a higher ranking available Negro applicant unless the latter is first interviewed and found unfit or unavailable.[12]

Local antidiscrimination programs commonly take the form of human rights commissions comprised mainly of civic leaders who utilize methods of persuasion to break down local industry prohibitions. They have been successful mainly in helping to negotiate agreements between black communities, industries, and unions, as in the Chicago and Los Angeles Plans which have been discussed earlier.

The following situations illustrate the existence of employment inequalities at the municipal level in various sectors of society. For example, only one black was found among the 1,867 persons holding policy-making positions in the private sector of Milwaukee, Wisconsin in 1968, according to a study released by the Milwaukee Urban League and the city's Community-Relations Social Development Commission. The study covered 44 Milwaukee-based businesses and industrial concerns with 1,000 or more employees or annual sales of more than $12 million, and companies not based in Milwaukee but employing at least 700 persons; 24 private hospitals; 7 major insurance companies; 26 banks with assets of at least $10 million; 26 law firms with six or more partners or at least two public-owned corporations as clients. Blacks compose 13 per cent of the city's population. The single black policy-maker was at an undisclosed private hospital. In 1968, 20 blacks held 42 of 856 (2.6%) city and county policy-making positions. (This included elected positions.) The report noted that blacks have a better chance of being appointed to policy posts than being elected. Five of 121 elected positions in the county (or 4.1%) are held by blacks who represent 9 per cent of the total population. 6.1 per cent of all county-appointed positions (36 out of 588) are held by blacks. In the city of Milwaukee, 8.3% of all elective positions and 7.2% of all appointive positions are held by blacks. The largest percentage of blacks was found in policy-making positions in the voluntary sector, particularly where policy was directly concerned with poverty problems. Out of 472 policy posts in the voluntary sector, 125 or 26.5% were held by blacks. Voluntary civic organizations, however, had only two blacks in policy-making positions, or 1.6%. Labor organizations had no blacks among 26 local policy-making posts and two in 36 regional policy-making jobs.[13]

Detroit's Commission on Community Relations has declared three Detroit-area businesses ineligible to bid for city business because they have failed to formulate plans for hiring minority workers. The three companies are Earle Equipment, General Riggers and Erectors, Inc., and Anderson's Vehicle Sales, Inc. The Commission said that all three companies have all-white work forces and have made no acceptable, positive efforts to alter the situation. At the same time, the Commission agreed to reinstate two companies which had previously been barred from city bidding in the same manner. The Commission is responsible for enforcement of the city's fair employment practices ordinance which says that all businesses bidding for city contracts must devise and carry out an affirmative action plan to hire, train and promote minority employees.[14]

THE EQUAL EMPLOYMENT OPPORTUNITY COMMISSION EXPERIENCE

At the federal level, the Equal Employment Opportunity Commission was established by Title VII of the Civil Rights Act of 1964. The Commission's responsibility is to assure that all Americans will be considered for hiring, firing and promotion on the basis of their ability and qualifications, without regard to race, color, religion, sex or national origin. The Commission is composed of five members appointed by the President by and with the consent of the Senate for terms of five years each. Under Title VII, the Commission is concerned with four major groups: employers, public and private employment agencies, labor organizations, and joint labor-management apprenticeship or training programs. Coverage broadened annually: beginning on July 2, 1965, Title VII applied to employers of 100 or more persons, labor unions with 100 or more members or those which operate hiring halls, and private employment agencies dealing with employers of 100 or more persons. On July 2, 1966, the provision applied to those with 75 or more employees or members; On July 2, 1967, to those with 50 or more employees or members; and on July 2, 1968, to those with 25 or more employees or members. Also covered are the U.S. Employment Service and the system of state and local employment services receiving federal assistance. Among those not covered are local, state and federal agencies, government-owned corporations, Indian tribes, religious organizations where the employee is engaged in religious activities, and educational institutions where the employee performs work connected with the institution's educational activities.[15]

The Commission has two basic responsibilities. First, it investigates complaints of discrimination, and if it finds they are justified, seeks a full remedy by the process of conciliation in which the alleged offender's identity is not publicly disclosed. Second, it promotes programs of voluntary compliance by employers, unions and community organizations to put the idea of equal opportunity into actual operation. If a person believes that he or she has been discriminated against by an employer, labor organization, employment agency or joint labor-management program, that person may file a complaint with the Commission. When such a complaint is received in Washington, it is handled by the Commision's Compliance Division. The analysis section assigns complaints to the following categories: Probable Jurisdiction, No Jurisdiction, Deferred for State Fair Employment Practice Action, and Returned for Additional Information. The Probable Jurisdiction complaints are assigned for investigation. Investigators first contact the complainant and his witnesses. If it appears that the complaint has grounds, the Commission sends conciliators to attempt to resolve the complaint to the satisfaction of all parties concerned. If conciliation efforts fail, the complainant may then take his complaint to the U.S. District Court.[16]

Individual Commissioners or the Commission as a whole may initiate complaints if they receive information they feel indicates the need for a complaint. For example, an individual may give a Commissioner information concerning an employer whom he suspects of using discriminatory practices. The individual may not personally wish to file a complaint because he fears retaliation by the employer. In this instance or any other instance where he has the necessary information, the Commissioner may file a complaint on his own. The EEOC does not have the authority to secure a court order to enjoin discriminatory employment practices before a case is heard. Such cases must be brought by the party charging discrimination. In certain cases, where the Commission feels that a pattern or practice of discrimination exists rather than a single instance, the Justice Department may be advised and the Attorney General of the United States may then undertake action in the appropriate U.S. District Court. The court, after a finding that Title VII has been violated by an organization, can demand the discontinuance of the discriminatory practices, affirmative action, the payment of back wages, reinstatement, and hiring.[17]

The Commission is allowed 60 days within which it must investigate a complaint, determine whether there is reasonable cause to believe it is true, and achieve voluntary compliance. At the end of this period, the complainant must be notified of the success or failure of the Commission's efforts, so that he may bring suit if he chooses to do so. However, the Commission may continue its efforts to resolve the dispute after the 60-day period has expired. The EEOC may require the production of records in order to make its investigation. It may serve a "Demand for Access to Evidence" in order to obtain the necessary information. This is done only after a charge has been filed.[18]

Title VII provides that the Equal Employment Opportunity

Commission must defer investigation of a case arising in a state with an enforceable fair employment practice law for a period of not less than 60 days, and in the case of a newly-established state Fair Employment Practice organization, for a period of not more than 120 days. The time limitation after the discriminatory action has taken place within which to file a complaint in a state which has no FEP laws is 90 days. In a state where there are FEP laws, the limit is 210 days from the date of the act or 30 days from disposition of the case by the State Fair Employment Practices Commission, whichever is sooner. In such a situation, the party cannot file a charge with the Commission until the state agency has had 60 days within which to act.[19] The Commission has determined that it will defer to the following states:

Alaska	Kansas	New York
California	Maryland	Ohio
Colorado	Massachusetts	Oregon
Connecticut	Michigan	Pennsylvania
Delaware	Minnesota	Puerto Rico
District of Columbia	Missouri	Rhode Island
Hawaii	Nebraska	Utah
Indiana	Nevada	Washington
Illinois	New Hampshire	Wisconsin
Iowa	New Jersey	Wyoming
	New Mexico	

Six states have laws which provide only for a criminal remedy. The Commission will not defer to these states and will assume immediate jurisdiction when a complaint is filed. These states are: Arizona, Idaho, Maine, Montana, North Dakota and Vermont. Three states have laws which contain no enforcement provisions. The EEOC will not defer to these states. They are: Oklahoma, Tennessee, and West Virginia.[20]

In Michigan, the state law covers employers with a minimum of 8 employees; in California, employers with at least 5 employees are included; in Maryland, employers with at least 25 employees are subject to the state FEP statute. Texas has no law presently.

The State and Local Liaison Office within the Commission is charged with the task of coordinating activities between the EEOC and various state and local Fair Employment Practices groups. Agreements of cooperation and information sharing are developed. Affirmative action programs are developed so that state agencies can aid those employers who want to change their employment practices to comply with the provisions of Title VII. These programs also help employers who practice discrimination in employment to change their policies before a complaint charge is filed against them. Liaison evaluates state and local agencies concerning enforcement powers so that EEOC members will know to which agencies complaints may be deferred. Cooperative agreements between the EEOC and other federal agencies are made in order to eliminate duplication of studies and to facilitate the gathering and exchange of information.[21]

Fair Employment Practice Commissions and state statutes in the Northern states had prohibited employment inequality before the federal law was passed. Moreover, many enterprises outside the South had voluntarily implemented fair employment policies since the end of World War II.

According to government sources, there are small employers who are still not aware of the existence of antidiscriminatory legislation. Also, prior to July 1968, employers of 25 or less were not compelled to file special reports with the EEOC relating to the racial composition of their work forces.

In addition, the Commission's power is limited largely to attempting to gain voluntary compliance with the law. Congress has refused to give the Commission authority to issue cease-and-desist orders to require compliance. If conciliation fails, the employee's only recourse is the federal courts.

As an example of the absence of employment equality, in 1965, the first year for the application of the civil rights legislation, the Equal Employment Opportunity Commission indicated that data from Akron, Ohio's four largest rubber companies showed Negroes representing 16.5 per cent of the unskilled and semiskilled employees, 2.6 per cent of the skilled craftsmen, 2.2 per cent of the female employees and only 0.8 per cent of the white-collar workers. The commission noted that 43 percent of the jobs at the four companies were white collar. Despite the low level at which Negroes were employed in the four largest companies, the report noted, "the record is even worse for smaller rubber companies." In 1965, Akron rubber plants with fewer than 500 employees "reported not a single Negro white-collar worker and only one Negro craftsman." This pattern in smaller companies was repeated throughout the state.[22]

One of the most important measures of the appropriateness of the corrective action provided in a conciliation agreement is the adequacy of the relief afforded to the charging party. EEOC is, after all, an agency created to serve people who come forward to file charges of discrimination. If this responsibility is not properly discharged, success in other areas pales by comparison. In accordance with this mandate, a number of agreements have been arranged through which the charging party not only was restored to employment in an improper discharge case but also was compensated for the period during which he was out of work as a result of the actions of the respondent company or union. A good example is a case involving a major steel producer in which the Commission decided that the discharge of one of the respondent's employees in 1966 was discriminatory. Pursuant to the Conciliation Agreement, the charging party was placed back at work at the going rate for his occupation and was compensated for the period of 1966, 1967 and 1968 at the rate he would have been earning had the company continued his employment. The emphasis here is on completeness of remedy. Likewise, promises of affirmative action must be viewed as an adjunct to, not a substitute for, complete satisfaction of the grievance at issue.[23]

Another area of improvement has been in the nature of the affirmative action provisions that do become incorporated into conciliation agreements. In place of general statements of good intentions, companies and unions have been persuaded to talk specifics. In the Commission's early history, for instance, conciliation clauses regarding affirmative recruitment programs simply stated that the respondent would "affirmatively recruit." Fiscal 1968, however, saw numerous agreements describing the details of just how respondent was going to recruit. Therefore, it was quite common to find agreements listing the persons, organizations and educational institutions to be contacted by the company, the frequency and mode of contact, or a listing of communications media to be used. Attention to particulars extended to other areas of affirmative action as well. Many agreements, for example, incorporated innovations such as the concept of "affirmative action files." Such a file maintains a "history" on each minority applicant for employment with the company, providing a continuing source for minority applicants when job vacancies occur. The file charts the result of each application by minority candidates: when they applied; whether or not they were considered; whether they were hired, and if so, for what occupations; how long they remained in the company's employ; what training they received; and a general prognosis of their experience with the company. Kept separate from conventional personnel files in order to prevent misuse, the "affirmative action file" makes possible the careful analysis and planning necessary to achieve positive results in affirmative action as in any other aspect of business enterprise.[24]

As in the past, the Equal Employment Opportunity Commission will try to achieve conciliation by talking with individual employers involved, but if investigators do not receive an immediate and receptive audience, an increase in the number of lawsuits filed under the 1964 Civil Rights Act charging a pattern or practice of discrimination will result.

In Fiscal Year 1968, the Commission successfully negotiated a variety of agreements reflecting refinement of the compliance process itself, along with advancement in specific areas of remedy. Thus, as the growing body of Commission decisions and court opinions shaped a more precise determination of what discrimination is, so in turn did they clarify the definition of what constitutes appropriate corrective action to be sought in conciliation.[25] AsTable 48 elaborates, nearly 45 per cent of all charges brought before the EEOC in fiscal 1968 involved race as the basis of discrimination, and were directed against employers, unions, private employment agencies, and state employment agencies.

Provisions regarding employment testing systems have also been strengthened. Of particular interest in Fiscal 1968 was the detailed test assessment system that a major aerospace company agreed in conciliation to undertake. In order to attain maximum relevancy between tests and jobs, selection and development of tests will follow a careful analysis of job and training requirements, screening carefully to avoid cultural content unrelated to employee performance, such as questions on etiquette or advanced metallurgy on a test for sheet metal workers. Meanwhile, to safeguard against unnecessary elimination of job applicants, the company adopted the policy of establishing cut-off scores whereby only those candidates with a high likelihood of failure will be screened out; further, test results will be viewed as only a single component of the applicant's qualifications, ensuring due consideration of other factors which might compensate for a low score. The new policy on testing enables the company to select a workforce whose abilities and skills are compatible with the level of work to be performed and provides an opportunity to persons who are "qualifiable" as well as to individuals presently qualified for job openings. This agreement, representing a new breakthrough in EEOC's efforts to promote nondiscriminatory employment testing procedures, stands as a model for other companies and industries to follow.[26]

In August of 1970, the EEOC issued revised guidelines on employee selection procedures, specifically testing. An evaluation of complaints filed with the Commission revealed that many testing procedures used by employers, unions, and employment agencies, although they appear fair and equitable on the surface, are in fact subtle and insidious tools used to exclude minorities and women from the mainstream of the labor force. The purpose of the guidelines is "to contribute to the implementation of nondiscriminatory personnel practices." They extend and amplify earlier testing guidelines issued by the Commission in August 1966. The guidelines affect employers, labor unions and employment agencies subject to EEOC's jurisdiction under Title VII of the 1964 Civil Rights Act. In addition to formal psychological tests, the guidelines apply to such other employment standards as scored application forms, personal interviews, educational requirements, and work experience. The guidelines state that, while professionally devised tests used in conjunction with other criteria may significantly aid in developing an efficient work force, they may also have a discriminatory effect. In many cases, minority job candidates experience disproportionately high rates of rejection because they fail to achieve a minimum test score. Yet, in many cases, there is no evidence that tests are valid predictors of good performance on the job. The guidelines were developed to provide "workable standards for employers, labor unions and employment agencies" in establishing nondiscriminatory employee selection procedures. A test is discriminatory when it screens out a disproportionately large number of classes protected by Title VII when it has not been shown to be valid for its intended purposes. Validation of a test requires the presentation of empirical data which demonstrate that the test accurately measures some skill, knowledge, aptitude, or characteristic which is relevant to the performance of the job in question. In certain cases, where there are job progression structures and seniority provisions for advancement, tests have been used at the entry level to predict ability to perform at the higher positions in the promotion ladder. The guidelines state that such tests are permissible only when "there is a high probability that persons employed will in fact attain that higher level job within a reasonable period of time." With respect to employment agencies, the guidelines cover not only tests given by the agencies but also those tests which employers or unions ask the agencies to administer for them. The guidelines state, "an employment agency or service will be expected to refuse to administer a test where the employer or union does not supply satisfactory evidence of validation." They urge employers, unions and employment agencies to provide an opportunity for retesting and reconsideration to earlier "failure" candidates who have availed themselves of more training or experience. These standards were developed in conjunction with the Office of Federal Contract Compliance of the Department of Labor which will also issue similar requirements for federal contractors and subcontractors subject to Executive Order 11246.[27]

Significant progress has also been observed in the matter of use of plant facilities, such as restrooms, locker rooms and drinking fountains. In early Commission conciliations, simple statements that facilities would be desegregated or that they were available to all employees were generally accepted. During the 1968 fiscal year, however, a more precise statement was required of respondents. For example, assignment of lockers in alphabetical surname order has been negotiated along with specific notices to all employees indicating that all facilities are open and available on a nondiscriminatory basis. Total desegregation of all facilities, then with immediate discharge set as the penalty for interference, is a provision common to agreements designed to eliminate separate facilities.[28]

REMEDIES IN THE FEDERAL COURTS

Title VII provides two methods for bringing matters before a Federal court in the event that conciliatory efforts should fail. If the case involves a pattern or practice of discrimination, and therefore is of general public importance, the Commission will discuss with the Department of Justice the possibility of the Attorney General bringing suit. In addition, the Commission will notify the charging party of his right under Section 706 of Title VII to maintain a civil action to compel compliance. EEOC has not only the right, uniformly recognized by all courts, but the duty to participate in such litigation where participation will tend to effectuate the policies of the Act. There is vital interaction here: the development of EEOC policies and procedures depend in some important respects on the resolution of issues raised in private cases and in actions by the Attorney General; similarly, the Commission's administrative process has a significant impact upon the rights of charging parties and respondents when litigation ensues. Thus, at the same time that it was strengthening the conciliation process, the Commission realized that, where litigation becomes necessary, the remedy available through the courts must be on a level consistent with that available through conciliation. Unless this parity is achieved and maintained, respondents would be encouraged to refuse to conciliate, and thereby frustrate the Congressional intent that conciliation be used as the primary vehicle for settling complaints of discrimination.[29]

PROCEDURAL AND JURISDICTIONAL PREREQUISITES

There are certain Title VII procedural requirements that must be fulfilled before a federal district court will entertain a cause of action. For example, under Section 706(a), at least some action by the Equal Employment Opportunity Commission in the form of a conciliation effort is required as a judicial prerequisite for the institution of a civil action.[30]

An aggrieved individual under Title VII may not maintain a civil action unless he first filed a charge with EEOC against the defendants named in the judicial complaint. There must be a congruence between the charge filed with EEOC and the complaint instituted in court. The receipt of a notice of failure to conciliate from the Commission is a condition precedent to the bringing of a civil action under Section 706(e). Only in exceptional circumstances may this requirement be waived, such as when the plaintiff can demonstrate that the Commission refuses to comply with his request for the notice of the right to bring suit. "Conciliation" or the notice of failure to achieve voluntary compliance does not refer to the agreement of the defendant firm to a Commission proposal, but to a mutually satisfactory agreement of the complainant and the respondent. By entering into an agreement with the company, the Commission cannot bind the rights of charging parties to judicial relief. To hold otherwise would prevent effective protection of individual rights guaranteed by the Civil Rights Act of 1964. It is settled law that the Commission's interpretation and application of the Act are to be accorded great weight by the court.[31]

For the purpose of bringing a civil action pursuant to Section 706(e), the potential plaintiff need only file a complaint with the court within thirty days from the date he received EEOC's "notice letter." There is no affirmative duty on the part of the plaintiff to expedite service of the complaint on the defendant, and the date of such service is irrelevant for meeting the thirty-day prescription. To illustrate, in a case in which the original charge was filed with EEOC in October 1966, and the state of Michigan did not pass a fair employment practice act until December 21, 1966, the EEOC would not ordinarily be required to defer to the state commission under Section 706(b). Similarly, when the original charge is amended subsequent to the passage of the Michigan statute, no deferral is necessary if the amended charge is substantially the same as the original, and merely serves to amplify the original. Pursuant to Section 1601.11(b) of the Commission's rules and regulations, the amendment related back to the original filing date. Such liberality of amending is in line with Rule 15 of the Federal Rules of Civil Procedure. The court also held that the failure of the Commission to attempt conciliation efforts did not bar the plaintiff from bringing a civil action, contrary to the ruling in *Mickel v. South Carolina State Employment Service*. Despite the provisions of Section 706(a) requiring the Commission to "endeavor to eliminate any such alleged unlawful practice by informal methods of conference, conciliation, and persuasion. . . ," the court held that the plaintiff, not responsible for the acts or omissions of the Commission, should not be denied judicial relief because of the Commission's inability to attempt conciliation.[32]

The complaint filed with a federal court must also indicate that the EEOC has attempted conciliation after a complainant has vainly sought relief in a state with a fair employment practice law, which bans racial discrimination in employment. If these facts are not included, the complaint will be dismissed as defective, with instructions for amendment, in order properly to establish the court's jurisdiction.[33]

In one case, the California Fair Employment Practice Commission had not been afforded the sixty days for processing the charge nor had it officially terminated its proceedings prior to the filing of the charge with the EEOC. The charge, therefore, was ruled as untimely and the jurisdictional prerequisite to bring suit under Section 706(e) was not satisfied. The court also found that initially a plaintiff may pursue his remedies under the collective bargaining agreement and those available to him under Title VII, but he may only pursue one of these remedies to completion. If a complainant accepts a grievance procedure award and returns to work, he is considered to have made a binding election.[34]

In order to maintain a civil action under Section 706(e), notice from

EEOC of its inability to obtain voluntary compliance is sufficient to show that administrative remedies have been exhausted. The plaintiff does not have to demonstrate that the Commission "actively" conciliated the claim.[35]

Title VII contemplates that a valid charge must be filed with the Commission within 90 days of the alleged unlawful violation, that conciliation efforts be completed within 60 days thereafter, and that the aggrieved individual must file a complaint within 30 days of notice that conciliation efforts have failed. As to the requirement of filing a charge within 90 days, there is no correlative requirement that the EEOC must serve a copy of that charge upon respondent within the 90-day period. EEOC's administrative delay in serving the charge should not be allowed to destroy the jurisdiction of the plaintiff's cause of action. In addition, the court would not combine these statutory time periods to arrive at an outside limit of 180 days within which the aggrieved party must file a complaint with the court. The 90- and 60-day time periods are considered directory and not jurisdictional requirements, and therefore EEOC's delay would not be the basis for destroying plaintiff's rights. Moreover, the 30-day period following "notice" that conciliation efforts have failed begins to run when the plaintiff receives the Commission's "30-day suit letter," and not when the plaintiff informally learns of such failure.[36] This requirement is applicable regardless of the delay which may occur before such notice is given him. In calculating the expiration of the 30-day statutory period, Rule 6(a) of the Federal Rules of Civil Procedure prevails and "the last day of the period so computed shall be included, unless it is a Saturday, a Sunday, or a legal holiday, in which event, the period runs until the end of the next day which is not a Saturday, Sunday, or a legal holiday." Thus, in one case in which the last two days of the 30-day statutory period fell on Saturday and Sunday, and plaintiff did not file his complaint until Monday, defendant's motion to dismiss due to untimely filing of the complaint was denied.[37]

Proper venue for a Title VII suit is a judicial district of the state in which the alleged unlawful employment practice was supposed to have occurred, and not the judicial district in which the defendant has its principal offices. However, the district court in which the case is brought may transfer the case to a more appropriate district court. In another case, since the parties either resided or did business in the Western District of Louisiana, the court felt compelled, in the interest of justice and for the convenience of the parties and witnesses, to transfer the case to the Western District.[38]

The courts have concurred with the EEOC that an employee may file charges of discrimination which affect not only his own interests but also the interests of the class of persons of which he is a member. Persons charging unlawful job discrimination may bring a class action under Title VII, and it is not necessary for each member of the class to have filed a charge with the Commission. Thus, in a case in which each of four Negroes brought suit on behalf of himself and all present and prospective Negro employees of the plant, as a class, seeking injunctive relief, the fact that only one of the four exhausted his administrative remedies before the Commission does not bar the other three from pursuing their legal action. It is sufficient, for purposes of being joined as coplaintiffs in a litigation, that the individuals who have not exhausted their administrative remedies are in a class and have asserted the same or some of the issues raised by the plaintiff that did exhaust his administrative remedies.[39]

However, certain types of alleged discrimination do not possess the characteristics required for class actions. In one case, the plaintiff, alleging a discriminatory discharge because of his race, sought back pay for the difference between his present (lower) wages and what he had been making while employed by the defendant. In addition, as the alleged representative of a class of Negroes, he sought an injunction for himself and his class against discriminatory job assignments and segregated facilities. A class action does not lie since the interests of the alleged class, as well as the questions of law and fact, are too disparate for such an action. The critical fact question as to the plaintiff would be whether he was discriminatorily discharged, a question not present as to the other members of the alleged class. Similarly, as a discharged employee, he could not effectively assert rights which only grow out of present employment. Without the existence of a class action and the equitable relief sought therefor, all that remains is plaintiff's claim for back wages, which is a simple contract claim.[40]

Despite the fact that a majority of plaintiffs in a class action had not complied with section 706(e) prerequisites for maintenance of a civil action, it is sufficient if prior to bringing the civil action the statute was complied with by some members of the class. The subsequent joining of additional class members does not vitiate the legitimate status of the action. However, where only the employer was named in the original charges filed with EEOC, the union cannot be made a party by being named in charges subsequent to the institution of a Section 706(e) civil action. It is a condition precedent to the bringing of a civil action against any party that the party be named in a charge filed with the EEOC by at least one member of the plaintiff class.[41]

The relationship between conciliation activities at the Commission and action in the courts was further defined by the determination, in litigation, that the existence of a conciliation agreement does not preclude a civil proceeding under Title VII by persons — even charging parties — who were not signatories to the agreement. Under Rule 23 (a) of the Federal rules of civil procedure, class action cannot be mooted *per se* by conciliation agreements to which the court is not a party. The class in whose behalf the plaintiffs were entitled to maintain the class action includes *all* Negro employees and Negro applicants. Therefore, in another case the defendant employer's motion to dismiss a class action as to persons other than the party plaintiffs was denied, despite the fact that the employer had entered into conciliation agreements with some of its aggrieved employees. The common questions of law or fact concern the company's maintenance of a pattern or practice of discriminatorily denying similarly situated Negroes equal employment opportunities.[42]

The EEOC is authorized under Section 709 (a) to issue a "Demand for Access to Evidence." The party so served has twenty days within which to seek an order in the District Court setting aside or modifying the demand of the Commission. Where such a party fails to seek the statutorily prescribed relief (Section 710(c)), it in effect waives its right to object on the basis of relevancy in a subsequent compliance proceeding instituted by the Commission under Section 710(b).[43]

When a court enforces the EEOC's Demand for Access to Evidence upon a defendant union, the union is given thirty days to make available to the Commission its records on applicants for membership, union members, persons to whom work permits were issued, union officers, the union constitution, by-laws, rules and regulations, minutes of meetings and dispatch records for the preceeding six months.[44]

Title VII does not exclude a union from utilizing the Act's remedial provisions. A union representing an employer's employees is an aggrieved person for the purpose of filing a charge with the EEOC and bringing a civil action under Title VII.[45]

A district court has held that Title VII conferred no jurisdiction to deal with alleged discrimination based on bargaining unit structures in the railroad industry. The National Mediation Board, established under the Railway Labor Act, is the appropriate administrative agency for dealing with an alleged discriminatory practice based on classification of employees for bargaining purposes, and this remedy must be exhausted prior to coming to federal court. Furthermore, if judicial redress is still needed, the representative unions and the National Mediation Board must be joined as necessary parties under Rule 19(a) of the Federal Rules of Civil Procedure.[46]

SUBSTANTIVE VIOLATIONS

In other cases, the prosecution of apparent substantive violations has been complicated by the fact of their origin prior to the effective date of the Act. For example, on March 9, 1966, an Alabama Negro filed a charge with the EEOC alleging that a union discriminated against him on account of race by denying him membership, the rejection occurring on May 8, 1965, prior to the effective date of Title VII. The court entered judgment for the defendant holding it lacked jurisdiction over an alleged unlawful employment practice which occurred before July 2, 1965.[47]

However, the courts have firmly established the concept of the "continuing act of discrimination" in order to rule on alleged offenses occurring prior to the effective date of the Act. The courts have recognized, as does the Commission, that certain kinds of conduct in themselves constitute an act of discrimination which has no particular boundaries in time, as for example, with a seniority system which has the intent or effect of discriminating on the basis of race. Because such discrimination is held to be continuing, and the event can be pinned to no particular date, a complaint based on the practice is timely whenever it is filed. In a leading decision, a number of Negroes sued the Phillip Morris Tobacco Company, charging racial discrimination, because of seniority and transfer provisions of collective bargaining contracts which adversely affected the conditions of employment and opportunities for advancement of the class. The court ruled that "Present discrimination may be found in contractual provisions that appear fair upon their face, but which operate unfairly because of the historical discrimination that undergirds them." In other words, they had an inherently discriminatory effect. Prior to January 1, 1966, the company's employment policy operated on "a token basis and racial segregation in hiring was the practice, if not the rule." Negroes had been restricted to specific departments. Opportunities for advancement and other privileges depended upon employment seniority, the date on which the employee was first permanently employed by the company. While the organization of the company's business on departmental lines with restrictive transfers serves legitimate functions, organization of the departments on a racially segregated basis prevented Negroes from advancing on their merits to jobs open only to white employees. Employment without regard to race since January 1, 1966 and the relaxation of departmental transfers only partly eliminated the competitive disadvantages imposed upon Negro employees and continued to subordinate Negroes to white employees regardless of employment seniority. The restrictions did not result from a lack of merit or qualification.

The present consequences of past discrimination, that is, a discriminatory seniority system devised before the effective date of the Act, are not outside the coverage of the Act. Congress did not intend to freeze an entire generation of Negro employees into discriminatory patterns that existed before the Act. A departmental seniority system that has its genesis in racial discrimination is not a bona fide seniority system under Section 703(h) of the Act.

In view of the discriminatory practices found and based upon the principle that the departmental seniority rights of white employees in the fabrication department are not vested rights but mere expectancies derived from the collective bargaining agreement subject to modification, the court ordered that all Negroes hired by the company before January 1, 1966, working in the prefabrication department be given the opportunity to transfer to the fabrication department or warehouse, shipping and receiving departments to fill vacancies. Members of the class transferring under the procedures set forth by the Court shall compute their departmental seniority from their employment seniority date. Negroes seeking to transfer were required to satisfy the same standard applied in hiring white employees for the fabrication and the warehouse, shipping and receiving departments. Transferees are to be allowed the normal probationary period of three months to perform adequately; unsuccessful transferees may be removed and returned to their old department and job classification with their seniority computed from their employment seniority date.

Defendant company committed an unlawful employment practice because of race with respect to two Negro employees by paying a higher wage to white employees who performed comparable jobs requiring equal skill and responsibility. However, the evidence did not support the allegation that Negroes as a class received lower wages than white employees doing substantially similar work. The company was required to adjust the wages of the two employees.[48]

Finding a pattern and practice of discrimination against Negroes in violation of Title VII, the U.S. Court of Appeals at St. Louis fashioned a broad order designed to eliminate the past violations. The court ordered the local unions involved to modify referral systems to permit Negroes who are reasonably qualified to register for employment at the locals' hiring halls and to be placed in the highest groups for which they qualify. They also were ordered to modify experience requirements for Negroes otherwise qualified and to take reasonable steps to publicize to the Negro community that all persons now were permitted to use the referral system. One local was also ordered to modify its journeyman's examination procedure so that the examination is objective in nature, is designed to test the ability of the applicant to perform journeyman's work, and is given and graded in such a manner as to permit review. In its decision, the appeals court reversed a federal district court holding and rejected a contention that the government is required to prove specific instances of discrimination after the effective date of the Act.[49]

A federal district court erred in denying a preliminary injunction sought by the Attorney General in a pattern-of-practice action brought against an employer charged with racial discrimination in hiring, transfer and promotion. The lower court answered the wrong question in deciding the issue, according to the appeals court. Shortly after the action was filed, the company was awarded a government contract that resulted in a substantial increase in its work force. So the company and the union negotiated a new agreement that loosened transfer procedures somewhat in favor of Negro employees. The lower court denied the injunction largely because it concluded that the new transfer program did not violate Title VII. But the appeals court said that the question was whether the fact that the new union contract and the transfer program partially corrected violations shown by the Attorney General negated the need for the injunction. It decided that it did not, finding the Attorney General could prevail on the merits. In holding that the injunction should have been issued, the appeals court said:

> We take the position that in such a case, irreparable injury should be presumed from the very fact that the statute has been violated. Whenever a qualified Negro employee is disciminatorily denied a chance to fill a position for which he is qualified and has the seniority to obtain it, he suffers irreparable injury and so does the labor force of the country as a whole.[50]

It is also established law that the Norris-LaGuardia Act does not prohibit a federal court from issuing an injunction against a labor union found to be involved in discriminatory practices, and the union can be enjoined from interfering with a court order eliminating a discriminatory "job seniority" system, where such system has the effect of "telescoping" past years or discrimination.[51]

In a Texas case, the defendant firm had engaged in an unlawful employment practice by limiting, segregating and discriminating against Negro employees because of their race. In addition to recovering lost wages, some of the plaintiffs were awarded compensatory damages on the grounds that they "were humiliated, relegated to a status below that of white persons and given only menial jobs. . . ."[52]

Despite affidavits by a company to the effect that its maintenance of separate classifications for "in town" and "on the road" drivers is applied in a nondiscriminatory manner, the court denied defendant's motion for summary judgment. In light of the facts that (1) seniority rights in one classification are not transferrable to the other classification, and (2) there are no Negroes in the "on the road" classification, the court felt that the system itself might be discriminatory. The court noted that in light of the opinion in *Quarles v. Phillip Morris, Inc.,* it was possible for the plaintiff to make a case based on the inherent discriminatory effect on the system.[53]

UNION BREACH OF FAIR REPRESENTATION OBLIGATION

Unions also run the risk of violating the Taft-Hartley Act when they practice racial discrimination. For instance, a segregated white local union that failed to process a grievance of a member of a Negro local at the same company violated its duty of fair representation under the Taft-Hartley Act and also engaged in unlawful restraint and coercion of employees under Section 8(b) (1)(A) of the same law. The union was stripped of its certification as bargaining representative and was ordered to cease and desist its unlawful practices, including a violation of its bargaining duty by refusing to process the grievance.[54] This landmark holding drew on the 1962 Miranda decision in which a Board majority held that the Taft-Hartley Act gives employees the right to be free from "unfair or irrelevant or invidious" treatment by their bargaining agent. If a union accords employees such treatment, the Board added, it commits an unfair labor practice; if the employer participates in or makes such treatment possible, he also commits an unfair labor practice.[55] The Miranda holding was denied enforcement by the U.S. Court of Appeals at New York in a decision in which there was no majority opinion, the three-judge panel splitting three ways.[56]

Two local unions violated the Taft-Hartley Act by maintaining and enforcing a 75-25 per cent distribution of work between an all-white local and an all Negro-local and by forbidding the assignment of white and Negro gangs to work together in ship hatches. The unions also violated their bargaining duty under the Act by negotiating a contract that discriminates against a group of employees on an unfair, invidious, or irrelevant basis. All five members agreed that the discrimination violated the Act insofar as it was based on the local an employee belonged to, but Chairman McCulloch and Member Fanning dissented to the holding that the racial discrimination was an unfair labor practice.[57] The division among the Board members in this case was the same as in the Hughes Tool case, with Chairman McCulloch and Member Fanning maintaining the Board may find unlawful discrimination under the Act only when it relates to union membership or activities. The decision of the Board was enforced in a brief per curiam order by the U.S. Court of Appeals at New Orleans.[58] The Supreme Court denied review of the case.[59]

A union violated the Taft-Hartley Act by failing to press back pay and integration grievances of Negro members of the union. An NLRB order directing the union not only to stop discriminating against the Negro members but also to go to the company and demand antidiscrimination contract clauses is enforced.[60] The court upheld this three-to-two decision of the NLRB. As they had in other similar cases, Chairman McCulloch and Member Fanning dissented. The Supreme Court denied review of the case.[61]

A union breached its duty of fair representation and violated the Act by discriminating on the basis of race in the operation of its hiring hall, and an employer's association also violated the Act by participating in the union's unlawful conduct. The decision was by a panel consisting of Members Brown, Jenkins, and Zagoria. Chairman McCulloch and Member Fanning have dissented in earlier cases involving findings of violation of the Act grounded upon discrimination based on race. As a remedy, the Board ordered the union to accept applications of rejected Negroes on the same terms and conditions applied to white applicants, with seniority as of a date six months before their unfair labor practice charges were filed.[62]

CONCURRENT NLRB JURISDICTION

The question of whether the NLRB can use its powers against racial discrimination in employment, even though Congress specifically addressed new legislation to the racial issue in the enactment of the Civil Rights Act, arose in a case involving Farmer's Cooperative Compress, a Lubbock, Texas concern that processes cotton. The concern at some times of the year employs up to 550 workers, many of whom are Negroes or Mexican-Americans. The workers are represented by the United Packinghouse Workers union. When the cotton processor and the union failed to agree on a contract in 1966, the union struck and also filed unfair practices charges with the NLRB. After a hearing, an NLRB examiner upheld the charges, ruling that Farmer's Cooperative Compress had encouraged employees to vote the union out, bargained in bad faith on wages and engaged in other practices of an economic nature. In addition, the examiner ruled that the concern had illegally refused to bargain with the union about the elimination of certain plant conditions that discriminated against the minority groups. The ruling was based on evidence that the cotton processor, for example, paid one Mexican-American $1.50 an hour on a job where the other workers were whites receiving $1.80. The board adopted the examiner's decision in a rather perfunctory order without saying much about the novel legal question of whether the 1935 law applies to job discrimination. The U.S. Circuit Court of Appeals for the District of Columbia, however, ruled flatly that the old law applies. The appeals court held that racial discrimination violates the National Labor Relations Act because an employer's bias "sets up a clash of interests between workers which tends to reduce the effectiveness of their working in concert to achieve their goals" under that act. Further, the appeals court decided that Congress hadn't denied the NLRB jurisdiction over racial matters when it created the Equal Employment Opportunity Commission. Both have jurisdiction, the court said. Farmer's Cooperative Compress asked the Supreme Court to review the appeals court's decision, and the Justices refused in a brief order without comment.[63] Although this is the first case in which the question of an employer's policy of discrimination as such was alleged to be a violation of the National Labor Relations Act, union discrimination on racial grounds has been before the board on numerous occasions. The courts have never experienced any difficulty in finding that unions have a duty of fair representation under both the Railway Labor Act and the National Labor Relations Act and that a union's failure in this respect constitutes an unfair labor practice. The final outcome of this case could be of major significance because of the administrative remedies, particularly cease and desist powers, presently available to the National Labor Relations Board which are not available to the Equal Employment Opportunity Commission.

PRIOR ARRESTS WITHOUT CONVICTION IN JOB DISQUALIFICATION

In another case, a federal district judge in Los Angeles ruled that an employer may not legally refuse to hire a Negro solely on the ground that he has an extensive arrest record without conviction. The jurist enjoined Litton Systems, Inc., from enforcing such a policy against a job applicant denied a position because of 14 arrests, and "all others similarly situated." The plaintiff was awarded $4,400 as the difference between what he earned and what he would have earned if he had been employed by Litton in 1968 as a structural sheet metal mechanic. He also was awarded $5,500 for attorney fees, but was denied punitive damages. Also, Litton was not ordered to award him the job because he no longer was asking for it. The court found that since Negroes are arrested more frequently than whites, any policy disqualifying them because of frequent arrests without convictions thus "discriminates in fact" against Negro job applicants. This is so even though the policy is applied fairly against both blacks and whites as was done by Litton. There is no evidence that persons arrested frequently can be expected to be less efficient or less honest on the job. Moreover, the judge maintained that to effectuate the policies of the Civil Rights Act, Litton must be restrained from seeking, obtaining and utilizing prior arrest records of job applicants which did not result in convictions.[64]

SEGREGATED LOCAL UNIONS

The Justice Department has also brought suit against Texas' 37 segregated longshoreman's local unions to condense them into 13 integrated ones. The custodian of funds of the West Gulf Maritime Association's labor relations office, as a witness, reported that weekly earnings of members of a white longshoreman's local in Galveston were higher in 1969 than weekly earnings of members of one Mexican-American and two Negro locals. Members of white Local 307 of the International Longshoreman's Association averaged $153.00 a week for the year ending September, 1969; members of black

Local 329 earned $100.60 per week, those in Negro Local 851 earned $138 and members of Mexican-American Local 1576 got $81.36 a week. Figures for two prior years indicated a similar comparison. Although the government is dealing only with the Texas locals in this suit, the court decision could affect longshoreman locals in Alabama, Florida, Louisiana, Mississippi, North Carolina and South Carolina. The government brought the action against the ILA after receiving complaints from an all-black Galveston Local and the Brownsville Negro Local. The government stated in its pretrial brief that 16 of the locals are all white, 19 are all Negro and 2 are predominantly Mexican-American. This segregated arrangement has been in effect since about 1900. Except for Local 329 in Galveston, most ILA unions work on a 50-50 basis with black and white work gangs often working separate sections of the same ship. Union attorneys contend that the mergers are opposed by a majority of the locals, black and white. An official of the all-black Local 872 in Houston stated that he is against a merger. "We've got 50 per cent of the work. Negroes in other crafts have less than 5 per cent."[65]

On August 1, 1970, a federal judge ruled that a union has no constitutional right to maintain separate locals for black and white workers. He said that unions are established for "economic advancement" and not to promote ideas and beliefs, and therefore cannot claim that practices of maintaining racially exclusive locals are covered by constitutional guarantees of freedom of association. The Justice Department had charged 15 months earlier that the International Longshoremen's Association was violating the 1964 Civil Rights Act by continuing to maintain virtually all white and virtually all black union locals on the Baltimore docks. Stipulations agreed to by the government and union lawyers showed that Baltimore Local 829 has 1,155 members, only four of whom are black, and that Local 858 has 1,226 members, only 5 of whom are white. This case, together with the Texas case noted above, were the first brought by the government to force unions to merge their virtually all-black and all-white locals. The Justice Department argued that the Constitution does not allow a union to exclude or segregate members in pursuit of economic benefits. The current dual local practices allegedly deny equal opportunities to black workers, despite defense contentions that the members of the two locals preferred associating with persons of their own race.[66]

TABLE 48.   Detailed Statistics on Charges of Racial Discrimination Brought Before the Equal Employment Opportunity Commission–Fiscal 1968.

Respondents and Types of Racial Discrimination Charges Recommended for Investigation

Employer Practices		Union Practices		Private Employment Agencies	
Hiring	612	Exclusion	106	Referral	15
Discharge	567	Discrimination	555		
Compensation	135	Classification	18	Subtotal, race	15
Terms	1,193				
Conditions	286	Subtotal, race	679	State Employment Agencies	
Classification	346			Referral	53
Miscellaneous	29	Labor–Management Practices		Testing	6
		Apprenticeship denial	7		
Subtotal, race	3,168	Training/retraining	44	Subtotal, race	59
Employer–Union–Agency Practices		Subtotal, race	51		
Retaliation	39				
Advertising	6				
Subtotal, race	45	Total race	4,017		

Respondents and Types of Charges Recommended for Deferral for State or Local FEPC Action

Employer Practices		Union Practices		Private Employment Agencies	
Hiring	234	Exclusion	36	Referral	3
Discharge	325	Discrimination	226		
Compensation	79	Classification	17	Subtotal, race	3
Terms	332				
Conditions	112	Subtotal, race	279	State Employment Agency Practices	
Classification	72			Referral	13
Miscellaneous	27	Labor–Management Practices			
		Apprenticeship denial	7	Subtotal, race	13
Subtotal, race	1,181	Training/retraining	2		
Employer–Union–Agency Practices		Subtotal, race	9		
Retaliation	1				
Subtotal, race	1	Total Race	1,486		

Respondents and Types of Charges Recommended for More Information

Employer Practices		*Union Practices*		*Private Employment*	
Hiring	240	Exclusion	21	*Agencies*	
Discharge	217	Discrimination	84	Referral	6
Compensation	63	Classification	16		
Terms	278			Subtotal, race	6
Conditions	54	Subtotal, race	121		
Classification	66			*State Employment*	
Miscellaneous	82			*Agencies*	
				Referral	13
Subtotal, race	1,000			Testing	3
				Subtotal, race	16

Labor-Management Practices		*Employer-Union-Agency Practices*	
Apprenticeship denial	1	Retaliation	1
Training/retraining	2		
		Subtotal, race	1
Subtotal race	3		

Total	1,147

Analysis of Charges of Racial Discrimination for Which There is no Probable Jurisdiction

Untimely	706
Less than 50 employees	23
Political subdivision	117
Educational institution	11
U. S. government	106
Not covered by Title VII	185
Subtotal	1,148

Disposition of All Title VII Charges — Involving Race

Recommended for investigation	6,056	4,017 or 66.3%
Deferred for state or local FEPC action	2,136	1,486 or 69.9%
Returned for additional information	2,980	1,147 or 38.5%
No probable jurisdiction	3,886	1,148 or 29.5%
Total charges brought	15,058 of which 6,650 or 44.2% involved race as the basis of discrimination	

Source: *Equal Employment Opportunity Commission, 3rd Annual Report*, Washington, D.C.: U. S. Government Printing Office, 1969.

REFERENCES

1. *Hearings Before the Subcommittee on Employment and Manpower of the Committee on Labor and Public Welfare on S. 773.* U.S. Senate, 88th Congress, 1st Sess., 1963. Washington, D.C.: U.S. Government Printing Office, 1963, p. 153 (statement by George Meany).

2. *Ibid.,* Note 17, p. 383 (colloquy among Senators Clark and Pell and Herman P. Miller, Bureau of Census); *H. R. Rep. No. 570,* 88th Cong., 1st Sess., p. 3 (1963); *H. R. Rep. No. 914,* 88th Cong., 1st Sess. (1963).

3. U.S. Commission on Civil Rights. *Cycle to   Nowhere.* Washington, D.C.: U.S. Government Printing Office, 1968, pp. 29-33.

4. Witmer, H. and Kotinsky, R. (editors). *Personality in the Making.* Cambridge, Mass.: Harvard University Press, 1952, Chapter VI.

5. Clark, Dr. Kenneth B. *Dark Ghetto: Dilemmas of Social Power.* New York: Harper & Row, Inc., 1965.

6. *Hearings before the General Subcommittee on Labor of the Committee on Education and Labor on H. R. 405.* U.S. House of Representatives, 88th Congress, 1st Sess., 1963. Washington, D.C.: U.S. Government Printing Office, 1963, pp. 66-67.

7. "Why Unions Can Bar Negroes." *U.S. News and World Report,* April 19, 1957, pp. 87-88.

8. "Briefs." *Engineering News Record,* January 22, 1970, p. 4.

9. *Ibid.*

10. "State Officials are Called Lax on Bias." *Engineering News Record,* November 20, 1969, p. 117.

11. *Ibid.,* p. 4.

12. McFadden, J. M. "Court Rules Against Alabama Hiring Policy, Orders Job Offers to 62 Blacks." *The Washington Post,* July 30, 1970, p. A-15.

13. *Urban Employment,* March 15, 1970, p. 4.

14. *Ibid.,* p. 6.

15. *Questions and Answers about Title VII of the Civil Rights Act of 1964 and the Equal Employment Opportunity Commission.* Washington, D.C.: Equal Employment Opportunity Commission, 1965, pp. 1-2 (mimeographed).

16. *Facts About Title VII of the Civil Rights Act of 1964 and the Equal Employment Opportunity Commission.* Washington, D.C.: Equal Employment Opportunity Commission, 1966.

17. *Ibid.*

18. *Questions and Answers About Title VII, op. cit.,* p. 5.

19. *Facts About Title VII, op. cit.,* p. 5.

20. *Ibid.,* p. 6.

21. *Questions and Answers About Title VII, op. cit.,* pp. 8-9.

22. "Study Asserts Ohio's Rubber Companies Evidence Discrimination in Negro Hiring." *The Wall Street Journal,* Nov. 20, 1967, p. 6.

23. Equal Employment Opportunity Commission, *3rd Annual Report, op. cit.,* p. 9.

24. *Ibid.,* p. 10.

25. *Ibid.,* p. 9.

26. *Ibid.,* p. 9.

27. "EEOC Announces Revised Guidelines on Employment Testing." *Labor Law Report — Employment Practices,* Report 47. Chicago: Commerce Clearing House, Inc., August 4, 1970.

28. Equal Employment Opportunity Commission, 3rd Annual Report, *op. cit.,* p. 11.

29. *Ibid.,* pp. 10, 11.

30. *Mickel v. South Carolina State Employment Service,* USDC, N.D. So. Car., No. 66-260, 57LC9111, February 22, 1968.

31. *Cox et al. v. United States Gypsum Company, et al.,* USDC, N.D. Indiana, Hammond Division, C.A. No. 4696, March 28, 968, 58 LC 9142.

32. *Wheeler et al. v. Bohn Aluminum and Brass Co.,* USDC, W.D. Mich. S. Div., C.A. No. 7, June 12, 1968, 68 LRRM 2769.

33. *Watts v. Douglas Aircraft Co.,* USDC, C.D. Cal., C.A. No. 68-389-S, June 26, 1968.

34. *Washington v. Aero-Jet General Corporation,* 282 F. Supp. 517, C.D. Cal. 1968.

35. *Pena v. Hunt Tool Company,* USDC, S.D. Tex., Corpus Christi Division, C.A. No. 67-C-110, February 27, 1968, 58 LC 9123.

36. *Pullen v. Otis Elevator Co.,* USDC, N.D. Ga., Atlanta Div., No. 11477, June 18, 1968, 58 LC 9133.

37. *Peurala v. United States Steel Corporation,* USDC, N.D. Ill. E. Div., No. 68-C-305, June 5, 1968, 58 LC 9135.

38. *Johnson et al. v. Continental Can Company, Inc., et al.,* USDC, E.D. La., New Orleans Div., No. 68-837, July 16, 1968.

39. *Oatis et al. v. Crown Zellerbach Corporation et al.,* Fifth Circuit, July 16, 1968, No. 25307, 68 LRRM 2782.

40. *Johnson v. Georgia Highway Express, Inc.,* USDC, N.D. Ga., Atlanta Div., C.A. No. 11598, June 24, 1968.

41. *Freese et al. v. John Morrell & Company et al.,* USDC, S.D. Iowa, C.A. No. 7-1823-C-1, November 16, 1966.

42. *Banks et al. v. Lockheed-Georgia Company,* USDC, N.D. Ga., Atlanta Div., C.A. No. 11675, June 12, 1968, 68 LRRM 2696m, 58 LC 9131.

43. *Overnite Transportation Company v. EEOC,* USDC, N.D. Ga., No. 11178, September 27, 1967. 66 LRRM 2407, aff'd 5th Cir., No. 25521, July 5, 1968, 58 LC 9136.

44. *EEOC v. Local 377, International Association of Bridge, Structural and Ornamental Ironworkers,* USDC, N.D. California, San Francisco Div., C.A. No. 49099, May 29, 1968, 58 LC 9127.

45. *Local Union No. 234 of the Wood, Wire and Metal Lathers International Union v. Acousti Engineering Company,* USDC, N.D. Ga., Atlanta Div., C.A. No. 10306, October 11, 1966.

46. *Norman v. Missouri Pacific Railroad,* USDC, E.D. Arkansas, No. LR-66-C-258, June 27, 1968, LRRM 2796.

47. *Banks v. Local Union 136, International Brotherhood of Electrical Workers, AFL-CIO,* USDC, N.D. Alabama, S. Div., C.A. No. 67-598, February 9, 1968.

48. *Quarles et al. v. Phillip Morris Inc. et al.,* USDC, E.D. Va., Richmond Division, No. 4544, September 26, 1966, 55 LC 9054, 271 F. Supp. 832 (F.A. Va. 1967).

49. *U.S. v. Sheet Metal Workers,* C.A. 8-1969, 2 FEP Cases 128.

50. *U.S. v. Hayes International Corp.,* C.A. 5-1969, 2 FEP Cases 67.

51. *U.S. v. United Papermakers and Paperworkers, Local 189* (Crown Zellerbach Corp.), 282 F. Supp. 39, E.D. La. 1968.

52. *Allen et al. v. Braswell Motor Freight Lines, Inc.,* USDC, N.D. Texas, Dallas Div. No. 3-2112-14, May 16, 1968.

53. *Bing v. Roadway Express Inc. and International Brotherhood of Teamsters, Chauffeurs, Warehousemen and Helpers of America,* USDC, N.D. Ga., Atlanta Div., C.A. No. 11144, February 7, 1968.

54. *Independent Metal Workers Union (Hughes Tool Co.),* NLRB 1964, 56 LRRM 1289.

55. *Miranda Fuel Co.,* NLRB-1962, 51 LRRM 1584.

56. *NLRB v. Miranda Fuel Co.,* C.A. 2-1963, 54 LRRM 2715.

57. *Local 1367, International Longshoremen's Association* (Galveston Maritime Association, Inc.), NLRB-1964, 57 LRRM 1083.

58. *NLRB v. Local 1367, International Longshoremen's Association* (Galveston Maritime Association, Inc.), C.A. 5-1966, 63 LRRM 2559.

59. *Local 1367, International Longshoremen's Association v. NLRB,* U.S. Sup. Ct-1967, 66 LRRM, 2307.

60. *Local 12, United Rubber Workers v. NLRB,* C.A. 5-1966, 63 LRRM 2395.

61. *Local 12, United Rubber Workers v. NLRB,* US Sup Ct-1967, 66 LRRM 2306.

62. *Houston Maritime Association, Inc., Local 1351, International Longshoremen's Association,* NLRB-1967, 66 LRRM 1337.

63. Kohlmeier, Louis M. "NLRB's Role in Job Bias Disputes Is Enhanced by the Supreme Court." *The Wall Street Journal,* November 11, 1969, p. 3.

64. "Judge Bans Arrests as Job Obstacle." *The Washington Post,* July 11, 1970, p. A-3.

65. "White Dockers Earned More, Court is Told." *The Washington Post,* July 14, 1970, p. A-9.

66. "Separate Union Locals for Races Ruled Illegal." *The Washington Post,* August 1, 1970, p. B-1.

Chapter 7
Conclusions and Recommendations

BUSINESS ATTITUDES TOWARD EQUAL EMPLOYMENT OPPORTUNITY

The surveys of large, medium-sized and small businesses indicated a general willingness to promote the goal of equal employment opportunity. Not unexpectedly, the medium-sized and small firms were more reluctant to contribute directly to necessary programs due to limited resources.

The significance of geographic location as an influential variable can be largely discounted since the responses from Baltimore and Houston were not markedly dissimilar in tone and content from employer opinions and attitudes in Detroit and Los Angeles, although Houston firms predictably were more critical of government efforts to help Negroes.

One might conclude, therefore, that the concept of employment equality has met with basic acceptance in all sections of the nation. However, several troubling contradictions surfaced throughout the empirical investigation. In the first place, sizeable numbers of respondents, while maintaining their adherence to the objective of equality, still refuse to recognize the pervasive influence of local racial employment customs, most of which perpetuate employment discrimination. Put more bluntly, they seem willing to pay lip service to Title VII of the 1964 Civil Rights Act rather than to conform fully to its requirements. In the second place, while the private sector, at least as expressed through two surveys, is cognizant that the ghetto background is the prime causative factor in explaining the black worker's performance deficiencies and that there is a need for motivational redirection and improved educational and training facilities and standards, nevertheless business still demonstrates a penchant for placing a large share of the blame for employment problems upon the black individual himself, who, it is felt, lacks the necessary incentive for self-improvement. This is tantamount to understanding the crucial reasons for the economic plight of the largest minority group while substituting self-serving rationalizations and continued reliance on the time-honored negative stereotypes and shibboleths for effective action.

Continuation of these unfortunate propensities toward self-deception will result in a less than total commitment to the elimination of discrimination and further frustrate effective implementation of corrective measures.

WORK ATTITUDES AND MOTIVATION

The significance of joblessness and of low-status, blind-alley employment to slum residents can be understood only in the context of the high value placed upon work by our society (confirmed by questionnaire comments against welfare) as the acceptable means of making a living and achieving success and social status. Preparing for work, getting a job, and moving up occupational ladders to better paying jobs are matters of crucial importance. For most people, the way to a more affluent and satisfying life is through meaningful work. But this way is all but closed to many slum residents. While too little is yet known regarding the effects of slum life and environment upon the aspirations and motivations of slum residents, scattered studies indicate a serious gap between their aspirations and opportunities for realizing them. Thus, the attitudes of some slum residents toward jobs and their work adjustment problems may arise not so much from the level of aspirations as from the frustrations experienced in efforts to achieve them. In many cases, the slum youth gets little or no help from schools, where efforts have frequently been directed at encouraging him to be realistic — to aspire to, or accept, the very types of low-income, low-prestige jobs from which he hopes to escape. The status which attaches to jobs is also important. White-collar or blue-collar jobs with companies of standing in the community may be accepted at lower wages than jobs as dishwashers, custodians, or janitors. When society places a low value on a job, in terms of pay and prestige, the slum resident is in complete agreement.

Ghetto employers offering low wages and low fringe benefits, debilitating production speeds, low-status work, unpleasant working conditions, unsympathetic supervision, inequitable industrial relations arrangements, low promotion opportunities, and unstable employment do not encourage worker loyalty, and turnover and frictional job vacancies are likely to be higher among these employers.

URBAN POVERTY AND THE CONDITION OF THE ECONOMY

It is possible to cite impressive statistics demonstrating that various programs of government and private enterprise for recruiting and training unemployed Negroes are working. However, it is questionable whether the hard-core unemployed ghetto resident is being affected by employment opportunities in suburban areas when he has no transportation out of the inner city or, due to functional illiteracy, is not aware that the opportunities exist.

There are two interrelated aspects causing the lack of effective implementation of equal employment opportunity policies at the firm level.

First, there is a serious shortage of qualified Negro job applicants. Second, very few Negroes apply for positions requiring experience, skill, training or combinations of these. In addition, small employers do not possess the financial resources for recruitment programs, and unions in skilled trades demand qualified persons and often engage in discriminatory hiring policies.

The income differentials between blacks and whites have narrowed appreciably in the last few years, with the greatest relative gains by Negroes being among those with the highest levels of education. Simultaneously, however, within the Negro community, two different classes are becoming increasingly evident as the best prepared are moving ahead rapidly while the least prepared are lagging behind. Unemployment problems are mainly concentrated among those with the least skill, work experience, education and training — notably the virtually unemployable disadvantaged ghetto resident.

With the continuing migration from rural areas to the cities, hard-core poverty problems persisted during the past decade. While many Negro families improved their incomes and living standards and moved out of city poverty slum areas, the urban ghetto slum communities remained crowded, were deteriorating, and had an increased concentration of social problems.

If the demand for certain types of unskilled or semiskilled labor is not sufficient, workers — white and Negro — are laid off. Furthermore, new jobseekers cannot really find work. The general economy's growth rate and the rising need for different or higher skills can thus adversely affect the socioeconomic status of poorly educated or unskilled Negroes, even if prejudice and discrimination are absent.

The pace of improvement in employment for any worker, of course, is governed by the rate at which the national economy grows and the demand for labor. But for Negro workers, a continuing strong demand for workers is critical, for it is often in the rapidly growing occupations that they can gain real ground. In growing occupations, or in occupations with high turnover, hiring needs are greater and upgrading is more prevalent than in declining fields. Furthermore, for Negro workers to gain a larger share of jobs in declining occupations might not necessarily be considered a favorable development if in the long run it led to unemployment or dead-end jobs. Similarly, Negro gains of the recent past could be lost if the economy fails to grow. The situation for Negro workers has long been one of "last hired, first fired."

COMPANY POLICIES TO PROMOTE UPWARD MOBILITY

Companies must begin to think seriously in terms of careers for their disadvantaged workers, rather than merely in terms of stop-gap, entry-level jobs. Characteristically, company expansion is impaired because of the failure to institute channels for the upward mobility of low-skilled workers. No adequate upgrading programs have been developed for them. This means that systems of manpower development are needed in companies, systems involving academic training, or skill training on the job, as well as extended orientation periods to acclimate the disadvantaged worker to company needs.

Convincing industry to become involved in the education and training of Negroes is difficult because companies find it more costly to recruit and train Negro employees than whites. In particular, small firms producing highly specialized products need skilled workers but do not possess the resources to train them, with the result that advancement potential for the disadvantaged inner city individual is all but nonexistent.

Placement of disadvantaged minority employees in entry-level jobs sometimes requires restructuring of jobs, with emphasis on the individual's willingness to do the work and reasonably good health as the basic requirements, rather than experience qualifications and skill level. By involving other members of the work force in a hard-core hiring program, resistance to such a program can be reduced.

It is fairly clear why Negroes will differ from whites when evaluated with respect to experience and education. In terms of experience, the Negro has been unable in the past to obtain many jobs that could provide him with worthwhile experience. It has only been in recent years that a few meaningful jobs have become available to him. For this reason trying to hire a Negro with ten years of supervisory experience is somewhat like trying to hire a high school graduate with ten years of sales experience. Neither is available. The difference is that in the case of the high school graduate, personnel people are at least aware of the fact.

Companies which analyze their job requirements may find that additional jobs, now held by whites, are also suitable for Negroes, given their current experience and education levels. Frequently, these jobs could offer a Negro sufficient experience to allow him to progress eventually to positions of significant responsibility. Far too few of these training positions are available for Negroes today.

The substantial gains in the occupational upgrading of the Negro work force are encouraging, but they cannot mask the fact that Negroes still constitute a disproportionate share of the workers in most low-paying, low-level occupations. It is not postulated here that Negroes, or any other population group, could or should achieve exactly proportional representation in each occupation. Many factors must be considered in understanding Negro occupational distributions: education, experience, training, geographic location, motivation, status, personal desires. Nevertheless, it is clear that the Negro's movement into better-paying, better-quality jobs must continue if equality of opportunity is to become a reality.

On-the-job upgrading training programs should aim at promoting Negroes to all levels of the firm. It is not enough merely to have a quantitatively representative minority work force. It should be qualitatively representative as well.

Sensitive management must realize that supervisors may not be the best judges of promotion decisions and must take action which objectifies the observations of the supervisor. Perhaps an industrial ombudsman, someone independent of both management and employees, could mediate differences and resolve disputes among coworkers, and between workers and supervisors.

PITFALLS IN "BLACK CAPITALISM"

Emphasizing black capitalism could further impede Negro gains, moreover, if the strategy comes to be seen as an alternative to more traditional programs designed to raise the educational level of blacks, improve their job skills, and reduce discrimination in employment and housing. Certainly, much of the white accomodation to separatist demands by black militants seems to reflect a desire to be rid of the Negro problem.

A black capitalism strategy designed to increase the number of black-owned businesses in the ghetto could backfire in another way. The ghetto offers a poor economic environment for business investment, whether in manufacturing plants or retail and service establishments. There is no need to exaggerate the obstacles to successful business development in slum areas. Many, if not most, of the "black capitalism" projects of the past several years have been disappointing, to say the least. Two notable examples are Aerojet-General's formation of Watts Manufacturing Company, and a metal-fabricating concern set up in Boston by E. G. & G., a nuclear and oceanographic research corporation. Neither has been able to turn a profit. Watts Manufacturing was forced to cut back on employment, and E. G. & G. abandoned the enterprise altogether.

In a society where 90 per cent of those at work are wage and salary earners, only a small number of people can move into the economic mainstream through self-employment and small business. Moreover, separatist economic schemes offer no hope for the advance of the overwhelming majority of disadvantaged minorities. Consistent commitment to the principles of integration and equal opportunity, accompanied by jobs, education, skills, and housing measures are essential.

A Detroit employer articulately summarized opposition to separatism in the following comment:

> The "black is best" attitude will drive people apart. There should
> be no reference to a black or white community, for it is all the same

community. The separate community concept violates the basic objective of equality. The present effect is to make one group "more equal" than the other. The longer the condition persists, the stronger the favored group becomes. The stronger the group becomes, the more demanding it will be, whether the demand is legitimate or not. . . . We must use present facilities and existing institutions to solve our problems, not create favored institutions that will destroy the orderly processes so necessary for stability in an era of constant change.

The emphasis on business in the ghetto is an understandable white response to recurrent black-nationalist demands for "community control" of all institutions located in black neighborhoods. The emphasis also stems from misleading analogies between the experiences of blacks and of white ethnic groups. Recalling the history of various immigrant groups, among whom ethnic solidarity and concentration in ghettos evoked a proliferation of small retail and service establishments, advocates of black capitalism have urged blacks to follow that path.

But this is not the way other ethnic groups "made it" into American society. Immigrants who succeeded in business may have begun by serving localized or specialized ethnic markets, but they quickly reached outward. The Greeks in the restaurant business, the Irish in port services, the Chinese in laundries and restaurants, the Armenians in the carpet business, Italians in construction and building, and in services such as shoemaking and barbering, Jews in the clothing industry — all catered to the larger market. If blacks are to succeed in business, they too will have to go where the customers are.

A strategy that equates black capitalism with business in the ghetto is doomed to failure. For one thing, it confuses quite separate goals: revitalizing rundown urban neighborhoods inhabited by blacks, wherever they live; and increasing the number of black businessmen. The last objective can contribute to the other two, of course, but is in no sense identical with them. Certainly, improvement in the Negro position in the economy does not depend on the growth of black-owned businesses. On the contrary, the Negro position improved dramatically during the 1960's with no significant increase, and quite possibly a decrease, in the number of black businesses.

EMPLOYER AND UNION ATTITUDES

In the long run, the attitudes of employers and unions toward Negro job applicants will prove decisive. Under the impetus of public opinion joined with federal mandate, official fair employment policies will undoubtedly be implemented by growing numbers of firms. Action will probably lag behind pronouncement, but should, nevertheless, be real. Until now, big business generally has been making the most concerted efforts, but many small companies have remained almost "lily white." State and local governments also frequently discriminate.

In some unions, such as the construction trades, the racial composition of membership and job levels is violently out of balance. Unions also often severely restrict Negro apprenticeships, and block the advancement of the few who are admitted. On the one hand, certain trades such as painting, could be learned in school or in the armed forces or "picked up" on the job, and excluding anyone capable of performing them is difficult. On the other hand, plumbing and electrical work require extensive formal apprenticeships and union control could be wielded. The availability or lack of skilled nonwhite craftsmen who could teach their own trade to other Negroes is also important. There are relatively large numbers of Negro plasterers, bricklayers, and cement finishers in the South because Negro craftsmen there have taught others these stable trades.

There has long been a difference in attitude and policy between the more discriminating craft unions and the more equalitarian industrial unions, and between the more liberal national unions and segregated locals. In 1955, the constitutions of both the AFL and CIO included nondiscrimination as a major objective. Late in 1961, this was augmented by a resolution to ask all affiliated unions to eliminate segregated locals, to negotiate for nondiscrimination clauses in all contracts, and to remove separate seniority listings based on race, religion, or national origin. Even the channels of complaint in case of noncompliance were outlined at that time. Now it is expected that Title VII of the Civil Rights Law will have considerable effect on union practices, but that the old local craft unions will continue to move slowly toward changes.

We will continue to see prejudices working to the disadvantage of the Negro as long as he is unequal in ability, education, work and personal habits or personality, to those with whom he competes for a given job opportunity. This prejudice exists against the less fitted.

The prospect for Negro employment improvements has many facets, but three variables dominate: (1) the condition of the general economy, (2) the availability of qualified Negro job applicants, and (3) the attitude of employers. Hopefully, in the future, trends in all three should combine to produce marked, if not dramatic, progress. There is little doubt that gains will be uneven and wide individual differences will persist at the industry and company levels. Despite stricter legislation, tokenism will be practiced by some, while hiring and promotions by other firms will be strictly on merit, and there may even be instances of discrimination in reverse. There will be no quick and easy solution in the quest for equal employment opportunity. Problems will persist until such time as the acceptance of the qualified Negro is replaced by the search for the qualifiable.

Appendix

TABLE 49.   Negro Employment by Occupation and Industry in the Baltimore Standard Metropolitan Statistical Area (SMSA), 1966.

	Total Employ- ment	White-Collar Occupations						Total Blue- Collar Em- ployment	Blue-Collar Occupations			
		Total White- Collar Em- ployment	Officials & Managers	Profes- sionals	Techni- cians	Sales Workers	Office & Clerical		Crafts- men	Opera- tives	Laborers	Service Workers
Primary metal industries												
Negro												
Total	9,597	115	56	0	7	0	52	9,195	579	4,601	4,015	287
Occupational distrib.	100.0	1.2	0.6	0.0	0.1	0.0	0.5	95.8	6.0	47.9	41.8	3.0
Participation rate	28.7	1.6	1.8	0.0	1.2	0.0	1.9	35.6	8.4	35.9	65.4	47.6
All employees												
Total (24 estab.)	33,496	7,070	3,093	571	597	117	2,692	25,823	6,863	12,818	6,142	603
Occupational distrib.	100.0	21.1	9.2	1.7	1.8	0.3	8.0	77.1	20.5	38.3	18.3	1.8
Printing & publishing, etc.												
Negro												
Total	622	125	8	23	0	23	71	429	43	251	135	68
Occupational distrib.	100.0	20.1	1.3	3.7	0.0	3.7	11.4	69.0	6.9	40.4	21.7	10.9
Participation rate	9.0	4.7	1.9	5.0	0.0	3.5	6.6	10.3	2.1	16.2	26.1	66.0
All employees												
Total (26 estab.)	6,928	2,676	419	461	57	665	1,074	4,149	2,087	1,545	517	103
Occupational distrib.	100.0	38.6	6.0	6.7	0.8	9.6	15.5	59.9	30.1	22.3	7.5	1.5
Paper & allied products												
Negro												
Total	1,100	25	10	0	1	1	13	1,007	95	454	458	68
Occupational distrib.	100.0	2.3	0.9	0.0	0.1	0.1	1.2	91.5	8.6	41.3	41.6	6.2
Participation rate	20.3	2.2	2.7	0.0	2.1	0.5	2.8	24.3	11.2	20.8	41.1	58.1
All employees												
Total (33 estab.)	5,413	1,153	369	83	47	185	469	4,143	847	2,181	1,115	117
Occupational distrib.	100.0	21.3	6.8	1.5	0.9	3.4	8.7	76.5	15.6	40.3	20.6	2.2
Retail trade												
Negro												
Total	2,283	696	35	1	1	388	271	583	70	335	178	1,004
Occupational distrib.	100.0	30.5	1.5	0.0	0.0	17.0	11.9	25.5	3.1	14.7	7.8	44.0
Participation rate	14.4	6.0	2.4	0.6	1.1	5.8	8.2	25.5	12.3	25.1	46.4	53.7
All employees												
Total (31 estab.)	15,811	11,657	1,439	163	94	6,641	3,320	2,286	569	1,333	384	1,868
Occupational distrib.	100.0	73.7	9.1	1.0	0.6	42.0	21.0	14.5	3.6	8.4	2.4	11.8

Table 49 continued

	Total Employment	White-Collar Occupations						Blue-Collar Occupations				
		Total White-Collar Employment	Officials & Managers	Professionals	Technicians	Sales Workers	Office & Clerical	Total Blue-Collar Employment	Craftsmen	Operatives	Laborers	Service Workers
Food & kindred products												
Negro												
Total	2,718	312	33	0	10	225	44	2,277	175	858	1,244	129
Occupational distrib.	100.0	11.5	1.2	0.0	0.4	8.3	1.6	83.8	6.4	31.6	45.8	4.7
Participation rate	19.2	6.4	2.7	0.0	7.9	11.1	3.3	25.5	9.9	20.3	45.2	41.5
All employees												
Total (58 estab.)	14,129	4,884	1,215	191	126	2,033	1,319	8,934	1,761	4,222	2,951	311
Occupational distrib.	100.0	34.6	8.6	1.4	0.9	14.4	9.3	63.2	12.5	29.9	20.9	2.2
Textile mill products												
Negro												
Total	262	12	2	0	0	0	10	237	8	127	102	13
Occupational distrib.	100.0	4.6	0.8	0.0	0.0	0.0	3.8	90.5	3.1	48.5	38.9	5.0
Participation rate	11.6	2.7	1.6	0.0	0.0	0.0	4.5	13.5	4.1	11.0	25.4	9.7
All employees												
Total (9 estab.)	2,263	445	125	22	28	49	221	1,752	197	1,153	402	66
Occupational distrib.	100.0	19.7	5.5	1.0	1.2	2.2	9.8	77.4	8.7	51.0	17.8	2.9
Rubber & plastic products												
Negro												
Total	281	16	0	0	6	0	10	254	35	119	100	11
Occupational distrib.	100.0	5.7	0.0	0.0	2.1	0.0	3.6	90.4	12.5	42.3	35.6	3.9
Participation rate	10.5	3.8	0.0	0.0	13.3	0.0	5.3	11.5	7.4	14.1	11.2	24.4
All employees												
Total (11 estab.)	2,675	418	141	34	45	10	188	2,212	475	843	894	45
Occupational distrib.	100.0	15.6	5.3	1.3	1.7	0.4	7.0	82.7	17.8	31.5	33.4	1.7
Stone, clay & glass products												
Negro												
Total	1,474	11	2	1	5	0	3	1,417	76	999	342	46
Occupational distrib.	100.0	0.7	0.1	0.1	0.3	0.0	0.2	96.1	5.2	67.8	23.2	3.1
Participation rate	31.6	1.4	0.8	1.1	4.5	0.0	1.1	36.9	7.8	44.8	53.8	83.6
All employees												
Total (16 estab.)	4,663	763	259	95	112	28	269	3,845	979	2,230	636	55
Occupational distrib.	100.0	16.4	5.6	2.0	2.4	0.6	5.8	82.5	21.0	47.8	13.8	1.2

Table 49 continued

	Total Employment	White-Collar Occupations						Blue-Collar Occupations				
		Total White-Collar Employment	Officials & Managers	Professionals	Technicians	Sales Workers	Office & Clerical	Total Blue-Collar Employment	Craftsmen	Operatives	Laborers	Service Workers
Fabricated metal products												
Negro												
Total	1,387	19	4	0	0	1	14	1,329	123	867	339	39
Occupational distrib.	100.0	1.4	0.3	0.0	0.0	0.1	1.0	95.8	8.9	62.5	24.4	2.8
Participation rate	11.6	0.7	0.5	0.0	0.0	0.3	1.4	14.6	4.1	17.8	26.8	28.1
All employees												
Total (35 estab.)	11,911	2,640	739	324	275	336	966	9,132	3,001	4,865	1,266	139
Occupational distrib.	100.0	22.2	6.2	2.7	2.3	2.8	8.1	76.7	25.2	40.8	10.6	1.2
Apparel & related products												
Negro												
Total	2,294	132	11	2	0	0	119	2,101	132	1,734	235	61
Occupational distrib.	100.0	5.8	0.5	0.1	0.0	0.0	5.2	91.6	5.8	75.6	10.2	2.7
Participation rate	23.1	7.3	2.2	5.6	0.0	0.0	10.7	26.3	5.9	32.0	72.1	64.2
All employees												
Total (29 estab.)	9,913	1,818	492	36	13	169	1,108	8,000	2,247	5,427	326	95
Occupational distrib.	100.0	18.3	5.0	0.4	0.1	1.7	11.2	80.7	22.7	54.7	3.3	1.0
Machinery (non-electrical)												
Negro												
Total	224	8	0	0	5	0	3	156	9	82	65	60
Occupational distrib.	100.0	3.6	0.0	0.0	2.2	0.0	1.3	69.6	4.0	36.6	29.0	26.8
Participation rate	3.4	0.4	0.0	0.0	1.6	0.0	0.4	3.4	0.4	3.8	14.3	45.8
All employees												
Total (17 estab.)	6,661	1,892	429	344	305	75	739	4,638	2,011	2,171	456	131
Occupational distrib.	100.0	28.4	6.4	5.2	4.6	1.1	11.1	69.6	30.2	32.6	6.8	2.0
Chemicals & allied products												
Negro												
Total	1,462	57	14	2	17	3	21	1,305	137	625	543	100
Occupational distrib.	100.0	3.9	1.0	0.1	1.2	0.2	1.4	89.3	9.4	42.7	37.1	6.8
Participation rate	15.6	1.7	1.5	0.4	3.3	0.8	2.0	22.8	9.9	22.7	34.4	43.3
All employees												
Total (42 estab.)	9,385	3,438	946	551	520	360	1,061	5,716	1,388	2,751	1,577	231
Occupational distrib.	100.0	36.6	10.1	5.9	5.5	3.8	11.3	60.9	14.8	29.3	16.8	2.5

Table 49 continued

	Total Employment	Total White-Collar Employment	White-Collar Occupations					Total Blue-Collar Employment	Blue-Collar Occupations			Service Workers
			Officials & Mangers	Professionals	Technicians	Sales Workers	Office & Clerical		Craftsmen	Operatives	Laborers	
Totals												
Negro employment	23,704	1,528	175	29	52	641	631	20,290	1,482	11,052	7,756	1,886
All employees	123,248	38,854	8,720	2,875	2,219	10,668	13,426	80,630	22,425	41,539	16,666	3,764
Negro participation rate	19.2	3.3	2.0	1.0	2.3	6.0	5.0	25.0	6.6	26.6	46.5	50.1

Note: Because of rounding, sums of individual items may not equal totals.

Source: Equal Employment Opportunity Report No. 1, Part III, Washington, D.C.: Equal Employment Opportunity Commission, 1966.

TABLE 50. Negro Employment by Occupation and Industry in the Detroit SMSA, 1966.

	Total Employment	White-Collar Occupations						Blue-Collar Occupations				
		Total White-Collar Employment	Officials & Managers	Professionals	Technicians	Sales Workers	Office & Clerical	Total Blue-Collar Employment	Craftsmen	Operatives	Laborers	Service Workers
Contract construction												
Negro												
Total	716	14	7	0	1	0	6	578	142	70	366	124
Occupational distrib.	100.0	2.0	1.0	0.0	0.1	0.0	0.8	80.7	19.8	9.8	51.1	17.3
Participation rate	9.3	0.8	1.1	0.0	0.6	0.0	0.9	10.0	3.5	10.4	36.7	66.7
All employees												
Total (86 estab.)	7,702	1,741	617	283	155	38	648	5,775	4,103	675	997	186
Occupational distrib.	100.0	22.6	8.0	3.7	2.0	0.5	8.4	75.0	53.3	8.8	12.9	2.4
Furnitures & fixtures												
Negro												
Total	808	13	9	1	1	0	2	794	18	509	267	1
Occupational distrib.	100.0	1.6	1.1	0.1	0.1	0.0	0.2	98.3	2.2	63.0	33.0	0.1
Participation rate	28.1	2.3	4.1	1.6	2.4	0.0	0.9	34.4	5.9	33.9	53.3	10.0
All employees												
Total (8 estab.)	2,877	558	218	63	42	24	211	2,309	305	1,503	501	10
Occupational distrib.	100.0	19.4	7.6	2.2	1.5	0.8	7.3	80.3	10.6	52.2	17.4	0.3
Printing & publishing ind.												
Negro												
Total	720	307	5	5	0	15	282	279	36	212	31	134
Occupational distrib.	100.0	42.6	0.7	0.7	0.0	2.1	39.2	38.8	5.0	29.4	4.3	18.6
Participation rate	8.4	7.2	0.8	1.1	0.0	1.3	15.3	6.9	1.9	11.9	8.6	48.9
All employees												
Total (30 estab.)	8,603	4,258	603	471	174	1,166	1,844	4,071	1,936	1,775	360	274
Occupational distrib.	100.0	49.5	7.0	5.5	2.0	13.6	21.4	47.3	22.5	20.6	4.2	3.2
Chemicals & allied products												
Negro												
Total	861	104	18	16	24	4	42	667	80	362	225	90
Occupational distrib.	100.0	12.1	2.1	1.9	2.8	0.5	4.9	77.5	9.3	42.0	26.1	10.5
Participation rate	5.1	1.2	1.1	1.3	3.0	0.2	1.9	8.4	3.7	9.2	12.1	19.9
All employees												
Total (44 estab.)	16,785	8,391	1,609	1,267	808	2,450	2,257	7,942	2,146	3,931	1,865	452
Occupational distrib.	100.0	50.0	9.6	7.5	4.8	14.6	13.4	47.3	12.8	23.4	11.1	2.7

Table 50 continued

Appendix 175

	Total Employment	White-Collar Occupations						Blue-Collar Occupations				
		Total White-Collar Employment	Officials & Managers	Professionals	Technicians	Sales Workers	Office & Clerical	Total Blue-Collar Employment	Craftsmen	Operatives	Laborers	Service Workers
Stone, clay & glass products												
Negro												
Total	434	2	1	0	0	0	1	427	11	208	208	5
Occupational distrib.	100.0	0.5	0.2	0.0	0.0	0.0	0.2	98.4	2.5	47.9	47.9	1.2
Participation rate	13.3	0.2	0.3	0.0	0.0	0.0	0.3	18.4	3.1	15.9	32.0	23.8
All employees												
Total (27 estab.)	3,261	925	359	73	73	59	361	2,315	356	1,309	650	21
Occupational distrib.	100.0	28.4	11.0	2.2	2.2	1.8	11.1	71.0	10.9	40.1	19.9	0.6
Primary metal industries												
Negro												
Total	6,670	102	49	1	16	0	36	6,563	1,081	4,067	1,415	105
Occupational distrib.	100.0	1.5	0.7	0.0	0.2	0.0	0.5	96.9	16.0	60.1	20.9	1.6
Participation rate	19.3	1.5	1.8	0.1	1.9	0.0	1.7	23.9	12.0	29.6	29.7	18.8
All employees												
Total (62 estab.)	35,010	6,942	2,752	750	840	421	2,179	27,510	9,035	13,718	4,757	558
Occupational distrib.	100.0	19.8	7.9	2.1	2.4	1.2	6.2	78.6	25.8	39.2	13.6	1.6
Fabricated metal products												
Negro												
Total	2,520	65	8	12	7	0	38	2,359	224	1,533	602	96
Occupational distrib.	100.0	2.6	0.3	0.5	0.3	0.0	1.5	93.6	8.9	60.8	23.9	3.8
Participation rate	9.2	0.8	0.4	0.7	0.7	0.0	1.4	12.4	4.7	15.2	14.7	18.5
All employees												
Total (99 estab.)	2,785	7,783	1,962	1,703	952	403	2,763	18,984	4,769	10,117	4,098	518
Occupational distrib.	100.0	28.5	7.2	6.2	3.5	1.5	10.1	69.6	17.5	37.1	15.0	1.9
Machinery (non-electrical)												
Negro												
Total	1,958	175	5	8	28	0	134	1,660	94	1,161	405	123
Occupational distrib.	100.0	8.9	0.3	0.4	1.4	0.0	6.8	84.8	4.8	59.3	20.7	6.3
Participation rate	4.3	1.2	0.2	0.3	0.9	0.0	2.7	5.5	0.9	7.1	14.2	18.0
All employees												
Total (127 estab.)	45,579	14,809	3,041	2,624	3,036	1,195	4,913	30,085	10,978	16,257	2,850	685
Occupational distrib.	100.0	32.5	6.7	5.8	6.7	2.6	10.8	66.0	24.1	35.7	6.3	1.5

Table 50 continued

	Total Employ-ment	Total White-Collar Employment	Officials & Managers	Profes-sionals	Techni-cians	Sales Workers	Office & Clerical	Total Blue-Collar Employment	Crafts-men	Opera-tives	Laborers	Service Workers
Electrical machinery, equipment & supplies												
Negro												
Total	561	24	2	3	7	0	12	508	9	481	18	29
Occupational distrib.	100.0	4.3	0.4	0.5	1.2	0.0	2.1	90.6	1.6	85.7	3.2	5.2
Participation rate	11.6	1.7	0.6	2.0	2.2	0.0	2.5	15.2	1.5	18.2	16.5	25.4
All employees												
Total (19 estab.)	4,830	1,379	333	151	324	95	476	3,337	588	2,640	109	114
Occupational distrib.	100.0		6.9	3.1	6.7	2.0	9.9	69.1	12.2	54.7	2.3	2.4
Transportation equipment												
Negro												
Total	60,222	1,844	350	100	96	0	1,298	55,300	1,959	49,432	3,909	3,078
Occupational distrib.	100.0	3.1	0.6	0.2	0.2	0.0	2.2	91.8	3.3	82.1	6.5	5.1
Participation rate	20.2	2.1	1.5	0.5	0.8	0.0	4.4	27.4	4.6	33.3	36.4	33.1
All employees												
Total (131 estab.)	297,627	86,461	23,759	20,592	11,959	800	29,351	201,874	42,860	148,261	10,753	9,292
Occupational distrib.	100.0	29.1	8.0	6.9	4.0	0.3	9.9	67.8	14.4	49.8	3.6	3.1
Instruments & related products												
Negro												
Total	117	12	0	1	1	0	10	99	5	85	9	6
Occupational distrib.	100.0	10.3	0.0	0.9	0.9	0.0	8.5	84.6	4.3	72.6	7.7	5.1
Participation rate	5.7	1.7	0.0	1.1	0.9	0.0	3.7	7.6	1.4	9.2	22.0	20.7
All employees												
Total (10 estab.)	2,048	712	148	87	107	103	267	1,307	347	919	41	29
Occupational distrib.	100.0	34.8	7.2	4.2	5.2	5.0	13.0	63.8	16.9	44.9	2.0	1.4
Motor freight transportation												
Negro												
Total	318	16	3	0	0	0	13	266	30	94	142	36
Occupational distrib.	100.0	5.0	0.9	0.0	0.0	0.0	4.1	83.6	9.4	29.6	44.7	11.3
Participation rate	2.8	0.7	0.4	0.0	0.0	0.0	0.9	3.0	3.3	1.4	10.2	24.2
All employees												
Total (84 estab.)	11,366	2,369	769	53	10	160	1,377	8,848	906	6,556	1,386	149
Occupational distrib.	100.0	20.8	6.8	0.5	0.1	1.4	12.1	77.8	8.0	57.7	12.2	1.3

White-Collar Occupations · *Blue-Collar Occupations*

Table 50 continued

	Total Employment	White-Collar Occupations						Blue-Collar Occupations				
		Total White-Collar Employment	Officials & Managers	Professionals	Technicians	Sales Workers	Office & Clerical	Total Blue-Collar Employment	Craftsmen	Operatives	Laborers	Service Workers
Wholesale trade												
Negro												
Total	1,329	272	30	7	20	51	164	988	110	355	523	69
Occupational distrib.	100.0	20.5	2.3	0.5	1.5	3.8	12.3	74.3	8.3	26.7	39.4	5.2
Participation rate	6.2	1.6	1.0	0.2	1.6	1.7	2.6	22.0	9.2	18.1	39.1	39.9
All employees												
Total (240 estab.)	21,481	16,814	3,122	3,032	1,248	3,056	6,356	4,494	1,193	1,964	1,337	173
Occupational distrib.	100.0	78.3	14.5	14.1	5.8	14.2	29.6	20.9	5.6	9.1	6.2	0.8
Retail trade												
Negro												
Total	3,361	1,597	45	3	7	1,080	462	493	99	234	160	1,271
Occupational distrib.	100.0	47.5	1.3	0.1	0.2	32.1	13.7	14.7	2.9	7.0	4.8	37.8
Participation rate	9.8	6.3	1.4	1.4	2.3	7.2	7.0	11.0	5.8	12.5	17.4	27.7
All employees												
Total (31 estab.)	34,375	25,299	3,243	215	303	14,979	6,559	4,493	1,700	1,872	921	4,583
Occupational distrib.	100.0	73.6	9.4	0.6	0.9	43.6	19.1	13.1	4.9	5.4	2.7	13.3
Personal services												
Negro												
Total	1,303	31	9	1	2	0	19	1,262	87	815	360	10
Occupational distrib.	100.0	2.4	0.7	0.1	0.2	0.0	1.5	96.9	6.7	62.5	27.6	0.8
Participation rate	60.5	6.0	7.9	100.0	33.3	0.0	16.7	77.8	83.7	71.1	96.5	76.9
All employees												
Total (8 estab.)	2,154	518	114	1	6	283	114	1,623	104	1,146	373	13
Occupational distrib.	100.0	24.0	5.3	0.0	0.3	13.1	5.3	75.3	4.8	53.2	17.3	0.6
Misc. business services												
Negro												
Total	1,687	768	7	8	34	1	718	520	26	67	427	399
Occupational distrib.	100.0	45.5	0.4	0.5	2.0	0.1	42.6	30.8	1.5	4.0	25.3	23.7
Participation rate	9.9	6.7	0.5	0.3	1.1	0.4	19.6	13.6	1.5	6.7	40.2	21.5
All employees												
Total (66 estab.)	17,076	11,387	1,466	2,881	3,131	241	3,668	3,836	1,777	966	1,063	1,853
Occupational distrib.	100.0	66.7	8.6	16.9	18.3	1.4	21.5	22.5	10.4	5.8	6.2	10.9

Table 50 continued

	Total Employ- ment	Total White- Collar Em- ployment	White-Collar Occupations					Total Blue- Collar Em- ployment	Blue-Collar Occupations			
			Officials & Managers	Profes- sionals	Techni- cians	Sales Workers	Office & Clerical		Crafts- men	Opera- tives	Laborers	Service Workers
Totals												
Negro employment	91,434	5,864	548	166	244	1,151	3,237	72,763	4,011	59,685	9,067	5,576
All employees	513,559	190,346	44,115	34,246	23,168	25,473	63,344	328,803	83,103	213,639	32,061	18,910
Negro participation rate	17.8	3.8	1.2	0.5	1.1	4.5	5.1	22.1	4.8	27.9	28.3	34.8

Note: Because of rounding, sums of individual items may not equal totals.

Source: Equal Employment Opportunity Report No. 1, Part III, Washington, D.C.: Equal Opportunity Employment Commission, 1966.

TABLE 51. Negro Employment by Occupation and Industry in the Houston SMSA, 1966.

	Total Employment	White-Collar Occupations						Blue-Collar Occupations				
		Total White-Collar Employment	Officials & Managers	Professionals	Technicians	Sales Workers	Office & Clerical	Total Blue-Collar Employment	Crafts-men	Opera-tives	Laborers	Service Workers
Crude petroleum & natural gas												
Negro												
Total	249	61	0	2	9	10	40	114	2	62	50	74
Occupational distrib.	100.0	24.5	0.0	0.8	3.6	4.0	16.1	45.8	0.8	24.9	20.1	29.7
Participation rate	2.0	0.6	0.0	0.1	0.6	9.7	1.1	3.2	0.2	3.5	6.3	47.1
All employees												
Total (68 estab.)	14,324	10,548	1,552	3,614	1,574	103	3,705	3,629	1,056	1,765	798	157
Occupational distrib.	100.0	73.6	10.8	25.2	11.0	0.7	25.9	25.3	7.4	12.3	5.6	1.1
Contract construction												
Negro												
Total	1,563	17	12	2	1	0	2	1,526	162	361	1,003	20
Occupational distrib.	100.0	1.1	0.8	0.1	0.1	0.0	0.1	97.6	10.4	23.1	64.2	1.3
Participation rate	8.9	0.4	1.0	0.2	0.1	0.0	0.2	12.0	2.6	11.7	29.0	8.2
All employees												
Total (105 estab.)	17,498	4,507	1,159	1,075	908	53	1,312	12,746	6,195	3,092	3,459	245
Occupational distrib.	100.0	25.8	6.6	6.1	5.2	0.3	7.5	72.8	35.4	17.7	19.8	1.4
Food & kindred products												
Negro												
Total	2,049	146	15	1	24	93	13	1,799	138	652	1,009	104
Occupational distrib.	100.0	7.1	0.7	0.0	1.2	4.5	0.6	87.8	6.7	31.8	49.2	5.1
Participation rate	22.3	4.2	1.8	0.6	16.0	6.1	1.6	33.0	13.8	27.6	48.0	47.1
All employees												
Total (50 estab.)	9,170	3,490	850	162	150	1,534	794	5,459	998	2,360	2,101	221
Occupational distrib.	100.0	38.1	9.3	1.8	1.6	16.7	8.7	59.5	10.9	25.7	22.9	2.4
Chemicals & allied products												
Negro												
Total	1,160	52	6	1	22	0	23	984	83	453	448	124
Occupational distrib.	100.0	4.5	0.5	0.1	1.9	0.0	2.0	84.8	7.2	39.1	38.6	10.7
Participation rate	5.7	0.6	0.2	0.0	1.5	0.0	1.2	8.9	1.8	8.2	53.2	27.8
All employees												
Total (84 estab.)	20,491	8,991	2,878	2,244	1,477	445	1,947	11,054	4,704	5,508	842	446
Occupational distrib.	100.0	43.9	14.0	11.0	7.2	2.2	9.5	53.9	23.0	26.9	4.1	2.2

TABLE 51 continued

	Total Employment	White-Collar Occupations						Blue-Collar Occupations				
		Total White-Collar Employment	Officials & Managers	Professionals	Technicians	Sales Workers	Office & Clerical	Total Blue-Collar Employment	Craftsmen	Operatives	Laborers	Service Workers
Primary metal industries												
Negro												
Total	1,787	43	26	1	10	0	6	1,712	178	1,098	436	32
Occupational distrib.	100.0	2.4	1.5	0.1	0.6	0.0	0.3	95.8	10.0	61.4	24.4	1.8
Participation rate	25.5	2.3	3.6	0.6	3.3	0.0	1.0	33.9	9.2	46.2	59.3	35.2
All employees												
Total (20 estab.)	7,003	1,855	721	156	304	83	591	5,057	1,944	2,378	735	91
Occupational distrib.	100.0	26.5	10.3	2.2	4.3	1.2	8.4	72.2	27.8	34.0	10.5	1.3
Fabricated metal products												
Negro												
Total	1,237	13	4	0	2	0	7	1,187	81	602	504	37
Occupational distrib.	100.0	1.1	0.3	0.0	0.2	0.0	0.6	96.0	6.5	48.7	40.7	3.0
Participation rate	12.7	0.5	0.5	0.0	0.4	0.0	0.7	16.9	3.6	18.1	35.1	39.8
All employees												
Total (45 estab.)	9,772	2,653	736	180	491	255	991	7,026	2,259	3,330	1,437	93
Occupational distrib.	100.0	27.1	7.5	1.8	5.0	2.6	10.1	71.9	23.1	34.1	14.7	1.0
Pipeline transportation												
Negro												
Total	6	5	0	0	3	0	2	0	0	0	0	1
Occupational distrib.	100.0	83.3	0.0	0.0	50.0	0.0	33.3	0.0	0.0	0.0	0.0	16.7
Participation rate	0.3	0.4	0.0	0.0	1.2	0.0	0.5	0.0	0.0	0.0	0.0	14.3
All employees												
Total (7 estab.)	2,052	1,210	297	280	252	2	379	835	440	324	71	7
Occupational distrib.	100.0	59.0	14.5	13.6	12.3	0.1	18.5	40.7	21.4	15.8	3.5	0.3
Wholesale trade												
Negro												
Total	1,315	82	2	3	6	13	58	1,168	252	555	361	65
Occupational distrib.	100.0	6.2	0.2	0.2	0.5	1.0	4.4	88.8	19.2	49.2	27.5	4.9
Participation rate	10.2	1.0	0.1	0.5	0.9	0.6	1.8	25.4	16.3	24.4	46.8	55.6
All employees												
Total (195 estab.)	12,884	8,174	1,346	610	634	2,284	3,300	4,593	1,548	2,273	772	117
Occupational distrib.	100.0	63.4	10.4	4.7	4.9	17.7	25.6	35.6	12.0	17.6	6.0	0.9

Table 51 continued

	Total Employment		White-Collar Occupations							Blue-Collar Occupations				
		Total White-Collar Employment	Officials & Managers	Professionals	Technicians	Sales Workers	Office & Clerical		Total Blue-Collar Employment	Crafts-men	Opera-tives	Laborers	Service Workers
Retail trade														
Negro														
Total	1,282	243	7	0	0	169	67		432	27	181	224	607
Occupational distrib.	100.0	19.0	0.5	0.0	0.0	13.2	5.2		33.7	2.1	14.1	17.5	47.3
Participation rate	10.5	2.6	0.6	0.0	0.0	3.0	3.0		23.0	5.0	24.6	37.7	57.9
All employees														
Total (32 estab.)	12,172	9,248	1,247	54	88	5,602	2,257		1,875	544	737	594	1,049
Occupational distrib.	100.0	76.0	10.2	0.4	0.7	46.0	18.5		15.4	4.5	6.1	4.9	8.6
Real estate														
Negro														
Total	133	0	0	0	0	0	0		32	5	6	21	101
Occupational distrib.	100.0	0.0	0.0	0.0	0.0	0.0	0.0		24.1	3.8	4.5	15.8	75.9
Participation rate	15.4	0.0	0.0	0.0	0.0	0.0	0.0		10.5	3.6	11.1	18.8	29.6
All employees														
Total (11 estab.)	864	218	38	33	8	1	138		305	139	54	112	341
Occupational distrib.	100.0	25.2	4.4	3.8	0.9	0.1	16.0		35.3	16.1	6.3	13.0	39.5
Banking														
Negro														
Total	497	188	8	3	123	0	54		21	0	2	19	288
Occupational distrib.	100.0	37.8	1.6	0.6	24.7	0.0	10.9		4.2	0.0	0.4	3.8	57.9
Participation rate	12.1	5.3	1.6	1.2	30.9	0.0	2.3		25.3	0.0	5.9	100.0	61.1
All employees														
Total (10 estab.)	4,098	3,544	499	247	398	6	2,394		83	30	34	19	471
Occupational distrib.	100.0	86.5	12.2	6.0	9.7	0.1	58.4		2.0	0.7	0.8	0.5	11.5
Totals														
Negro employment	11,278	850	581	13	200	285	272		8,975	928	3,972	4,015	1,453
All employees	110,328	54,438	11,323	8,655	6,284	10,368	17,808		52,652	17,679	21,855	10,940	3,238
Negro participation rate	10.2	1.6	5.1	0.2	3.2	2.7	1.5		17.1	5.3	13.6	36.7	44.9

Note: Because of rounding, sums of individual items may not equal totals.

Source: Equal Employment Opportunity Report No. 1, Part III. Washington, D.C.: Equal Employment Opportunity Commission, 1966.

TABLE 52. Negro Employment by Occupation and Industry in the Los Angeles SMSA, 1966.

	Total Employment	White-Collar Occupations						Blue-Collar Occupations				
		Total White-Collar Employment	Officials & Managers	Professionals	Technicians	Sales Workers	Office & Clerical	Total Blue-Collar Employment	Craftsmen	Operatives	Laborers	Service Workers
Crude petroleum & natural gas												
Negro												
Total	25	21	0	3	0	0	18	4	2	1	1	0
Occupational distrib.	100.0	84.0	0.0	12.0	0.0	0.0	72.0	16.0	8.0	4.0	4.0	0.0
Participation rate	0.7	1.0	0.0	0.5	0.0	0.0	1.8	0.3	0.3	0.2	0.5	0.0
All employees												
Total (25 estab.)	3,501	2,196	361	561	209	48	1,017	1,245	630	429	186	60
Occupational distrib.	100.0	62.7	10.3	16.0	6.0	1.4	29.0	35.6	18.0	12.3	5.3	1.7
Contract construction												
Negro												
Total	946	63	11	11	10	1	30	845	309	169	367	38
Occupational distrib.	100.0	6.7	1.2	1.2	1.1	0.1	3.2	89.3	32.7	17.9	38.8	4.0
Participation rate	4.5	0.9	0.6	0.5	1.2	0.2	1.3	6.4	3.6	7.0	16.5	18.4
All employees												
Total (221 estab.)	20,807	7,388	1,730	2,201	820	409	2,228	13,212	8,588	2,398	2,226	207
Occupational distrib.	100.0	35.5	8.3	10.6	3.9	2.0	10.7	63.5	41.3	11.5	10.7	1.0
Food & kindred products												
Negro												
Total	2,408	249	20	3	12	144	70	1,881	289	645	947	278
Occupational distrib.	100.0	10.3	0.8	0.1	0.5	6.0	2.9	78.1	12.0	26.8	39.3	11.5
Participation rate	7.0	1.9	0.8	0.6	3.2	2.2	2.3	9.3	6.9	6.7	14.6	21.8
All employees												
Total (164 estab.)	34,418	12,912	2,454	484	371	6,527	3,076	20,228	4,184	9,559	6,485	1,278
Occupational distrib.	100.0	37.5	7.1	1.4	1.1	19.0	8.9	58.8	12.2	27.8	18.8	3.7
Apparel & related products												
Negro												
Total	1,157	82	10	1	6	0	65	978	136	715	127	97
Occupational distrib.	100.0	7.1	0.9	0.1	0.5	0.0	5.6	84.5	11.8	61.8	11.0	8.4
Participation rate	13.1	6.0	2.7	1.1	6.3	0.0	11.2	13.5	6.8	16.1	16.3	52.2
All employees												
Total (60 estab.)	8,801	1,378	375	88	96	237	582	7,237	2,009	4,449	779	186
Occupational distrib.	100.0	15.7	4.3	1.0	1.1	2.7	6.6	82.2	22.8	50.6	8.9	2.1

Table 52 continued

	Total Employment	White-Collar Occupations						Blue-Collar Occupations				
		Total White-Collar Employment	Officials & Managers	Professionals	Technicians	Sales Workers	Office & Clerical	Total Blue-Collar Employment	Craftsmen	Operatives	Laborers	Service Workers
Furniture & fixtures												
Negro												
Total	734	28	7	0	3	0	18	685	116	256	313	21
Occupational distrib.	100.0	3.8	1.0	0.0	0.4	0.0	2.5	93.3	15.8	34.9	42.6	2.9
Participation rate	12.1	2.0	1.8	0.0	4.7	0.0	3.1	14.8	9.4	11.7	26.5	21.4
All employees												
Total (37 estab.)	6,087	1,376	383	101	64	256	572	4,613	1,239	2,194	1,180	98
Occupational distrib.	100.0	22.6	6.3	1.7	1.1	4.2	9.4	75.8	20.4	36.0	19.4	1.6
Paper & allied products												
Negro												
Total	790	18	2	0	1	1	14	727	107	416	204	45
Occupational distrib.	100.0	2.3	0.3	0.0	0.1	0.1	1.8	92.0	13.5	52.7	25.8	5.7
Participation rate	6.9	0.6	0.2	0.0	0.7	0.2	1.2	8.7	4.9	10.3	9.7	29.6
All employees												
Total (73 estab.)	11,521	3,029	874	222	146	573	1,214	8,340	2,170	4,057	2,113	152
Occupational distrib.	100.0	26.3	7.6	1.9	1.3	5.0	10.5	72.4	18.8	35.2	18.3	1.3
Printing & pub. industries												
Negro												
Total	724	125	4	4	4	12	101	234	35	126	73	365
Occupational distrib.	100.0	17.3	0.6	0.6	0.6	1.7	14.0	32.3	4.8	17.4	10.1	50.4
Participation rate	4.2	1.8	0.4	0.3	1.3	0.8	3.4	2.5	0.7	3.5	7.0	37.8
All employees												
Total (67 estab.)	17,401	7,000	1,030	1,145	303	1,531	2,991	9,436	4,834	3,558	1,044	965
Occupational distrib.	100.0	40.2	5.9	6.6	1.7	8.8	17.2	54.2	27.8	20.4	5.0	5.5
Chemicals & allied products												
Negro												
Total	626	94	4	25	14	8	43	444	64	202	178	88
Occupational distrib.	100.0	15.0	0.6	4.0	2.2	1.3	6.9	70.9	10.2	32.3	28.4	14.1
Participation rate	3.2	0.9	0.2	1.9	1.4	0.4	1.3	4.8	2.8	4.5	7.1	25.8
All employees												
Total (135 estab.)	19,693	10,088	2,102	1,322	1,030	2,259	3,375	9,264	2,319	4,443	2,502	341
Occupational distrib.	100.0	51.2	10.7	6.7	5.2	11.5	17.1	47.0	11.8	22.6	12.7	1.7

Table 52 continued

	Total Employment	White-Collar Occupations						Blue-Collar Occupations				
		Total White-Collar Employment	Officials & Managers	Professionals	Technicians	Sales Workers	Office & Clerical	Total Blue-Collar Employment	Craftsmen	Operatives	Laborers	Service Workers
Rubber & plastic products												
Negro												
Total	1,466	28	7	1	7	0	13	1,366	117	824	425	72
Occupational distrib.	100.0	1.9	0.5	0.1	0.5	0.0	0.9	93.2	8.0	56.2	29.0	4.9
Participation rate	11.0	0.9	0.6	0.3	2.3	0.0	1.1	14.0	5.7	16.1	16.3	22.9
All employees												
Total (71 estab.)	13,272	3,207	1,079	391	306	228	1,203	9,751	2,037	5,111	2,603	314
Occupational distrib.	100.0	24.2	8.1	2.9	2.3	1.7	9.1	73.5	15.3	38.5	19.6	2.4
Stone, clay, & glass products												
Negro												
Total	506	43	4	7	8	0	24	443	21	286	136	20
Occupational distrib.	100.0	8.5	0.8	1.4	1.6	0.0	4.7	87.5	4.2	56.5	26.9	4.0
Participation rate	4.3	1.3	0.4	1.7	2.8	0.0	2.0	5.3	1.2	6.2	7.2	18.5
All employees												
Total (57 estab.)	11,643	3,240	1,016	421	285	304	1,214	8,295	1,760	4,641	1,894	108
Occupational distrib.	100.0	27.8	8.7	3.6	2.4	2.6	10.4	71.2	15.1	39.9	16.3	0.9
Fabricated metal products												
Negro												
Total	1,701	53	11	2	14	3	23	1,582	345	750	487	66
Occupational distrib.	100.0	3.1	0.6	0.1	0.8	0.2	1.4	93.0	20.3	44.1	28.6	3.9
Participation rate	5.9	0.7	0.5	0.3	1.5	0.3	0.8	7.6	4.2	8.0	14.7	20.6
All employees												
Total (151 estab.)	28,877	7,698	2,146	745	936	1,093	2,778	20,858	8,174	9,367	3,317	321
Occupational distrib.	100.0	26.7	7.4	2.6	3.2	3.8	9.6	72.2	28.3	32.4	11.5	1.1
Electrical machinery, equipment, supplies												
Negro												
Total	7,737	1,628	79	422	525	6	596	5,510	938	3,846	726	599
Occupational distrib.	100.0	21.0	1.0	5.5	6.8	0.1	7.7	71.2	12.1	49.7	9.4	7.7
Participation rate	5.1	1.8	0.6	1.2	3.4	0.3	2.3	9.4	4.5	11.8	13.5	29.3
All employees												
Total (249 estab.)	152,909	92,155	13,273	36,323	15,275	1,788	25,496	58,708	20,788	32,562	5,358	2,046
Occupational distrib.	100.0	60.3	8.7	23.8	10.0	1.2	16.7	38.4	13.6	21.3	3.5	1.3

Table 52 continued

	Total Employment	White-Collar Occupations						Blue-Collar Occupations				
		Total White-Collar Employment	Officials & Managers	Professionals	Technicians	Sales Workers	Office & Clerical	Total Blue-Collar Employment	Crafts-men	Opera-tives	Laborers	Service Workers
Transportation equipment												
Negro												
Total	8,328	732	41	134	121	0	436	7,205	1,735	4,950	520	391
Occupational distrib.	100.0	8.8	0.5	1.6	1.5	0.0	5.2	86.5	20.8	59.4	6.2	4.7
Participation rate	6.7	1.5	0.5	0.8	2.3	0.0	2.4	9.9	5.0	13.9	16.9	18.4
All employees												
Total (155 estab.)	124,898	49,720	8,295	17,682	5,178	554	18,011	73,056	34,449	35,534	3,073	2,122
Occupational distrib.	100.0	39.8	6.6	14.2	4.1	0.4	14.4	58.5	27.6	28.5	2.5	1.7
Instruments & related products												
Negro												
Total	468	79	9	20	21	2	27	337	46	191	100	52
Occupational distrib.	100.0	16.9	1.9	4.3	4.5	0.4	5.8	72.0	9.8	40.8	21.4	11.1
Participation rate	2.3	0.8	0.5	0.6	1.0	0.6	0.9	3.5	1.4	4.2	5.5	22.5
All employees												
Total (70 estab.)	20,457	10,505	1,883	3,253	2,016	354	2,999	9,721	3,373	4,541	1,807	231
Occupational distrib.	100.0	51.4	9.2	15.9	9.9	1.7	14.7	47.5	16.5	22.2	8.8	1.1
Miscellaneous mfrg. industries												
Negro												
Total	1,386	71	12	6	1	1	51	1,297	52	546	699	18
Occupational distrib.	100.0	5.1	0.9	0.4	0.1	0.1	3.7	93.6	3.8	39.4	50.4	1.3
Participation rate	15.8	2.4	1.6	1.1	0.7	0.3	4.2	22.6	6.9	20.3	30.5	30.5
All employees												
Total (37 estab.)	8,785	2,984	743	531	153	347	1,210	5,742	759	2,694	2,289	59
Occupational distrib.	100.0	34.0	8.5	6.0	1.7	3.9	13.8	65.4	8.6	30.7	26.1	0.7
Motor freight transportation												
Negro												
Total	910	33	3	4	0	0	26	837	53	466	318	40
Occupational distrib.	100.0	3.6	0.3	0.4	0.0	0.0	2.9	92.0	5.8	51.2	34.9	4.4
Participation rate	5.6	0.8	0.3	1.8	0.0	0.0	1.2	6.8	3.6	5.4	15.3	33.1
All employees												
Total (95 estab.)	16,314	3,963	1,149	224	39	408	2,143	12,230	1,476	8,669	2,085	121
Occupational distrib.	100.0	24.3	7.0	1.4	0.2	2.5	13.1	75.0	9.0	53.1	12.8	0.7

Table 52 continued

	Total Employment	White-Collar Occupations						Blue-Collar Occupations				
		Total White-Collar Employment	Officials & Managers	Professionals	Technicians	Sales Workers	Office & Clerical	Total Blue-Collar Employment	Crafts-men	Opera-tives	Laborers	Service Workers
Transportation services												
Negro												
Total	121	34	0	0	0	0	34	87	0	0	87	0
Occupational distrib.	100.0	28.1	0.0	0.0	0.0	0.0	28.1	71.9	0.0	0.0	71.9	0.0
Participation rate	12.8	4.7	0.0	0.0	0.0	0.0	6.4	38.5	0.0	0.0	38.7	0.0
All employees												
Total (22 estab.)	943	717	88	5	0	96	528	226	0	1	225	0
Occupational distrib.	100.0	76.0	9.3	0.5	0.0	10.2	56.0	24.0	0.0	0.1	23.9	0.0
Wholesale trade												
Negro												
Total	1,348	423	7	9	83	83	241	778	62	387	329	147
Occupational distrib.	100.0	31.4	0.5	0.7	6.2	6.2	17.9	57.7	4.6	28.7	24.4	10.9
Participation rate	3.5	1.6	0.2	0.7	3.7	1.0	2.5	6.1	2.1	6.4	8.9	28.3
All employees												
Total (483 estab.)	39,072	25,825	4,082	1,309	2,226	8,454	9,754	12,727	2,994	6,024	3,709	520
Occupational distrib.	100.0	66.1	10.4	3.4	5.7	21.6	25.0	32.6	7.7	15.4	9.5	1.3
Retail trade												
Negro												
Total	4,411	2,392	90	3	50	1,310	939	988	130	483	375	1,031
Occupational distrib.	100.0	54.2	2.0	0.1	1.1	29.7	21.3	22.4	2.9	10.9	8.5	23.4
Participation rate	7.5	5.2	1.5	0.8	14.4	4.9	7.8	10.8	5.6	14.5	10.6	25.6
All employees												
Total (76 estab.)	58,860	45,649	6,089	377	348	26,760	12,075	9,186	2,319	3,324	3,543	4,025
Occupational distrib.	100.0	77.6	10.3	0.6	0.6	45.5	20.5	15.6	3.9	5.6	6.0	6.8
Miscellaneous business services												
Negro												
Total	5,531	929	52	153	355	2	367	1,046	388	536	122	3,556
Occupational distrib.	100.0	16.8	0.9	2.8	6.4	0.0	6.6	18.9	7.0	9.7	2.2	64.3
Participation rate	13.0	3.6	1.5	1.7	10.0	0.3	4.0	11.8	7.7	16.9	20.1	44.8
All employees												
Total (156 estab.)	42,665	25,895	3,403	9,189	3,557	633	9,113	8,837	5,050	3,180	607	7,933
Occupational distrib.	100.0	60.7	8.0	21.5	8.3	1.5	21.4	20.7	11.8	7.5	1.4	18.6

Table 52 continued

	Total Employ-ment	White-Collar Occupations						Blue-Collar Occupations				
		Total White-Collar Em-ployment	Officials & Managers	Profes-sionals	Techni-cians	Sales Workers	Office & Clerical	Total Blue-Collar Em-ployment	Crafts-men	Opera-tives	Laborers	Service Workers
Totals												
Negro employment	41,323	7,125	461	808	1,235	1,573	3,136	27,274	4,945	15,795	6,534	6,924
All employees	640,924	316,925	52,555	76,574	33,358	52,859	101,579	295,121	109,152	146,735	47,025	21,087
Negro participation rate	6.4	2.2	0.9	1.1	3.7	3.0	3.1	9.2	4.5	10.8	13.9	32.8

Note: Because of rounding, sums of individual items may not equal totals.

Source: Equal Employment Opportunity Report No. 1, Part III, Washington, D.C.: Equal Employment Opportunity Commission, 1966.

TABLE 53.   Minority Group Employment by Occupation in the Baltimore SMSA, 1969.

	Total Empl.	White-Collar	Off. Mgrs.	Prof.	Tech.	Sales Wkrs.	Off. Cler.	Blue-Collar	Craft.	Oper.	Labor.	Serv. Wkrs.
All T	343,754	165,298	30,765	27,079	16,448	29,429	61,577	157,151	52,599	75,241	29,311	21,305
All M	236,534	95,222	27,679	21,098	12,654	17,134	16,657	129,973	50,119	58,231	21,623	11,339
All F	107,220	70,076	3,086	5,981	3,794	12,295	44,920	27,178	2,480	17,010	7,688	9,966
Ang T[1]	276,950	151,949	29,840	25,552	14,576	26,918	55,063	115,432	47,556	52,343	15,533	9,569
Ang M	191,151	89,856	26,950	20,173	11,676	16,013	15,044	95,510	45,385	39,625	10,500	5,785
Ang F	85,799	62,093	2,890	5,379	2,900	10,905	40,019	19,922	2,171	12,718	5,033	3,784
Neg T[2]	63,742	11,736	817	829	1,644	2,381	6,065	40,406	4,313	22,481	13,612	11,600
Neg M	43,196	4,420	639	399	817	1,071	1,494	33,306	4,011	18,288	11,007	5,470
Neg F	20,546	7,316	178	430	827	1,310	4,571	7,100	302	4,193	2,605	6,130
SSA T[3]	967	576	50	197	106	98	125	330	87	175	68	61
SSA M	668	372	46	151	88	41	46	257	84	120	53	39
SSA F	299	204	4	46	18	57	79	73	3	55	15	22
Ori T[4]	1,491	770	27	495	116	25	107	658	590	56	12	63
Ori M	1,183	505	23	370	67	7	38	639	590	41	8	39
Ori F	308	265	4	125	49	18	69	19		15	4	24
AmI T[5]	604	267	31	6	6	7	217	325	53	186	86	12
AmI M	336	69	21	5	6	2	35	261	49	157	55	6
AmI F	268	198	10	1		5	182	64	4	29	31	6
Ang T PR*	80.6	91.9	97.0	94.4	88.6	91.5	89.4	73.5	90.4	69.6	53.0	44.9
Ang M PR	80.8	94.4	97.4	95.6	92.3	93.5	90.3	73.5	90.6	68.0	48.6	51.0
Ang F PR	80.0	88.6	93.6	89.9	76.4	88.7	89.1	73.3	87.5	74.8	65.5	38.0
Neg T PR	18.5	7.1	2.7	3.1	10.0	8.1	9.8	25.7	8.2	29.9	46.4	54.4
Neg M PR	18.3	4.6	2.3	1.9	6.5	6.3	9.0	25.6	8.0	31.4	50.9	48.2
Neg F PR	19.2	10.4	5.8	7.2	21.8	10.7	10.2	26.1	12.2	24.7	33.9	61.5
SSA T PR	0.3	0.3	0.2	0.7	0.6	0.3	0.2	0.2	0.2	0.2	0.2	0.3
SSA M PR	0.3	0.4	0.2	0.7	0.7	0.2	0.3	0.2	0.2	0.2	0.2	0.3
SSA F PR	0.3	0.3	0.1	0.8	0.5	0.5	0.2	0.3	0.1	0.3	0.2	0.2

Table 53 continued

	Total Empl.	White-Collar	Off. Mgrs.	Prof.	Tech.	Sales Wkrs.	Off. Cler.	Blue-Collar	Craft.	Oper.	Labor.	Serv. Wkrs.
Ori T PR	0.4	0.5	0.1	1.8	0.7	0.1	0.2	0.4	1.1	0.1	0.0	0.3
Ori M PR	0.5	0.5	0.1	1.8	0.5	0.0	0.2	0.5	1.2	0.1	0.0	0.3
Ori F PR	0.3	0.4	0.1	2.1	1.3	0.1	0.2	0.1		0.1	0.1	0.2
AmI T PR	0.2	0.2	0.1	0.0	0.0	0.0	0.4	0.2	0.1	0.2	0.3	0.1
AmI M PR	0.1	0.1	0.1	0.0	0.0	0.0	0.2	0.2	0.1	0.3	0.3	0.1
AmI F PR	0.2	0.3	0.3	0.0		0.0	0.4	0.2	0.2	0.2	0.4	0.1

[1] All other.
[2] Negro,
[3] Spanish surnamed.
[4] Oriental.
[5] American Indian.
*Participation rates.

Source: Equal Employment Opportunity Report No. 1, Washington, D.C.: Equal Employment Opportunity Commission, 1969.

TABLE 54. Minority Group Employment by Occupation in the Detroit SMSA, 1969.

	Total Empl.	White-Collar	Off. Mgrs.	Prof.	Tech.	Sales Wkrs.	Off. Cler.	Blue-Collar	Craft.	Oper.	Labor.	Serv. Wkrs.
All T	659,809	312,614	59,750	48,844	30,193	55,700	118,127	297,495	82,643	172,688	42,164	49,700
All M	456,916	174,057	53,553	39,188	24,117	30,003	27,196	260,003	80,537	148,016	31,450	22,856
All F	202,893	138,557	6,197	9,656	6,076	25,697	90,931	37,492	2,106	24,672	10,714	26,844
Ang T[1]	542,448	285,373	57,716	46,227	26,981	51,157	103,292	226,123	77,661	119,434	29,028	30,952
Ang M	377,652	165,450	51,976	37,714	23,000	28,069	24,691	197,777	76,031	100,389	21,357	14,425
Ang F	164,796	119,923	5,740	8,513	3,981	23,088	78,601	28,346	1,630	19,045	7,671	16,527
Neg T[2]	110,823	24,986	1,781	1,825	2,946	4,297	14,137	67,985	4,429	51,324	12,232	17,852
Neg M	74,432	7,262	1,352	866	919	1,816	2,309	59,283	3,991	45,919	9,373	7,887
Neg F	36,391	17,724	429	959	2,027	2,481	11,828	8,702	438	5,405	2,859	9,965
SSA T[3]	4,381	1,008	153	143	111	148	453	2,649	360	1,549	740	724
SSA M	3,388	578	137	115	98	78	150	2,352	347	1,404	601	458
SSA F	993	430	16	28	13	70	303	297	13	145	139	266
Ori T[4]	1,420	1,009	52	630	143	50	134	289	55	163	71	122
Ori M	947	660	44	479	90	22	25	225	51	132	42	62
Ori F	473	349	8	151	53	28	109	64	4	31	29	60
Aml T[5]	737	238	48	19	12	48	111	449	138	218	93	50
Aml M	497	107	44	14	10	18	21	366	117	172	77	24
Aml F	240	131	4	5	2	30	90	83	21	46	16	26
Ang T PR*	82.2	91.3	96.6	94.6	89.4	91.8	87.4	76.0	94.0	69.2	68.8	62.3
Ang M PR	82.7	95.1	97.1	96.2	95.4	93.6	90.8	76.1	94.4	67.8	67.9	63.1
Ang F PR	81.2	86.6	92.6	88.2	65.5	89.8	86.4	75.6	77.4	77.2	71.6	61.6
Neg T PR	16.8	8.0	3.0	3.7	9.8	7.7	12.0	22.9	5.4	29.7	29.0	35.9
Neg M PR	16.3	4.2	2.5	2.2	3.8	6.1	8.5	22.8	5.0	31.0	29.8	34.5
Neg F PR	17.9	12.8	6.9	9.9	33.4	9.7	13.0	23.2	20.8	21.9	26.7	37.1
SSA T PR	0.7	0.3	0.3	0.3	0.4	0.3	0.4	0.9	0.4	0.9	1.8	1.5
SSA M PR	0.7	0.3	0.3	0.3	0.4	0.3	0.6	0.9	0.4	0.9	1.9	2.0
SSA F PR	0.5	0.3	0.3	0.3	0.2	0.3	0.3	0.8	0.6	0.6	1.3	1.0

Table 54 continued

	Total Empl.	White-Collar	Off. Mgrs.	Prof.	Tech.	Sales Wkrs.	Off. Cler.	Blue-Collar	Craft.	Oper.	Labor.	Serv. Wkrs.
Ori T PR	0.2	0.3	0.1	1.3	0.5	0.1	0.1	0.1	0.1	0.1	0.2	0.2
Ori M PR	0.2	0.4	0.1	1.2	0.4	0.1	0.1	0.1	0.1	0.1	0.1	0.3
Ori F PR	0.2	0.3	0.1	1.6	0.9	0.1	0.1	0.2	0.2	0.1	0.3	0.2
AmI T PR	0.1	0.1	0.1	0.0	0.0	0.1	0.1	0.2	0.2	0.1	0.2	0.1
AmI M PR	0.1	0.1	0.1	0.0	0.0	0.1	0.1	0.1	0.1	0.1	0.2	0.1
AmI F PR	0.1	0.1	0.1	0.1	0.0	0.1	0.1	0.2	1.0	0.2	0.1	0.1

[1] All other.
[2] Negro.
[3] Spanish surnamed.
[4] Oriental.
[5] American Indian.
*Participation rates.

Source: Equal Employment Opportunity Report No. 1, Washington, D.C.: Equal Employment Opportunity Commission, 1969.

TABLE 55. Minority Group Employment by Occupation in the Houston SMSA, 1969.

	Total Empl.	White-Collar	Off. Mgrs.	Prof.	Tech.	Sales Wkrs.	Off. Cler.	Blue-Collar	Craft.	Oper.	Labor.	Serv. Wkrs.
All T	310,025	173,531	29,831	33,530	19,725	32,959	57,486	114,593	45,763	48,741	20,089	21,901
All M	223,671	106,823	27,850	27,985	15,408	19,851	15,729	105,881	44,593	43,723	17,565	10,967
All F	86,354	66,708	1,981	5,545	4,317	13,108	41,757	8,712	1,170	5,018	2,524	10,934
Ang T[1]	244,443	158,033	28,830	31,762	17,065	29,004	51,372	77,059	39,330	30,425	7,304	9,351
Ang M	176,773	99,434	26,991	26,832	14,198	17,577	13,836	72,366	38,488	27,577	6,301	4,973
Ang F	67,670	58,599	1,839	4,930	2,867	11,427	37,536	4,693	842	2,848	1,003	4,378
Neg T[2]	44,030	8,244	420	633	1,689	2,150	3,352	26,170	3,504	13,166	9,500	9,616
Neg M	31,428	3,473	348	301	552	1,155	1,117	23,537	3,296	11,824	8,417	4,418
Neg F	12,602	4,771	72	332	1,137	995	2,235	2,633	208	1,342	1,083	5,198
SSA T[3]	19,505	5,846	437	578	846	1,525	2,460	10,848	2,652	4,969	3,227	2,811
SSA M	14,076	3,009	391	437	562	910	709	9,557	2,554	4,199	2,804	1,510
SSA F	5,429	2,837	46	141	284	615	1,751	1,291	98	770	423	1,301
Ori T[4]	934	792	41	484	86	63	118	70	24	39	7	72
Ori M	644	561	36	369	62	50	44	51	21	24	6	32
Ori F	290	231	5	115	24	13	74	19	3	15	1	40
AmI T[5]	1,113	616	103	73	39	217	184	446	253	142	51	51
AmI M	750	346	84	46	34	159	23	370	234	99	37	34
AmI F	363	270	19	27	5	58	161	76	19	43	14	17
Ang T PR*	78.8	91.1	96.6	94.7	86.5	88.0	89.4	67.2	85.9	62.4	36.4	42.7
Ang M PR	79.0	93.1	96.9	95.9	92.1	88.5	88.0	68.3	86.3	63.1	35.9	45.3
Ang F PR	78.4	87.8	92.8	88.9	66.4	87.2	89.9	53.9	72.0	56.8	39.7	40.0
Neg T PR	14.2	4.8	1.4	1.9	8.6	6.5	5.8	22.8	7.7	27.0	47.3	43.9
Neg M PR	14.1	3.3	1.2	1.1	3.6	5.8	7.1	22.2	7.4	27.0	47.9	40.3
Neg F PR	14.6	7.2	3.6	6.0	26.3	7.6	5.4	30.2	17.8	26.7	42.9	47.5
SSA T PR	6.3	3.4	1.5	1.7	4.3	4.6	4.3	9.5	5.8	10.2	16.1	12.8
SSA M PR	6.3	2.8	1.4	1.6	3.6	4.6	4.5	9.0	5.7	9.6	16.0	13.8
SSA F PR	6.3	4.3	2.3	2.5	6.6	4.7	4.2	14.8	8.4	15.3	16.8	11.9

Table 55 continued

	Total Empl.	White-Collar	Off. Mgrs.	Prof.	Tech.	Sales Wkrs.	Off. Cler.	Blue-Collar	Craft.	Oper.	Labor.	Serv. Wkrs.
Ori T PR	0.3	0.5	0.1	1.4	0.4	0.2	0.2	0.1	0.1	0.1	0.0	0.3
Ori M PR	0.3	0.5	0.1	1.3	0.4	0.3	0.3	0.0	0.0	0.1	0.0	0.3
Ori F PR	0.3	0.3	0.3	2.1	0.6	0.1	0.2	0.3	0.3	0.3	0.0	0.4
AmI T PR	0.4	0.4	0.3	0.2	0.2	0.7	0.3	0.4	0.6	0.3	0.3	0.2
AmI M PR	0.3	0.3	0.3	0.2	0.2	0.8	0.1	0.3	0.5	0.2	0.2	0.3
AmI F PR	0.4	0.4	1.0	0.5	0.1	0.4	0.4	0.9	1.6	0.9	0.6	0.2

[1] All other.
[2] Negro.
[3] Spanish surnamed.
[4] Oriental.
[5] American Indian.
*Participation rates.

Source: Equal Employment Opportunity Report No. 1, Washington, D.C.: Equal Employment Opportunity Commission, 1969.

TABLE 56. Minority Group Employment by Occupation in the Los Angeles SMSA, 1969.

	Total Empl.	White-Collar	Off. Mgrs.	Prof.	Tech.	Sales Wkrs.	Off. Cler.	Blue-Collar	Craft.	Oper.	Labor.	Serv. Wkrs.
All T	994,390	575,913	94,657	124,482	54,624	86,958	215,192	357,522	130,590	168,170	58,762	60,955
All M	660,151	333,751	83,918	104,433	42,812	52,813	49,775	290,326	122,871	126,455	41,000	36,074
All F	334,239	242,162	10,739	20,049	11,812	34,145	165,417	67,196	7,719	41,715	17,762	24,881
Ang T[1]	776,991	501,846	89,147	114,335	45,403	77,180	175,781	237,065	105,005	104,227	27,833	38,080
Ang M	519,098	299,773	79,318	96,837	36,289	47,056	40,273	198,150	99,659	79,209	19,282	21,175
Ang F	257,893	202,073	9,829	17,498	9,114	30,124	135,508	38,915	5,346	25,018	8,551	16,905
Neg T[2]	79,947	26,201	1,557	2,422	3,456	3,876	14,890	40,331	7,310	22,927	10,094	13,415
Neg M	50,431	10,278	1,159	1,632	1,944	2,135	3,408	31,476	6,657	17,482	7,337	8,677
Neg F	29,516	15,923	398	790	1,512	1,741	11,482	8,855	653	5,445	2,757	4,738
SSA T[3]	110,956	30,384	2,583	2,787	3,399	4,176	17,439	72,665	15,668	37,774	19,223	7,907
SSA M	74,417	13,984	2,261	2,125	2,711	2,478	4,409	55,178	14,208	27,617	13,353	5,255
SSA F	36,539	16,400	322	662	688	1,698	13,030	17,487	1,460	10,157	5,870	2,652
Ori T[4]	23,536	16,366	1,186	4,801	2,190	1,616	6,573	5,814	2,059	2,407	1,348	1,356
Ori M	14,087	9,103	1,028	3,723	1,732	1,069	1,551	4,135	1,825	1,489	821	849
Ori F	9,449	7,263	158	1,078	458	547	5,022	1,679	234	918	527	507
AmI T[5]	2,960	1,116	184	137	176	110	509	1,647	548	835	264	197
AmI M	2,118	613	152	116	136	75	134	1,387	522	658	207	118
AmI F	842	503	32	21	40	35	375	260	26	177	57	79
Ang T PR*	78.1	87.1	94.2	91.8	83.1	88.8	81.7	66.3	80.4	62.0	47.4	62.5
Ang M PR	78.6	89.8	94.5	92.7	84.8	89.1	80.9	68.3	81.1	62.6	47.0	58.7
Ang F PR	77.2	83.4	91.5	87.3	77.2	88.2	81.9	57.9	69.3	60.0	48.1	67.9
Neg T PR	8.0	4.5	1.6	1.9	6.3	4.5	6.9	11.3	5.6	13.6	17.2	22.0
Neg M PR	7.6	3.1	1.4	1.6	4.5	4.0	6.8	10.8	5.4	13.8	17.9	24.1
Neg F PR	8.8	6.6	3.7	3.9	12.8	5.1	6.9	13.2	8.5	13.1	15.5	19.0
SSA T PR	11.2	5.3	2.7	2.2	6.2	4.8	8.1	20.3	12.0	22.5	32.7	13.0
SSA M PR	11.3	4.2	2.7	2.0	6.3	4.7	8.9	19.0	11.6	21.8	32.6	14.6
SSA F PR	10.9	6.8	3.0	3.3	5.8	5.0	7.9	26.1	18.9	24.3	33.0	10.7

Table 56 continued

	Total Empl.	White-Collar	Off. Mgrs.	Prof.	Tech.	Sales Wkrs.	Off. Cler.	Blue-Collar	Craft.	Oper.	Labor.	Serv. Wkrs.
Ori T PR	2.4	2.8	1.3	3.9	4.0	1.9	3.1	1.6	1.6	1.4	2.3	2.2
Ori M PR	2.1	2.7	1.2	3.6	4.0	2.0	3.1	1.4	1.5	1.2	2.0	2.4
Ori F PR	2.8	3.0	1.5	5.4	3.9	1.6	3.0	2.5	3.0	2.2	3.0	2.0
Aml T PR	0.3	0.2	0.2	0.1	0.3	0.1	0.2	0.5	0.4	0.5	0.4	0.3
Aml M PR	0.3	0.2	0.2	0.1	0.3	0.1	0.3	0.5	0.4	0.5	0.5	0.3
Aml F PR	0.3	0.2	0.3	0.1	0.3	0.1	0.2	0.4	0.3	0.4	0.3	0.3

[1] All other.
[2] Negro.
[3] Spanish surnamed.
[4] Oriental.
[5] American Indian.
*Participation rates.

Source: Equal Employment Opportunity Report No. 1, Washington, D.C.: Equal Employment Opportunity Commission, 1969.

FROM: EQUAL EMPLOYMENT OPPORTUNITY COMMISSION
        1800 G Street, N.W.
        Washington, D.C. 20506

PUBLIC LAW 88-352

88th Congress, H.R. 7152
July 2,1964

AN ACT

TITLE VII—EQUAL EMPLOYMENT OPPORTUNITY

DEFINITIONS

Sec. 701. For the purposes of this title—
(a) The term "person" includes one or more individuals, labor "Person."
unions, partnerships, associations, corporations, legal representatives,
mutual companies, joint-stock companies, trusts, unincorporated
organizations, trustees, trustees in bankruptcy, or receivers.
(b) The term "employer" means a person engaged in an industry "Employer."
affecting commerce who has twenty-five or more employees for each
working day in each of twenty or more calendar weeks in the current
or preceding calendar year, and any agent of such a person, but such
term does not include (1) the United States, a corporation wholly
owned by the Government of the United States, an Indian tribe, or a
State or political subdivision thereof, (2) a bona fide private membership club (other than a labor organization) which is exempt from
taxation under section 501(c) of the Internal Revenue Code of 1954:   68A Stat. 163;
Provided, That during the first year after the effective date prescribed   74 Stat. 534.
in subsection (a) of section 716, persons having fewer than one hun-   26 USC 501.

dred employees (and their agents) shall not be considered employers, and, during the second year after such date, persons having fewer than seventy-five employees (and their agents) shall not be considered employers, and, during the third year after such date, persons having fewer than fifty employees (and their agents) shall not be considered employers: *Provided further*, That it shall be the policy of the United States to insure equal employment opportunities for Federal employees without discrimination because of race, color, religion, sex or national origin and the President shall utilize his existing authority to effectuate this policy.

"Employment agency."

(c) The term "employment agency" means any person regularly undertaking with or without compensation to procure employees for an employer or to procure for employees opportunities to work for an employer and includes an agent of such a person; but shall not include an agency of the United States, or an agency of a State or political subdivision of a State, except that such term shall include the United States Employment Service and the system of State and local employment services receiving Federal assistance.

"Labor organization."

(d) The term "labor organization" means a labor organization engaged in an industry affecting commerce, and any agent of such an organization, and includes any organization of any kind, any agency, or employee representation committee, group, association, or plan so engaged in which employees participate and which exists for the purpose, in whole or in part, of dealing with employers concerning grievances, labor disputes, wages, rates of pay, hours, or other terms or conditions of employment, and any conference, general committee, joint or system board, or joint council so engaged which is subordinate to a national or international labor organization.

(e) A labor organization shall be deemed to be engaged in an industry affecting commerce if (1) it maintains or operates a hiring hall or hiring office which procures employees for an employer or procures for employees opportunities to work for an employer, or (2) the number of its members (or, where it is a labor organization composed of other labor organizations or their representatives, if the aggregate number of the members of such other labor organization) is (A) one hundred or more during the first year after the effective date prescribed in subsection (a) of section 716, (B) seventy-five or more during the second year after such date or fifty or more during the third year, or (C) twenty-five or more thereafter, and such labor organization—

61 Stat. 136.
29 USC 167.
44 Stat. 577;
49 Stat. 1189.
45 USC 151.

(1) is the certified representative of employees under the provisions of the National Labor Relations Act, as amended, or the Railway Labor Act, as amended;

(2) although not certified, is a national or international labor organization or a local labor organization recognized or acting as the representative of employees of an employer or employers engaged in an industry affecting commerce; or

(3) has chartered a local labor organization or subsidiary body which is representing or actively seeking to represent employees of employers within the meaning of paragraph (1) or (2); or

(4) has been chartered by a labor organization representing or actively seeking to represent employees within the meaning of paragraph (1) or (2) as the local or subordinate body through which such employees may enjoy membership or become affiliated with such labor organization; or

(5) is a conference, general committee, joint or system board, or joint council subordinate to a national or international labor organization, which includes a labor organization engaged in an

industry affecting commerce within the meaning of any of the preceding paragraphs of this subsection.

(f) The term "employee" means an individual employed by an employer.   "Employee."

(g) The term "commerce" means trade, traffic, commerce, transportation, transmission, or communication among the several States; or between a State and any place outside thereof; or within the District of Columbia, or a possession of the United States; or between points in the same State but through a point outside thereof.   "Commerce."

(h) The term "industry affecting commerce" means any activity, business, or industry in commerce or in which a labor dispute would hinder or obstruct commerce or the free flow of commerce and includes any activity or industry "affecting commerce" within the meaning of the Labor-Management Reporting and Disclosure Act of 1959.   "Industry affecting commerce."

73 Stat. 519.
29 USC 401 note.

(i) The term "State" includes a State of the United States, the District of Columbia, Puerto Rico, the Virgin Islands, American Samoa, Guam, Wake Island, the Canal Zone, and Outer Continental Shelf lands defined in the Outer Continental Shelf Lands Act.   "State."

67 Stat. 462.
43 USC 1331 note.

EXEMPTION

SEC. 702. This title shall not apply to an employer with respect to the employment of aliens outside any State, or to a religious corporation, association, or society with respect to the employment of individuals of a particular religion to perform work connected with the carrying on by such corporation, association, or society of its religious activities or to an educational institution with respect to the employment of individuals to perform work connected with the educational activities of such institution.   Religious organizations, etc.

DISCRIMINATION BECAUSE OF RACE, COLOR, RELIGION, SEX, OR NATIONAL ORIGIN

SEC. 703. (a) It shall be an unlawful employment practice for an employer—   Unlawful practices.
Employers.

(1) to fail or refuse to hire or to discharge any individual, or otherwise to discriminate against any individual with respect to his compensation, terms, conditions, or privileges of employment, because of such individual's race, color, religion, sex, or national origin; or

(2) to limit, segregate, or classify his employees in any way which would deprive or tend to deprive any individual of employment opportunities or otherwise adversely affect his status as an employee, because of such individual's race, color, religion, sex, or national origin.

(b) It shall be an unlawful employment practice for an employment agency to fail or refuse to refer for employment, or otherwise to discriminate against, any individual because of his race, color, religion, sex, or national origin, or to classify or refer for employment any individual on the basis of his race, color, religion, sex, or national origin.   Employment agency.

(c) It shall be an unlawful employment practice for a labor organization—   Labor organization.

(1) to exclude or to expel from its membership, or otherwise to discriminate against, any individual because of his race, color, religion, sex, or national origin;

(2) to limit, segregate, or classify its membership, or to classify or fail or refuse to refer for employment any individual, in any

way which would deprive or tend to deprive any individual of employment opportunities, or would limit such employment opportunities or otherwise adversely affect his status as an employee or as an applicant for employment, because of such individual's race, color, religion, sex, or national origin; or

(3) to cause or attempt to cause an employer to discriminate against an individual in violation of this section.

Training programs.

(d) It shall be an unlawful employment practice for any employer, labor organization, or joint labor-management committee controlling apprenticeship or other training or retraining, including on-the-job training programs to discriminate against any individual because of his race, color, religion, sex, or national origin in admission to, or employment in, any program established to provide apprenticeship or other training.

Exceptions.

(e) Notwithstanding any other provision of this title, (1) it shall not be an unlawful employment practice for an employer to hire and employ employees, for an employment agency to classify, or refer for employment any individual, for a labor organization to classify its membership or to classify or refer for employment any individual, or for an employer, labor organization, or joint labor-management committee controlling apprenticeship or other training or retraining programs to admit or employ any individual in any such program, on the basis of his religion, sex, or national origin in those certain instances where religion, sex, or national origin is a bona fide occupational qualification reasonably necessary to the normal operation of that particular business or enterprise, and (2) it shall not be an unlawful employment practice for a school, college, university, or other educational institution or institution of learning to hire and employ employees of a particular religion if such school, college, university, or other educational institution or institution of learning is, in whole or in substantial part, owned, supported, controlled, or managed by a particular religion or by a particular religious corporation, association, or society, or if the curriculum of such school, college, university, or other educational institution or institution of learning is directed toward the propagation of a particular religion.

(f) As used in this title, the phrase "unlawful employment practice" shall not be deemed to include any action or measure taken by an employer, labor organization, joint labor-management committee, or employment agency with respect to an individual who is a member of the Communist Party of the United States or of any other organization required to register as a Communist-action or Communist-front organization by final order of the Subversive Activities Control Board pursuant to the Subversive Activities Control Act of 1950.

64 Stat. 987.
50 USC 781 note.

(g) Notwithstanding any other provision of this title, it shall not be an unlawful employment practice for an employer to fail or refuse to hire and employ any individual for any position, for an employer to discharge any individual from any position, or for an employment agency to fail or refuse to refer any individual for employment in any position, or for a labor organization to fail or refuse to refer any individual for employment in any position, if—

(1) the occupancy of such position, or access to the premises in or upon which any part of the duties of such position is performed or is to be performed, is subject to any requirement imposed in the interest of the national security of the United States under any security program in effect pursuant to or administered under any statute of the United States or any Executive order of the President; and

(2) such individual has not fulfilled or has ceased to fulfill that requirement.

(h) Notwithstanding any other provision of this title, it shall not be an unlawful employment practice for an employer to apply different standards of compensation, or different terms, conditions, or privileges of employment pursuant to a bona fide seniority or merit system, or a system which measures earnings by quantity or quality of production or to employees who work in different locations, provided that such differences are not the result of an intention to discriminate because of race, color, religion, sex, or national origin, nor shall it be an unlawful employment practice for an employer to give and to act upon the results of any professionally developed ability test provided that such test, its administration or action upon the results is not designed, intended or used to discriminate because of race, color, religion, sex or national origin. It shall not be an unlawful employment practice under this title for any employer to differentiate upon the basis of sex in determining the amount of the wages or compensation paid or to be paid to employees of such employer if such differentiation is authorized by the provisions of section 6(d) of the Fair Labor Standards Act of 1938, as amended (29 U.S.C. 206(d)). 77 Stat. 56.
29 USC 206.
Indians.

(i) Nothing contained in this title shall apply to any business or enterprise on or near an Indian reservation with respect to any publicly announced employment practice of such business or enterprise under which a preferential treatment is given to any individual because he is an Indian living on or near a reservation.

(j) Nothing contained in this title shall be interpreted to require Preferential
any employer, employment agency, labor organization, or joint labor- treatment.
management committee subject to this title to grant preferential treatment to any individual or to any group because of the race, color, religion, sex, or national origin of such individual or group on account of an imbalance which may exist with respect to the total number or percentage of persons of any race, color, religion, sex, or national origin employed by any employer, referred or classified for employment by any employment agency or labor organization, admitted to membership or classified by any labor organization, or admitted to, or employed in, any apprenticeship or other training program, in comparison with the total number or percentage of persons of such race, color, religion, sex, or national origin in any community, State, section, or other area, or in the available work force in any community, State, section, or other area.

OTHER UNLAWFUL EMPLOYMENT PRACTICES

Sec. 704. (a) It shall be an unlawful employment practice for an employer to discriminate against any of his employees or applicants for employment, for an employment agency to discriminate against any individual, or for a labor organization to discriminate against any member thereof or applicant for membership, because he has opposed any practice made an unlawful employment practice by this title, or because he has made a charge, testified, assisted, or participated in any manner in an investigation, proceeding, or hearing under this title.

(b) It shall be an unlawful employment practice for an employer, labor organization, or employment agency to print or publish or cause to be printed or published any notice or advertisement relating to employment by such an employer or membership in or any classification or referral for employment by such a labor organization, or relating to any classification or referral for employment by such an employment agency, indicating any preference, limitation, specification, or discrimination, based on race, color, religion, sex, or national origin, except that such a notice or advertisement may indicate a preference, limitation, specification, or discrimination based on religion, sex, or national origin when religion, sex, or national origin is a bona fide occupational qualification for employment.

EQUAL EMPLOYMENT OPPORTUNITY COMMISSION

Establishment.

Term of office.

SEC. 705. (a) There is hereby created a Commission to be known as the Equal Employment Opportunity Commission, which shall be composed of five members, not more than three of whom shall be members of the same political party, who shall be appointed by the President by and with the advice and consent of the Senate. One of the original members shall be appointed for a term of one year, one for a term of two years, one for a term of three years, one for a term of four years, and one for a term of five years, beginning from the date of enactment of this title, but their successors shall be appointed for terms of five years each, except that any individual chosen to fill a vacancy shall be appointed only for the unexpired term of the member whom he shall succeed. The President shall designate one member to serve as Chairman of the Commission, and one member to serve as Vice Chairman. The Chairman shall be responsible on behalf of the Commission for the administrative operations of the Commission, and shall appoint, in accordance with the civil service laws, such officers, agents, attorneys, and employees as it deems necessary to assist it in the performance of its functions and to fix their compensation in accordance with the Classification Act of 1949, as amended. The Vice Chairman shall act as Chairman in the absence or disability of the Chairman or in the event of a vacancy in that office.

63 Stat. 954;
76 Stat. 843.
5 USC 1071 note.

(b) A vacancy in the Commission shall not impair the right of the remaining members to exercise all the powers of the Commission and three members thereof shall constitute a quorum.

(c) The Commission shall have an official seal which shall be judicially noticed.

Reports to the
President and
Congress.

(d) The Commission shall at the close of each fiscal year report to the Congress and to the President concerning the action it has taken; the names, salaries, and duties of all individuals in its employ and the moneys it has disbursed; and shall make such further reports on the cause of and means of eliminating discrimination and such recommendations for further legislation as may appear desirable.

70 Stat. 736.
5 USC 2201 note.

(e) The Federal Executive Pay Act of 1956, as amended (5 U.S.C. 2201–2209), is further amended—

(1) by adding to section 105 thereof (5 U.S.C. 2204) the following clause:

"(32) Chairman, Equal Employment Opportunity Commission"; and

70 Stat. 737.
5 USC 2205.

(2) by adding to clause (45) of section 106(a) thereof (5 U.S.C. 2205(a)) the following: "Equal Employment Opportunity Commission (4)."

(f) The principal office of the Commission shall be in or near the District of Columbia, but it may meet or exercise any or all its powers at any other place. The Commission may establish such regional or State offices as it deems necessary to accomplish the purpose of this title.

Powers.

(g) The Commission shall have power—

(1) to cooperate with and, with their consent, utilize regional, State, local, and other agencies, both public and private, and individuals;

(2) to pay to witnesses whose depositions are taken or who are summoned before the Commission or any of its agents the same witness and mileage fees as are paid to witnesses in the courts of the United States;

(3) to furnish to persons subject to this title such technical assistance as they may request to further their compliance with this title or an order issued thereunder;

(4) upon the request of (i) any employer, whose employees or some of them, or (ii) any labor organization, whose members or some of them, refuse or threaten to refuse to cooperate in effectuating the provisions of this title, to assist in such effectuation by conciliation or such other remedial action as is provided by this title;

(5) to make such technical studies as are appropriate to effectuate the purposes and policies of this title and to make the results of such studies available to the public;

(6) to refer matters to the Attorney General with recommendations for intervention in a civil action brought by an aggrieved party under section 706, or for the institution of a civil action by the Attorney General under section 707, and to advise, consult, and assist the Attorney General on such matters.

(h) Attorneys appointed under this section may, at the direction of the Commission, appear for and represent the Commission in any case in court.

(i) The Commission shall, in any of its educational or promotional activities, cooperate with other departments and agencies in the performance of such educational and promotional activities.

(j) All officers, agents, attorneys, and employees of the Commission shall be subject to the provisions of section 9 of the Act of August 2, 1939, as amended (the Hatch Act), notwithstanding any exemption contained in such section. 53 Stat. 1148; 64 Stat. 475. 5 USC 1181.

PREVENTION OF UNLAWFUL EMPLOYMENT PRACTICES

SEC. 706. (a) Whenever it is charged in writing under oath by a person claiming to be aggrieved, or a written charge has been filed by a member of the Commission where he has reasonable cause to believe a violation of this title has occurred (and such charge sets forth the facts upon which it is based) that an employer, employment agency, or labor organization has engaged in an unlawful employment practice, the Commission shall furnish such employer, employment agency, or labor organization (hereinafter referred to as the "respondent") with a copy of such charge and shall make an investigation of such charge, provided that such charge shall not be made public by the Commission. If the Commission shall determine, after such investigation, that there is reasonable cause to believe that the charge is true, the Commission shall endeavor to eliminate any such alleged unlawful employment practice by informal methods of conference, conciliation, and persuasion. Nothing said or done during and as a part of such endeavors may be made public by the Commission without the written consent of the parties, or used as evidence in a subsequent proceeding. Any officer or employee of the Commission, who shall make public in any manner whatever any information in violation of this subsection shall be deemed guilty of a misdemeanor and upon conviction thereof shall be fined not more than $1,000 or imprisoned not more than one year.

(b) In the case of an alleged unlawful employment practice occurring in a State, or political subdivision of a State, which has a State or local law prohibiting the unlawful employment practice alleged and establishing or authorizing a State or local authority to grant or seek relief from such practice or to institute criminal proceedings with respect thereto upon receiving notice thereof, no charge may be filed under subsection (a) by the person aggrieved before the expira- Legal proceedings.

tion of sixty days after proceedings have been commenced under the State or local law, unless such proceedings have been earlier terminated, provided that such sixty-day period shall be extended to one hundred and twenty days during the first year after the effective date of such State or local law. If any requirement for the commencement of such proceedings is imposed by a State or local authority other than a requirement of the filing of a written and signed statement of the facts upon which the proceeding is based, the proceeding shall be deemed to have been commenced for the purposes of this subsection at the time such statement is sent by registered mail to the appropriate State or local authority.

Time requirements.

(c) In the case of any charge filed by a member of the Commission alleging an unlawful employment practice occurring in a State or political subdivision of a State, which has a State or local law prohibiting the practice alleged and establishing or authorizing a State or local authority to grant or seek relief from such practice or to institute criminal proceedings with respect thereto upon receiving notice thereof, the Commission shall, before taking any action with respect to such charge, notify the appropriate State or local officials and, upon request, afford them a reasonable time, but not less than sixty days (provided that such sixty-day period shall be extended to one hundred and twenty days during the first year after the effective day of such State or local law), unless a shorter period is requested, to act under such State or local law to remedy the practice alleged.

(d) A charge under subsection (a) shall be filed within ninety days after the alleged unlawful employment practice occurred, except that in the case of an unlawful employment practice with respect to which the person aggrieved has followed the procedure set out in subsection (b), such charge shall be filed by the person aggrieved within two hundred and ten days after the alleged unlawful employment practice occurred, or within thirty days after receiving notice that the State or local agency has terminated the proceedings under the State or local law, whichever is earlier, and a copy of such charge shall be filed by the Commission with the State or local agency.

(e) If within thirty days after a charge is filed with the Commission or within thirty days after expiration of any period of reference under subsection (c) (except that in either case such period may be extended to not more than sixty days upon a determination by the Commission that further efforts to secure voluntary compliance are warranted), the Commission has been unable to obtain voluntary compliance with this title, the Commission shall so notify the person aggrieved and a civil action may, within thirty days thereafter, be brought against the respondent named in the charge (1) by the person claiming to be aggrieved, or (2) if such charge was filed by a member of the Commission, by any person whom the charge alleges was aggrieved by the alleged unlawful employment practice. Upon application by the complainant and in such circumstances as the court may deem just, the court may appoint an attorney for such complainant and may authorize the commencement of the action without the payment of fees, costs, or security. Upon timely application, the court may, in its discretion, permit the Attorney General to intervene in such civil action if he certifies that the case is of general public importance. Upon request, the court may, in its discretion, stay further proceedings for not more than sixty days pending the termination of State or local proceedings described in subsection (b) or the efforts of the Commission to obtain voluntary compliance.

Courts. Jurisdiction.

(f) Each United States district court and each United States court of a place subject to the jurisdiction of the United States shall have jurisdiction of actions brought under this title. Such an action may be brought in any judicial district in the State in which the unlawful employment practice is alleged to have been committed, in the judicial district in which the employment records relevant to such practice are maintained and administered, or in the judicial district in which the plaintiff would have worked but for the alleged unlawful employment practice, but if the respondent is not found within any such district, such an action may be brought within the judicial district in which the respondent has his principal office. For purposes of sections 1404 and 1406 of title 28 of the United States Code, the judicial district in which the respondent has his principal office shall in all cases be considered a district in which the action might have been brought. 62 Stat. 937.
74 Stat. 912;
76A Stat. 699.

(g) If the court finds that the respondent has intentionally engaged in or is intentionally engaging in an unlawful employment practice charged in the complaint, the court may enjoin the respondent from engaging in such unlawful employment practice, and order such affirmative action as may be appropriate, which may include reinstatement or hiring of employees, with or without back pay (payable by the employer, employment agency, or labor organization, as the case may be, responsible for the unlawful employment practice). Interim earnings or amounts earnable with reasonable diligence by the person or persons discriminated against shall operate to reduce the back pay otherwise allowable. No order of the court shall require the admission or reinstatement of an individual as a member of a union or the hiring, reinstatement, or promotion of an individual as an employee, or the payment to him of any back pay, if such individual was refused admission, suspended, or expelled or was refused employment or advancement or was suspended or discharged for any reason other than discrimination on account of race, color, religion, sex or national origin or in violation of section 704(a).

(h) The provisions of the Act entitled "An Act to amend the Judicial Code and to define and limit the jurisdiction of courts sitting in equity, and for other purposes," approved March 23, 1932 (29 U.S.C. 101–115), shall not apply with respect to civil actions brought under this section. 47 Stat. 70.

(i) In any case in which an employer, employment agency, or labor organization fails to comply with an order of a court issued in a civil action brought under subsection (e), the Commission may commence proceedings to compel compliance with such order.

(j) Any civil action brought under subsection (e) and any proceedings brought under subsection (i) shall be subject to appeal as provided in sections 1291 and 1292, title 28. United States Code. 62 Stat. 929.

(k) In any action or proceeding under this title the court, in its discretion, may allow the prevailing party, other than the Commission or the United States, a reasonable attorney's fee as part of the costs, and the Commission and the United States shall be liable for costs the same as a private person. 65 Stat. 726;
72 Stat. 348,
1770.
Costs, fees.

SEC. 707. (a) Whenever the Attorney General has reasonable cause to believe that any person or group of persons is engaged in a pattern or practice of resistance to the full enjoyment of any of the rights secured by this title, and that the pattern or practice is of such a nature and is intended to deny the full exercise of the rights herein described, the Attorney General may bring a civil action in the appropriate district court of the United States by filing with it a complaint (1) signed by him (or in his absence the Acting Attorney General), (2) setting forth facts pertaining to such pattern or practice, and (3) requesting such relief, including an application for a permanent or temporary injunction, restraining order or other order against the Suits by Attorney General.

person or persons responsible for such pattern or practice, as he deems necessary to insure the full enjoyment of the rights herein described.

(b) The district courts of the United States shall have and shall exercise jurisdiction of proceedings instituted pursuant to this section, and in any such proceeding the Attorney General may file with the clerk of such court a request that a court of three judges be convened to hear and determine the case. Such request by the Attorney General shall be accompanied by a certificate that, in his opinion, the case is of general public importance. A copy of the certificate and request for a three-judge court shall be immediately furnished by such clerk to the chief judge of the circuit (or in his absence, the presiding circuit judge of the circuit) in which the case is pending. Upon receipt of such request it shall be the duty of the chief judge of the circuit or the presiding circuit judge, as the case may be, to designate immediately three judges in such circuit, of whom at least one shall be a circuit judge and another of whom shall be a district judge of the court in which the proceeding was instituted, to hear and determine such case, and it shall be the duty of the judges so designated to assign the case for hearing at the earliest practicable date, to participate in the hearing and determination thereof, and to cause the case to be in every way expedited. An appeal from the final judgment of such court will lie to the Supreme Court.

In the event the Attorney General fails to file such a request in any such proceeding, it shall be the duty of the chief judge of the district (or in his absence, the acting chief judge) in which the case is pending immediately to designate a judge in such district to hear and determine the case. In the event that no judge in the district is available to hear and determine the case, the chief judge of the district, or the acting chief judge, as the case may be, shall certify this fact to the chief judge of the circuit (or in his absence, the acting chief judge) who shall then designate a district or circuit judge of the circuit to hear and determine the case.

It shall be the duty of the judge designated pursuant to this section to assign the case for hearing at the earliest practicable date and to cause the case to be in every way expedited.

EFFECT ON STATE LAWS

SEC. 708. Nothing in this title shall be deemed to exempt or relieve any person from any liability, duty, penalty, or punishment provided by any present or future law of any State or political subdivision of a State, other than any such law which purports to require or permit the doing of any act which would be an unlawful employment practice under this title.

INVESTIGATIONS, INSPECTIONS, RECORDS, STATE AGENCIES

SEC. 709. (a) In connection with any investigation of a charge filed under section 706, the Commission or its designated representative shall at all reasonable times have access to, for the purposes of examination, and the right to copy any evidence of any person being investigated or proceeded against that relates to unlawful employment practices covered by this title and is relevant to the charge under investigation.

Agreements, State and local agencies.

(b) The Commission may cooperate with State and local agencies charged with the administration of State fair employment practices laws and, with the consent of such agencies, may for the purpose of carrying out its functions and duties under this title and within the limitation of funds appropriated specifically for such purpose, utilize the services of such agencies and their employees and, notwithstanding any other provision of law, may reimburse such agencies and their employees for services rendered to assist the Commission in carrying out this title. In furtherance of such cooperative efforts, the Commission may enter into written agreements with such State or local agencies and such agreements may include provisions under which the Commission shall refrain from processing a charge in any cases or class of cases specified in such agreements and under which no person may bring a civil action under section 706 in any cases or class of cases so specified, or under which the Commission shall relieve any person or class of persons in such State or locality from requirements imposed under this section. The Commission shall rescind any such agreement whenever it determines that the agreement no longer serves the interest of effective enforcement of this title.

(c) Except as provided in subsection (d), every employer, employment agency, and labor organization subject to this title shall (1) make and keep such records relevant to the determinations of whether unlawful employment practices have been or are being committed, (2) preserve such records for such periods, and (3) make such reports therefrom, as the Commission shall prescribe by regulation or order, after public hearing, as reasonable, necessary, or appropriate for the enforcement of this title or the regulations or orders thereunder. The Commission shall, by regulation, require each employer, labor organization, and joint labor-management committee subject to this title which controls an apprenticeship or other training program to maintain such records as are reasonably necessary to carry out the purpose of this title, including, but not limited to, a list of applicants who wish to participate in such program, including the chronological order in which such applications were received, and shall furnish to the Commission, upon request, a detailed description of the manner in which persons are selected to participate in the apprenticeship or other training program. Any employer, employment agency, labor organization, or joint labor-management committee which believes that the application to it of any regulation or order issued under this section would result in undue hardship may (1) apply to the Commission for an exemption from the application of such regulation or order, or (2) bring a civil action in the United States district court for the district where such records are kept. If the Commission or the court, as the case may be, finds that the application of the regulation or order to the employer, employment agency, or labor organization in question would impose an undue hardship, the Commission or the court, as the case may be, may grant appropriate relief. *(Records.)*

(d) The provisions of subsection (c) shall not apply to any employer, employment agency, labor organization, or joint labor-management committee with respect to matters occurring in any State or political subdivision thereof which has a fair employment practice law during any period in which such employer, employment agency, labor organization, or joint labor-management committee is subject to such law, except that the Commission may require such notations on records which such employer, employment agency, labor organization, or joint labor-management committee keeps or is required to keep as are necessary because of differences in coverage or methods of enforcement between the State or local law and the provisions of this title. Where an employer is required by Executive Order 10925, issued March 6, 1961, or by any other Executive order prescribing fair employment practices for Government contractors and subcontractors, or by rules or regulations issued thereunder, to file reports relating to his employment practices with any Federal agency or committee, and he is substantially in compliance with such requirements, the Commission shall not require him to file additional reports pursuant to subsection (c) of this section. *(Exceptions.)* *(3 CFR, 1961 Supp., p. 86. 5 USC 631 note.)*

Prohibited
disclosures.

(e) It shall be unlawful for any officer or employee of the Commission to make public in any manner whatever any information obtained by the Commission pursuant to its authority under this section prior to the institution of any proceeding under this title involving such information. Any officer or employee of the Commission who shall make public in any manner whatever any information in violation of this subsection shall be guilty of a misdemeanor and upon conviction thereof, shall be fined not more than $1,000, or imprisoned not more than one year.

INVESTIGATORY POWERS

Sec. 710. (a) For the purposes of any investigation of a charge filed under the authority contained in section 706, the Commission shall have authority to examine witnesses under oath and to require the production of documentary evidence relevant or material to the charge under investigation.

(b) If the respondent named in a charge filed under section 706 fails or refuses to comply with a demand of the Commission for permission to examine or to copy evidence in conformity with the provisions of section 709(a), or if any person required to comply with the provisions of section 709 (c) or (d) fails or refuses to do so, or if any person fails or refuses to comply with a demand by the Commission to give testimony under oath, the United States district court for the district in which such person is found, resides, or transacts business, shall, upon application of the Commission, have jurisdiction to issue to such person an order requiring him to comply with the provisions of section 709 (c) or (d) or to comply with the demand of the Commission, but the attendance of a witness may not be required outside the State where he is found, resides, or transacts business and the production of evidence may not be required outside the State where such evidence is kept.

Petitions.

(c) Within twenty days after the service upon any person charged under section 706 of a demand by the Commission for the production of documentary evidence or for permission to examine or to copy evidence in conformity with the provisions of section 709(a), such person may file in the district court of the United States for the judicial district in which he resides, is found, or transacts business, and serve upon the Commission a petition for an order of such court modifying or setting aside such demand. The time allowed for compliance with the demand in whole or in part as deemed proper and ordered by the court shall not run during the pendency of such petition in the court. Such petition shall specify each ground upon which the petitioner relies in seeking such relief, and may be based upon any failure of such demand to comply with the provisions of this title or with the limitations generally applicable to compulsory process or upon any constitutional or other legal right or privilege of such person. No objection which is not raised by such a petition may be urged in the defense to a proceeding initiated by the Commission under subsection (b) for enforcement of such a demand unless such proceeding is commenced by the Commission prior to the expiration of the twenty-day period, or unless the court determines that the defendant could not reasonably have been aware of the availability of such ground of objection.

(d) In any proceeding brought by the Commission under subsection (b), except as provided in subsection (c) of this section, the defendant may petition the court for an order modifying or setting aside the demand of the Commission.

NOTICES TO BE POSTED

SEC. 711. (a) Every employer, employment agency, and labor organization, as the case may be, shall post and keep posted in conspicuous places upon its premises where notices to employees, applicants for employment, and members are customarily posted a notice to be prepared or approved by the Commission setting forth excerpts from or, summaries of, the pertinent provisions of this title and information pertinent to the filing of a complaint.

(b) A willful violation of this section shall be punishable by a fine of not more than $100 for each separate offense.

VETERANS' PREFERENCE

SEC. 712. Nothing contained in this title shall be construed to repeal or modify any Federal, State, territorial, or local law creating special rights or preference for veterans.

RULES AND REGULATIONS

SEC. 713. (a) The Commission shall have authority from time to time to issue, amend, or rescind suitable procedural regulations to carry out the provisions of this title. Regulations issued under this section shall be in conformity with the standards and limitations of the Administrative Procedure Act.

60 Stat. 237. 5 USC 1001 note.

(b) In any action or proceeding based on any alleged unlawful employment practice, no person shall be subject to any liability or punishment for or on account of (1) the commission by such person of an unlawful employment practice if he pleads and proves that the act or omission complained of was in good faith, in conformity with, and in reliance on any written interpretation or opinion of the Commission, or (2) the failure of such person to publish and file any information required by any provision of this title if he pleads and proves that he failed to publish and file such information in good faith, in conformity with the instructions of the Commission issued under this title regarding the filing of such information. Such a defense, if established, shall be a bar to the action or proceeding, notwithstanding that (A) after such act or omission, such interpretation or opinion is modified or rescinded or is determined by judicial authority to be invalid or of no legal effect, or (B) after publishing or filing the description and annual reports, such publication or filing is determined by judicial authority not to be in conformity with the requirements of this title.

FORCIBLY RESISTING THE COMMISSION OR ITS REPRESENTATIVES

SEC. 714. The provisions of section 111, title 18, United States Code, shall apply to officers, agents, and employees of the Commission in the performance of their official duties.

62 Stat. 688.

SPECIAL STUDY BY SECRETARY OF LABOR

SEC. 715. The Secretary of Labor shall make a full and complete study of the factors which might tend to result in discrimination in employment because of age and of the consequences of such discrimination on the economy and individuals affected. The Secretary of Labor shall make a report to the Congress not later than June 30, 1965, containing the results of such study and shall include in such report such recommendations for legislation to prevent arbitrary discrimination in employment because of age as he determines advisable.

Report to Congress.

EFFECTIVE DATE

SEC. 716. (a) This title shall become effective one year after the date of its enactment.

(b) Notwithstanding subsection (a), sections of this title other than sections 703, 704, 706, and 707 shall become effective immediately.

Presidential conferences.

(c) The President shall, as soon as feasible after the enactment of this title, convene one or more conferences for the purpose of enabling the leaders of groups whose members will be affected by this title to become familiar with the rights afforded and obligations imposed by its provisions, and for the purpose of making plans which will result in the fair and effective administration of this title when all of its provisions become effective.

Membership.

The President shall invite the participation in such conference or conferences of (1) the members of the President's Committee on Equal Employment Opportunity, (2) the members of the Commission on Civil Rights, (3) representatives of State and local agencies engaged in furthering equal employment opportunity, (4) representatives of private agencies engaged in furthering equal employment opportunity, and (5) representatives of employers, labor organizations, and employment agencies who will be subject to this title.

STATE FAIR EMPLOYMENT PRACTICE LAWS
AUGUST 1965

| State | Date of Enactment | State Law Prohibits Discrimination Based On: | | | Federal Commission Will Defer to State Agency for Period of:* |
		Race, Color, Creed or National Origin	Sex	Age	
ALABAMA					
ALASKA	6/18/63	x	x	x	60 days#
ARIZONA	4/ 1/65	x	x		NONE
ARKANSAS	1960	x	x		
CALIFORNIA	9/18/59	x	x	x	60 days
COLORADO	3/13/57	x	x	x	60 days#
CONNECTICUT	T5/19/47	x	x	x	60 days
DELAWARE	7/ 9/60	x		x	60 days
DIST. OF COL.	7/ 2/65	x	x		120 days#
FLORIDA					
GEORGIA					
HAWAII	1/ 1/64	x	x	x	60 days#
IDAHO	1961	x		x	NONE
ILLINOIS	7/21/61	x	x		60 days
INDIANA	3/ 9/63	x		x	60 days
IOWA	5/ 7/65	x			120 days
KANSAS	4/13/61	x			60 days
KENTUCKY					
LOUISIANA	1950			x	
MAINE	6/ 4/65	x	x	x	NONE
MARYLAND	7/ 1/65	x	x	x	120 days#
MASSACHUSETTS	8/21/46	x	x	x	60 days#
MICHIGAN	1/ 1/64	x	x	x	60 days
MINNESOTA	7/ 1/55	x			60 days
MISSISSIPPI					
MISSOURI	10/13/61	x	x		60 days
MONTANA	3/ 6/65	x	x	x	NONE
NEBRASKA	8/ 4/65	x	x	x	
NEVADA	7/ 1/65	x			120 days
NEW HAMPSHIRE	1965	x	x		
NEW JERSEY	4/16/45	x	x	x	60 days
NEW MEXICO	3/17/49	x			
NEW YORK	7/ 1/52	x	x	x	60 days#
NORTH CAROLINA					
NORTH DAKOTA	1965		x	x	

STATE FAIR EMPLOYMENT PRACTICE LAWS AUGUST 1965 (Continued)

State	Date of Enactment	State Law Prohibits Discrimination Based On:			Federal Commission Will Defer to State Agency for Period of:
		Race, Color, Creed or National Origin	Sex	Age	
OHIO	7/29/59	x	x	x	60 days
OKLAHOMA	1963	x	x		NONE
OREGON	8/13/49	x	x	x	60 days
PENNSYLVANIA	11/28/55	x	x	x	60 days
RHODE ISLAND	9/ 1/59	x	x	x	60 days
SOUTH CAROLINA					
SOUTH DAKOTA					
TENNESSEE					
TEXAS	1919		x	x	
UTAH	3/18/65	x	x		120 days#
VERMONT	1963	x	x		NONE
VIRGINIA					
WASHINGTON	3/19/49	x	x	x	60 days
WEST VIRGINIA	1961	x	x		NONE
WISCONSIN	7/ 5/57	x	x	x	60 days#
WYOMING	7/ 1/65	x	x		120 days#
PUERTO RICO	6/30/59	x		x	60 days

*Federal Commission will not accept a charge of discrimination based on race, color, creed or national origin from individuals in these states unless they have filed charges under the state law and the period of time indicated has elapsed.

The 120 day period of deference is extended to states whose laws were enacted in 1965; in all others the period is 60 days.

No deference to Arizona, Oklahoma and West Virginia because their laws contain no enforcement provisions. No deference to Idaho, Maine, Montana and Vermont because their laws are enforced only under criminal procedures.

#Period of deference also applies to charges of discrimination based on sex.

SUMMARY OF STATE FAIR EMPLOYMENT PRACTICE LAWS

ALASKA

Administered by:
Commissioner of Labor
Box 2141
Juneau, Alaska

Covered by the Act:
Employers of one or more - Labor organizations - Employment agencies

Excluded from the Act:
Nonprofit charitable, educational, religious and fraternal enterprises -
Domestic servants

Illegal practices:
Discrimination on the grounds of race, religion, color, ancestry,
national origin or age by: employers, labor organizations, employment
agencies - Refusal to work with members of minority groups - Reprisals
against persons filing complaints or testifying - Aiding or inciting or
coercing others to violate the Act

Who may file complaint:
The aggrieved person - Employers whose employees refuse or threaten to
refuse to comply with the law

Complaints to be filed within:
Not specified

Commissioner empowered to:
Receive, investigate and pass upon complaints - Conciliate complaints -
Conduct hearings - Issue cease and desist orders

Review and enforcement:
By the Courts - Violation of the law is a misdemeanor

CALIFORNIA

Administered by:
Division of Fair Employment Practices
455 Golden Gate Avenue   107 Broadway
San Francisco 2, California   Los Angeles, California

2550 Mariposa Street   1350 Front Street
Fresno, California   San Diego, California

Covered by th Act:
Private employers of five or more - Labor organizations - Employment
agencies - State and its political subdivisions

Excluded from the Act:
 Nonprofit social, fraternal, charitable, educational or religious
 associations or corporations - Persons employed by family - Domestic
 servants - Agricultural workers residing on farms where employed.

Illegal practices:
 Discrimination on the grounds of race, religious creed, color, national
 origin, ancestry or age by: employers, labor organizations, employment
 agencies, government agencies - Advertisements, inquiries or employment
 applications specifying race, etc. - Reprisals against persons filing
 complaints - Action to obstruct employer's compliance with the Act -
 Aiding, inciting or coercing others to violate the Act.

Who may file complaint:
 The aggrieved person - The Attorney General - The Division Employers whose
 employees refuse or threaten to refuse to comply with the law.

Complaints to be filed within:
 One year

Division empowered to:
 Initiate, receive, investigate and pass upon complaints - Conciliate
 complaints - Conduct hearings - Subpoena witnesses and records - Issue
 cease and desist orders - Order affirmative action - Adopt rules and
 regulations - Seek injunctions - Create advisory agencies and
 conciliation councils - Use the services of other governmental
 departments and agencies. Issue publications - Report annually to
 Governor and Legislature - Formulate policies to eliminate discriminatio
 Make recommendations to the state and local agencies.

Review and enforcement:
 By the courts - Resisting, impeding or violating a division order or
 activity is a misdemeanor.

COLORADO

Administered by:
 Colorado Anti-Discrimination Commission
 306 State Services Building
 1525 Sherman Street
 Denver 3, Colorado

Covered by the Act:
 Private employers of six or more - Labor organizations - Employment
 agencies - State and its political subdivisions - Religious associations
 supported in whole or in part by tax funds or public borrowing.

Excluded from the Act:
 Domestic servants

Illegal practices:
    Discrimination on the grounds of race, color, creed, ancestry or national
    origin by: public or private employers, labor organizations, employment
    agencies, vocational educational institutions, government agencies -
    Discrimination in any apprenticeship or on-the-job training programs or
    vocational school - Refusal to work with members of minority groups -
    Advertisements, inquiries or employment applications specifying race,
    etc. - Aiding, inciting or coercing others to violate the Act

Who may file complaint:
    The aggrieved person - The Commission - The Attorney General - Any
    employer, labor organization or vocational school whose employees or
    members refuse to comply with Act

Complaints to be filed within:
    Six months

Commission empowered to:
    Receive, initiate and investigate complaints - Conciliate complaints -
    Conduct hearings - Subpoena witnesses and records - Issue cease and
    desist orders - Order affirmative action - Formulate educational programs
    to eliminate discrimination - Investigate discrimination and recommend
    further legislation - Issue publications and reports

Review and endorcement:
    By the courts

CONNECTICUT

Administered by:
    Commission on Civil Rights
    State Office Building
    Hartford 15, Connecticut

Covered by the Act:
    All enterprises, including charitable and nonprofit, employing five or
    more - Labor organizations - Employment agencies - State and its
    political subdivisions

Excluded from the Act:
    Domestic servants

Illegal practices:
    Discrimination on the grounds of race, color, religious creed, age,
    (between age of 40 and 65 years) ancestry or national origin by: employers,
    labor organizations, employment agencies - Advertisements or inquiries
    specifying race, etc. - Refusal to work with members of minority groups -
    Reprisals against persons filing complaints - Aiding, inciting or coercing
    others to violate the Act

Who may file complaint:
> The aggrieved person - The Commission - Employers whose employees refuse or threaten to refuse to comply with the law

Complaints to be filed within:
> 90 days

Commission empowered to:
> Receive, initiate and investigate complaints - Conciliate complaints - Appoint hearing tribunal to conduct hearings - Issue cease and desist orders - Order affirmative action - Subpoena witnesses and records - Adopt rules and regulations - Develop educational programs - Conduct research - Recommend policies and legislation for the elimination of discrimination - Issue publications and reports

Review and enforcement:
> By the courts

DELAWARE

Administered by:
> Division Against Discrimination
> Department of Labor and Industrial Relations
> 824 West Street
> Wilmington, Delaware

Covered by the Act:
> Employers - Employment agencies - Labor organizations - Religious, fraternal, sectarian or charitable organizations supported in whole or part by government funds

Excluded from the Act:
> Religious, fraternal, sectarian or charitable organizations if race or creed constitutes a bona fide occupational qualification

Illegal practices:
> Discrimination on grounds of race, creed, color or national origin or age (between 45 and 65 years) by: employer, employment agency, labor organization - Print or circulate any advertisement, application form or make an inquiry which expresses race, etc., unless based on bona fide occupational qualification - Reprisal against person opposing unlawful Act, files a complaint or assists in proceeding - Aiding, abetting or coercing others to violate the law

Who may file complaint:
> The aggrieved person

Complaints to be filed within:
> 90 days

Division empowered to:
    Receive and investigate complaints - Conciliate complaints - Issue
    regulations to enforce Act

Review and enforcement:
    First violation, a $200 fine; second violation, a fine up to $500 and
    imprisonment up to 90 days, or both

HAWAII

Administered by:
    Hawaii Department of Labor
    825 Mililani Street
    Honolulu 13, Hawaii

Covered by the Act:
    All enterprises conducted for profit - Employment agencies - Charitable
    and nonprofit enterprises

Excluded from the Act:
    Religious institutions, and charitable or educational organizations
    operated or controlled by religious institutions may give preference
    to persons of same religion

Illegal practices:
    Discrimination on the grounds of race, sex, age, religion, color or
    ancestry by: employers, employment agencies, labor unions - Advertise-
    ments, inquiries or employment applications specifying race, etc. -
    Reprisals against persons filing complaints or testifying - Aiding or
    inciting others to violate the Act

Who may file complaint:
    The aggrieved person - The Attorney General

Complaints to be filed within:
    90 days

Department empowered to:
    Receive and investigate complaints - Conciliate complaints - Conduct
    hearings - Issue supoenas - Issue cease and desist orders - Order
    affirmative action - Formulate rules and regulations

Review and enforcement:
    By the courts - Penalty for first violation is fine up to $200; and for
    second violation up to $500 fine and 90 days in prison, or both

IDAHO

Administered by:
    Department of Labor
    Industrial Administration Building
    317 Main
    Boise, Idaho

Covered by the Act:
    All enterprises including charitable, religious and nonprofit organization
    State and political subdivisions

Excluded from the Act:
    None specified

Illegal practices:
    Discriminate on grounds of race, creed, color, ancestry or national
    origin by: employers, employment agencies, labor unions, individuals,
    government agencies

Review and enforcement:
    Violation of Act is a misdemeanor and is punished as any other legal
    violation

ILLINOIS

Administered by:
    Fair Employment Practices Commission
    205 West Wacker Drive
    Chicago 6, Illinois

Covered by the Act:
    Employers of 75 or more during 1964; thereafter, employers of 50
    or more - Employers and subcontractors on all public works contracts -
    Employment agencies - Labor organizations - State and its political
    subdivisions and agencies (if employing the minimum number of
    employees)

Excluded from the Act:
    Nonprofit corporation or association organized for fraternal, social or
    religious purposes - Educational or charitable institutions affiliated
    with a church or religious institution - Domestic servants -
    Agricultural workers

Illegal practices
    Discrimination based on race, color, religion, national origin, or
    ancestry by: employer, employment agencies, labor organizations,
    government agencies, apprenticeship training programs - Reprisals
    against persons filing complaints or testifying - Compel or coerce
    anyone to violate the Act

<u>Who may file complaint</u>:
    The aggrieved person

<u>Complaints to be filed within</u>:
    120 days

<u>Commission empowered to</u>:
    Receive and investigate complaints - Conciliation of complaints -
    Subpoenas witnesses and records - Hold public hearings - Issue cease
    and desist orders - Order affirmative action - Issue publications -
    Conduct research and surveys

<u>Review and endorcement</u>:
    By the courts

INDIANA

<u>Administered by</u>:
    Civil Rights Commission
    State Office Building
    101 North Senate Street
    Indianapolis, Indiana

<u>Covered by the Act</u>:
    All enterprises conducted for profit employing 6 or more - Social clubs,
    nonprofit fraternal, charitable, and educational institutions, and
    religious institutions drawing some support from public funds -
    Employment agencies - Employers holding public contracts - State
    government

<u>Excluded from the Act</u>:
    Nonprofit enterprises organized for religious, fraternal or social
    purposes - Schools conducted or affiliated with churches - Persons
    employed by family - Domestic servants

<u>Illegal practices</u>:
    Discrimination on grounds of race, creed, color, national origin or
    ancestry by: employers, labor organizations, employment agencies, state
    and its subdivisions - Reprisals for filing a complaint or testifying

<u>Who may file complaint</u>:
    The aggrieved person - The Commission - Any person with knowledge of
    discriminatory practices

<u>Complaints to be filed within</u>:
    90 days

Commission empowered to:
    Receive, initiate and investigate complaints - Investigate
    discrimination in State agencies and recommend corrective
    legislation - Conciliate complaints - Hold hearings - Issue cease
    and desist orders - Order affirmative action - Develop rules and
    regulations - Provide technical assistance to employers and public
    and private organizations - Create local advisory and conciliation
    councils - Conduct research and issue publications - Develop
    educational program with State Department of Public Instruction and
    universities - Recommend legislation and formulate plans for the
    elimination of prejudice and discrimination - Subpoena witnesses and
    records from employers and state and local agencies and departments

Review and enforcement:
    By the courts

IOWA

Administered by:
    No administrative agency is established, law makes discrimination a mis-
    demeanor enforced by police and law enforcement agencies

Covered by the Act:
    All employers - Labor organizations - State and political subdivisions

Excluded from the Act:
    None

Illegal practices:
    Discrimination on grounds of race, religion, color, national origin or
    ancestry by: employers, labor organization, state and subdivision -
    Inquiring into religious affiliation for employment in public schools
    and other public institutions

Who may file a complaint:
    Not specified

Complaints must be filed within:
    Not specified

Review and enforcement:
    Violation is a misdeameanor punished by fine and imprisonment

KANSAS

Administered by:
>   Commission on Civil Rights
>   State Office Building
>   Topeka, Kansas

Covered by the Act:
>   Employers of eight or more - Labor organizations - Employment agencies -
>   State and its political subdivisions

Excluded from the Act:
>   Nonprofit religious, charitable, fraternal, social, educational and
>   sectarian associations or corporations - Persons employed by family -
>   Domestic servants - Any person whose religious creed and practices
>   include a refusal to recognize U.S. flag or serve in Armed Forces

Illegal practices:
>   Discrimination on grounds of race, religion, color, national origin or
>   ancestry by: employers, labor organizations, employment agencies, State
>   and political subdivisions - Advertisements, inquiries or employment
>   applications specifying race, etc. - Reprisals for filing complaint or
>   testifying - Aiding, inciting or coercing persons to violate Act

Who may file complaint:
>   The aggrieved person - The Attorney General - Employer whose employees
>   refuse or threaten to refuse to cooperate with the Act

Complaints to be filed within:
>   6 months

Commission empowered to:
>   Receive and investigate complaints - Conciliate complaints - Hold
>   public hearings - Issue cease and desist orders - Order affirmative
>   actions - Create advisory agencies and conciliation councils - Issue
>   rules and regulations - Study existence, character and causes of
>   discrimination, and ways of eliminating it - Cooperate with, and
>   furnish technical and mediation assistance to, employers, labor unions
>   and other groups - Make recommendations - Prepare comprehensive
>   educational program in cooperation with State Department of Education -
>   Conduct research and issue publications

Review and enforcement:
>   By the courts - Anyone willfully resisting or impeding work of
>   Commission is guilty of a misdemeanor

MASSACHUSETTS

Administered by:
>   Massachusetts Commission Against Discrimination
>   41 Fremont Street
>   Boston 8, Massachusetts

Covered by the Act:
    All enterprises conducted for profit and employing six or more - Labor
    organizations - Employment agencies - State and its political subdivisions

Excluded from the Act:
    Nonprofit charitable, educational, religious or fraternal enterprises -
    Persons employed by family - Domestic servants

Illegal practices:
    Discrimination on the grounds of race, color, religious creed, ancestry,
    national origin or age (between 45 and 65 years) by: employers, labor
    organizations, employment agencies - Advertisements, inquiries or
    application forms specifying race, etc. - Failure to post provisions
    of the Act - Reprisals against persons filing complaints, giving
    testimony or opposing discriminatory practices - Aiding, inciting or
    coercing others to violate the Act

Who may file complaint:
    The aggrieved person - The Commission - The Attorney General - Employers
    whose employees refuse or threaten to refuse to comply with the law

Complaints to be filed within:
    Six months

Commission empowered to:
    Receive, initiate and investigate complaints - Conciliate complaints -
    Subpoena witnesses and records - Conduct hearings - Issue cease and
    desist orders - Order affirmative action - Adopt rules and regulations -
    Create advisory agencies and conciliation councils - Develop educational
    programs - Issue publications and Annual Reports

Review and enforcement:
    By the courts - Willful violation of Commission orders or interfering
    with work of Commission shall be penalized by not more than 1 year
    imprisonment and $500 fine, or both

MICHIGAN

Administered by:
                      Michigan Civil Rights Commission
        129 Mason Building   900 Cadillac Square Building   328 S. Saginaw St.
        Lansing, Michigan   Detroit 26, Michigan   Flint , Michigan

Covered by the Act:
    Employers of eight or more - Labor organizations - Employment agencies -
    State and its political subdivisions - Contractors and subcontractors
    with the State or its political subdivisions

Excluded from the Act:
    Domestic servants

Illegal practices:
    Discrimination on the grounds of race, color, religion, ancestry or
    national origin by: employers, labor organizations, employment agencies -
    Advertisments, inquiries or application forms specifying race, etc. -
    Establishing a quota system based on race, etc. - Failure to post
    provisions of the Act - Reprisals against persons filing complaints or
    testifying - Using an employment agency, training school or registry
    known to discriminate - Aiding or inciting others to violate the Act

Who may file complaint:
    The aggrieved person - Employers whose employees refuse or threaten to
    refuse to comply with the law

Complaints to be filed within:
    90 days

Commission empowered to:
    Receive, investigate and pass upon complaints - Conciliate complaints -
    Conduct hearings - Petition court for subpoena if witness refuses to
    appear, testify or produce records - Issue cease and desist orders -
    Order affirmative action - Adopt rules and regulations - Create
    advisory agencies - Develop and carry out educational programs - Issue
    publications and conduct research - Report annually to Governor and
    legislature on activities and make recommendations

Review and enforcement:
    By the courts - Failure to post notice of Act punishable by fine

MINNESOTA

Administered by:
    Minnesota Commission Against Discrimination
    55 State Office Building
    St. Paul 1, Minnesota

Covered by the Act:
    Employers of eight or more - Labor organizations - Employment agencies -
    State and its political subdivisions

Excluded from the Act:
    persons employed by family - Domestic servants - Religious or fraternal
    associations where religion is a bona fide occupational qualification

Illegal practices:
    Discrimination on the grounds of race, color, creed, religion or national
    origin by: employers, labor organizations, employment agencies - Adver-
    tisements or inquiries specifying race, etc. - Requiring photographs
    prior to employment - Reprisals against persons filing complaints or
    testifying - Aiding, inciting or coercing others to violate the Act

Who may file complaint:
    The aggrieved person - The Commission - Employers whose employees refuse or threaten to refuse to comply with the law - Labor unions whose members refuse or threaten to refuse to comply with the law

Complaints to be filed within:
    Six months

Commission empowered to:
    Receive, initiate and investigate complaints - Conciliate complaints - Subpoena witnesses and records - Adopt rules and regulations - Utilize records of states departments of employment security - Notify Governor of failure to eliminate discriminatory practice and request appointment of board of review - Develop education programs - Conduct research - Issue publications - Report annually to Governor and to each legislative session - Make recommendations to agencies of State and its subdivisions

Board of Review empowered to:
    Hold hearings - Subpoena witnesses and records - Adopt rules of practice with respect to hearings - Issue cease and desist orders - Order affirmative action

Review and enforcement:
    By the courts - Violation of court injunction punishable by maximum of six months imprisonment, a fine of $250, or both

MISSOURI

Administered by:
    Missouri Commission on Human Rights
    State Office Building
    Jefferson City, Missouri

Covered by the Act:
    Employers of more than 50 persons - State and political or civil subdivisions

Excluded from the Act:
    Corporations or associations owned and operated by a religious group

Illegal practices:
    Discrimination based on race, creed, color, religion, national origins or ancestry by: employers, labor organizations and employment agencies - Advertisements, inquiries or application forms specifying race, etc. - Reprisals against persons filing complaints or testifying - Aiding, inciting or coercing others to violate Act

Who may file complaint:
   The aggrieved person - The Attorney General - The Commission - Any employer
   whose employees refuse or threaten to refuse to comply with the law

Complaints to be filed within:
   90 days

Commission empowered to:
   Receive, initiate and investigate complaints - Conciliate complaints -
   Hold hearings - Subpoena witnesses and records - Issue cease and desist
   orders - Order affirmative action - Adopt rules and regulations - Publish
   studies and research - Report annually to Governor and Legislature - Make
   recommendations to agencies and officers of State and subdivisions

Review and enforcement:
   By the courts - Willful violation of law and Commission orders is a
   misdemeanor

                              NEVADA

Administered by:
   Commission on Equal Rights of Citizens
   Department of Labor
   Carson City, Nevada

Covered by the Act:
   All citizens and employers

Excluded from the Act:
   None

Illegal practices:
   No actions are declared illegal but it is declared public policy to
   foster the right of all persons reasonably to seek, obtain and hold
   employment without discrimination, distinction, or restriction because of
   race, religious creed, color, national origins, or ancestry

Who may file complaint:
   Not specified but any citizen who is aggrieved probably can file

Complaints to be filed within:
   Not specified

Commission is empowered to:
   Receive, initiate and investigate complaints - Conciliate complaints -
   Conduct private or public hearings - Subpoena witnesses and records - Report
   findings of fact and recommendations to Governor - Cooperate with private
   and public organizations - Carry out educational programs - Make studies
   and disseminate information

Review and enforcement:
    The Act is without any enforcement powers

                            NEW JERSEY

Administered by:
                    Division on Civil Rights
                    New Jersey Department of Education
    1100 Raymond Boulevard   162 West State Street
    Newark 2, New Jersey   Trenton 25, New Jersey

Covered by the Act:
    All enterprises conducted for profit and employing six or more - Labor
    organizations - Employment agencies - State and its political subdivisions

Excluded from the Act:
    Nonprofit charitable, religious, educational or fraternal enterprises -
    Persons employed by family - Domestic servants

Illegal practices:
    Discrimination on the grounds of race, creed, color, national origin, age
    or liability for military service by: employers, labor organizations,
    employment agencies - Discrimination in any apprenticeship or training
    program by a labor union - Refusal to work with members of minority
    groups - Advertisements, inquiries or application forms specifying race,
    etc. - Reprisals against persons filing complaints or testifying -- Aiding,
    inciting or coerce others to violate the Act

Who may file complaint:
    The aggrieved person - The Commissioner of Labor - The Commission of
    Education - Attorney General - Employers whose employees refuse or
    threaten to refuse to comply with the law

Complaints to be filed within:
    90 days

Division empowered to:
    Receive, initiate and investigate complaints - Conciliate complaints -
    Subpoena witnesses and records - Conduct hearings - Issue cease and
    desist orders - Order affirmative actions - Adopt rules and regulations -
    Develop educational programs - Issue publications and results of
    research - File Annual Reports - Maintain liaison with appropriate local,
    state and federal agencies and officials

Review and enforcement:
    By the courts - Willful violation of law shall be a misdemeanor punishable
    by imprisonment of up to 1 year, a $500 fine, or both

NEW MEXICO

Administered by:
  Fair Employment Practice Commission
  137 E. De Vargas Street
  Santa Fe, New Mexico

Covered by the Act:
  Employers of four or more - Labor organizations - Employment agencies -
  The State and its political subdivisions - Employers holding contracts
  with or political subdivisions

Excluded from the Act:
  Religious corporations or associations - Nonprofit social or fraternal
  clubs - Persons employed by family - Domestic servants

Illegal practices:
  Discrimination on the grounds of race, color, religion, national origin
  or ancestry - Advertisements, inquiries or application forms specifying
  race, etc. - Reprisals against persons filing complaints or testifying -
  Aiding, inciting or coercing others to violate the Act

Who may file complaint:
  The aggrieved person, or anyone acting in his behalf - The Labor
  Commissioner - The Attorney General - Employers whose employees refuse
  or threaten to refuse to comply with the law

Complaints to be filed within:
  No time limit specified

Commission empowered to:
  Receive, investigate and pass upon complaints - Conciliate complaints -
  Conduct hearings - Subpoena witnesses and records - Issue cease and
  desist orders - Order affirmative action - Develop educational programs -
  Adopt rules and regulations - Create advisory agencies and conciliation
  councils - Make recommendations to State and local government agencies -
  Issue publications and conduct research - Report annually to Governor
  and to Legislature with legislative recommendations

Review and enforcement:
  By the courts - Willful violation of law is a misdemeanor punishable by
  imprisonment of up to 90 days, up to a $500 fine, or both

NEW YORK

Administered by:
New York State Commission for Human Rights
270 Broadway
New York 7, New York

Branch Offices:

62 East 125th St. New York, New York	248 State Street Albany 7, New York	6 Broadway Buffalo, New York
118 Court Street Brooklyn 1, New York	333 East Washington Street Syracuse, New York	61 Mitchell Place White Plains, N.Y.
	244 Mineola Boulevard Mineola, New York	

Covered by the Act:
All enterprises conducted for profit and employing six or more - Labor
organizations - Employment agencies - Advertisements, inquiries or
application forms specifying race, etc. - Licensing agencies with
respect to age qualifications - State and its political subdivisions

Excluded from the Act:
Nonprofit charitable, educational, religious, fraternal or social
enterprises - Persons employed by family - Domestic servants

Illegal practices:
Discrimination on the grounds of race, creed, color, age (between 40
and 65 years) ancestry or national origin by: employers, labor
organizations, employment agencies - Discrimination in any apprenticeship, on-the-job training or occupational training program - Refusing
to post notices about law - Advertisements or inquiries specifying race,
etc. - Reprisals against persons filing complaints or testifying - Aiding,
inciting or coerce others to violate the Act

Who may file complaint:
The aggrieved person - The Industrial Commissioner - The Attorney General -
Employers whose employees refuse or threaten to refuse to comply with the
law

Complaints to be filed within:
90 days by the aggrieved person - Six months by Attorney General and
Industrial Commissioner.

Powers of Commission:
Receive, investigate and pass upon complaints - Conciliate complaints -
Subpoena witnesses and records - Conduct hearings - Issue cease and
desist orders - Order affirmative actions - Adopt rules and regulations -
Develop educational programs - Create advisory agencies and counciliation
councils - Use the services of all government departments and agencies -
Make recommendations to agencies and officers of State and its
subdivisions - Issue publications and conduct research - Make annual
reports to Governor and Legislature

Review and enforcement:
By the courts - Willful violation of laws or interference with Commission's
work is a misdemeanor punishable by up to 1 year imprisonment, up to a
$500 fine, or both

OHIO

Administered by:

Ohio Civil Rights Commission

222 East Gay Street	1302 Ontario Street	431 Main Street
Columbus 15, Ohio	Cleveland, Ohio	Cincinnati, Ohio

Covered by the Act:
Private employers of four or more - Labor organizations - Employment
agencies - The State and its political subdivisions

Excluded from the Act:
Domestic servants

Illegal practices:
Discrimination on the grounds of race, color, religion, ancestry,
national origin or age* by: employers, labor organizations, employment
agencies - Discrimination in apprentice training programs - Advertisements, inquiries or application forms specifying race, etc. - Use of
recruitment or training facilities which are known to discriminate -
Refusing to post notices about law - Reprisals against persons filing
complaint or testifying - Aiding, inciting or coercing others to
violate the Act

Who may file complaint:
Anyone with knowledge of an unlawful practice - The Commission

Complaints to be filed within:
Six months

*Discrimination based on age is enforced by the Department of Industrial
Relations

Commission empowered to:
 Receive, investigate and pass upon complaints - Initiate investigations
of discriminatory practices - Conciliate complaints - Subpoena witnesses
and records - Conduct hearings - Issue cease and desist orders - Order
affirmative action - Adopt rules and regulations - Make periodic surveys
of the existence and effects of discrimination based on race, etc. -
Make recommendations to agencies and officers of State and its subdivisions - Prepare comprehensive educational programs - Create advisory
agencies and conciliation councils - Issue publications and conduct
research - Make annual reports to Governor and legislature

Review and enforcement:
 By the courts

OREGON

Administered by:
 Civil Rights Division
 Oregon Bureau of Labor
 1400 S.W. 5th Avenue
 Portland 1, Oregon

Covered by the Act:
 Employers of six or more - Labor organizations - Employment agencies

Excluded from the Act:
 Nonprofit social, fraternal, charitable, educational or religious associations or corporations - Persons employed by family - Domestic servants

Illegal practices:
 Discrimination on the grounds of race, color, religion, national origin
or age (between 25-65 years) by: employers, labor organizations, employment agencies, vocational and professional schools - Discrimination on
grounds of age by public agencies - Refusal to work with members of
minority groups - Advertisements, inquiries, application forms specifying
race, etc. - Reprisals against persons filing complaints or testifying -
Aiding, inciting or coercing others to violate the Act

Who may file complaint:
 The aggrieved person - The Attorney General - Employers whose employees
refuse or threaten to refuse to comply with the law

Complaints to be filed within:
 90 days

Division empowered to:
Receive, investigate and pass upon complaints - Conciliate complaints -
Conduct hearings - Issue cease and desist orders - Investigate existence,
causes and extent of discrimination - Study ways and formulate plans to
eliminate discrimination - Publish and disseminate reports of findings -
Create advisory agencies and intergroup relations councils - Transmit
recommendations to Governor and Legislature

Review and enforcement:
By the courts

PENNSYLVANIA

Administered by:
Pennsylvania Human Relations Commission
Department of Labor and Industry   State Office Building
1401 Labor and Industry Building   1400 Spring Garden Street
Harrisburg, Pennsylvania   Philadelphia, Pennsylvania

State Office Building
300 Liberty Avenue
Pittsburgh 22, Pennsylvania

Covered by the Act:
Employers of twelve or more - Labor organizations - Employment agencies -
The State and its political subdivisions

Excluded from the Act:
Religious, fraternal, charitable or sectarian corporations or associations,
unless supported in whole or in part by public appropriation - Agricultural
employment - Persons employed by family - Domestic servants

Illegal practices:
Discrimination on the grounds of race, color, religious creed, age (between
40 and 62 years), ancestry or national origin by: employers, labor organizations, employment agencies - Refusal to work with members of minority
groups - Advertisements, inquiries or application forms specifying race,
etc. - Use of recruitment facilities which are known to discriminate -
"Position Wanted" ads specifying race, etc. - Reprisals against persons
filing complaints or testifying - Aiding, inciting or coercing others to
violate the Act

Who may file complaint:
The aggrieved person - The Commission - The Attorney General - Employers
whose employees refuse or threaten to refuse to comply with the law

Complaints to be filed within:
90 days

Commission empowered to:
> Receive, initiate and investigate complaints - Conciliate complaints - Subpoena witnesses and records - Conduct hearings - Issue cease and desist orders - Order affirmative action - Adopt rules and regulations - Create advisory agencies and conciliation councils - Develop educational programs - Conduct research - Issue publications and Annual Reports - Make recommendations to agencies and officers of State and political subdivisions - Recommend legislation to Governor and Legislature

Review and enforcement:
> By the courts - Willful interference with or violation of Commission order is a misdemeanor punishable by fine and/or imprisonment

PUERTO RICO

Administered by:
> Department of Labor
> Barbosa Avenue
> Santurce, Puerto Rico

Covered by the Act:
> All employers - Government agencies operating as private businesses or enterprises

Excluded from the Act:
> None specified

Illegal practices:
> Discrimination on grounds of race, color, creed, birth, social position or age (between 30 and 60 years) by: employers, labor unions

Who may file complaint:
> The aggrieved person - Secretary of Labor

Complaints to be filed within:
> Not specified

Department of Labor is empowered to:
> Order employer or labor union to pay damages for loss of income - Initiate court action for civil damages for monetary payments - Seek cease and desist order in court - Order affirmative action - Initiate criminal charges in court

Review by:
> The act is enforced by civil liability suits for damages incurred by discrimination - Violation is also a misdemeanor punishable by fine and/or imprisonment

<u>RHODE ISLAND</u>

<u>Administered by</u>:
    Rhode Island Commission Against Discrimination
    State House
    Providence 2, Rhode Island

<u>Covered by the Act</u>:
    Employers of four or more - Labor organizations - Employment agencies

<u>Excluded from the Act</u>:
    Nonprofit religious, charitable, fraternal, social, educational, sectarian
    corporations or associations - Persons employed by family - Domestic
    servants

<u>Illegal practices</u>:
    Discrimination on the grounds of race, color, religion, national origin
    or age* by: employers, labor organizations, employment agencies, training
    school or employee referring organizations - Employment or referring
    agencies complying with discriminatory job requests - Refusal to work with
    members of minority groups - Refusing to post notices of law - Advertise-
    ments or inquiries specifying race, etc - Reprisals against persons filing
    complaints or assisting in proceedings under the Act - Aiding, inciting or
    coercing others to violate the Act

<u>Who may file complaint</u>·
    The aggrieved person - The Commission - Organizations combating
    discrimination, or promoting full or equal employment opportunities

<u>Complaints to be filed within</u>:
    One year

<u>Commission empowered to</u>:
    Receive, initiate, investigate and pass upon complaints - Conciliate
    complaints - Subpoena witnesses and records - Conduct hearings - Issue
    cease and desist orders - Order affirmative action - Adopt rules and
    regulations - Formulate educational programs - Create advisory agencies
    and conciliation councils - Issue publications and Annual Reports -
    Make recommendations to Governor and legislature

<u>Review and enforcement</u>:
    By the courts

*The State Department of Labor has jurisdiction over charges of discrimination
based on age.

VERMONT

Administered by:
>The act is not enforced through an administrative agency - Violations
>are prosecuted as criminal action by law enforcement agencies

Covered by the Act:
>All employers

Excluded from the Act:
>Persons employed by a family - domestic servants

Illegal practices:
>Discrimination by employer, employment, labor unions on grounds of race
>color, religion, ancestry, national origin or place of birth -
>Discrimination in rates of pay by reason of sex - Advertisements
>indicating preference of race, etc.

Enforcement and review:
>Any employer, labor organization or employment agency willfully
>violating act shall be fined up to $500 for each violation - Act is
>enforced in courts as a violation of criminal code

WASHINGTON

Administered by:
>Washington State Board Against Discrimination
>1411 Fourth Avenue Building   1005 West Third Street
>Seattle, Washington   Spokane, Washington
>
>   General Administration Building
>   Olympia, Washington

Covered by the Act:
>Employers of eight or more - Labor organizations - Employment agencies -
>The State and its political subdivisions

Excluded from the Act:
>Nonprofit religious or sectarian organizations - Persons employed by
>family - Domestic servants

Illegal practices:
    Discrimination on the grounds of race, creed, color, ancestry, national
    origin or age by: employers, labor organizations, employment agencies -
    Advertisements, inquiries or application forms specifying race, etc. -
    Reprisals against persons filing complaints or testifying - Aiding or
    inciting others to violate the Act

Who may file complaint:
    The aggrieved person - The Board Against Discrimination - Employers whose
    employees refuse or threaten to refuse to comply with the law

Complaints to be filed within:
    Six months

Board empowered to:
    Receive, initiate and investigate complaints - Conciliate complaints -
    Subpoena witnesses and records - Conduct hearings - Issue cease and
    desist orders - Order affirmative actions - Adopt rules and regulations
    - Develop educational programs - Conduct research - Create advisory
    agencies and conciliation councils - Issue publications and reports -
    Recommend further legislation

Review and enforcement:
    By the courts - Willful violation of Board order is a misdemeanor

WISCONSIN

Administered by:
    Wisconsin Fair Employment Practices Division Industrial Commission
    1 W. Wilson Street   3190 Plankenton Building
    Madison, Wisconsin   Milwaukee, Wisconsin

Covered by the Act:
    All employers except nonprofit social clubs, fraternal or religious
    associations - Labor organizations - Employment agencies

Excluded from the Act:
    Persons employed by family

Illegal practices:
    Discrimination on the grounds of race, color, creed, age, (between 40
    and 65 years) sex, ancestry or national origin by: employers, labor
    organizations, employment agencies - Reprisals against any one filing
    a complaint or testifying

Who may file complaint:
    Any person with knowledge of discriminatory practices

Complaints to be filed within:
    No time limit specified

Division empowered to:
    Receive and investigate complaints - Conciliate complaints - Subpoena
    witnesses - Conduct hearings - Issue cease and desist orders - Adopt
    rules and regulations - Conduct studies - Make findings and issue
    recommendations and orders - Recommend legislation - Formulate educational
    programs to eliminate discrimination - Issue publications and reports

Review and enforcement:
    By the courts

Index

5